The Idol and Distance

Perspectives in Continental Philosophy
John D. Caputo, series editor

The Idol and Distance

FIVE STUDIES

Jᴇᴀɴ-Lᴜᴄ Mᴀʀɪᴏɴ

Translated and with an introduction by
Tʜᴏᴍᴀs A. Cᴀʀʟsᴏɴ

FORDHAM UNIVERSITY PRESS
New York • 2001

Perspectives in Continental Philosophy, No. 17
ISSN 1089–3938

Library of Congress Cataloging-in-Publication Data

Marion, Jean-Luc, 1946–
    [Idole et la distance. English]
    The idol and distance : five studies / Jean-Luc Marion ; translated and
with an introduction by Thomas A. Carlson.
        p.   cm.—(Perspectives in continental philosophy ; no 17)
    Originally published: Paris : B. Grasset, 1977.
    Includes bibliographical references and index.
    ISBN 0-8232-2077-X (hardcover)—ISBN 0-8232-2078-8 (pbk.)
    1. Metaphysics.   2. Death of God.   3. God.   I. Title.   II. Series.
B2430.   283 I3613   2001
194—dc21   00-061690

Printed in the United States of America
01 02 03 04 05 5 4 3 2 1

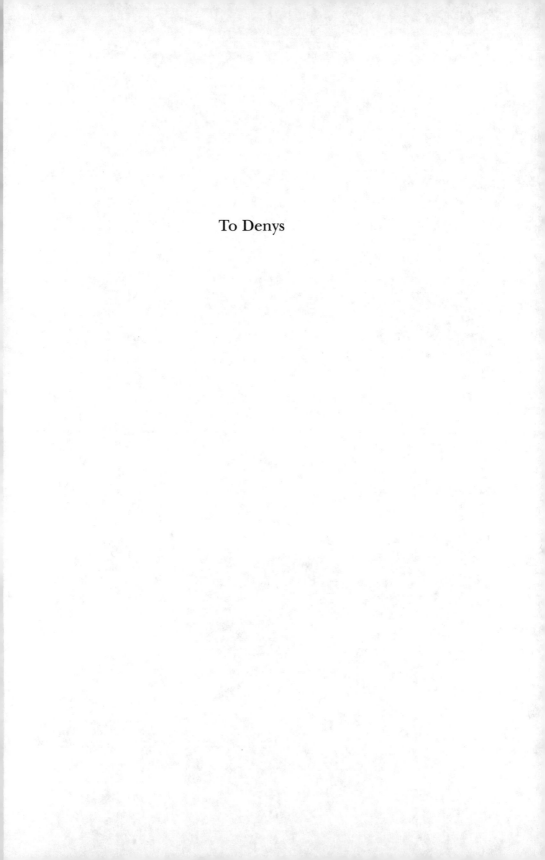

To Denys

For union, in setting separation apart, has in no way under-mined difference.

Maximus the Confessor (*Ambigua*, PG 91, 1056 c)

Every concept formed in order to reach and encompass the divine nature succeeds only in fashioning an idol of God and not at all in making him known.

Gregory of Nyssa (*Life of Moses*, II, 165, PG 44, 337b)

CONTENTS

TRANSLATOR'S INTRODUCTION
Converting the Given into the Seen: Introductory Remarks on Theological and Phenomenological Vision

Nearly a quarter century old, and marked sharply by its time and place (Paris in the 1970s), this early theological text by Jean-Luc Marion nevertheless maintains a strikingly deep resonance with his most recent, groundbreaking, and ever more widely discussed phenomenology. Indeed, one can see emerging here already, in Marion's theological meditation on "distance," the core concerns that will define his mature phenomenology of "donation."[1] And while Marion will want to insist on a clear distinction between the theological and phenomenological projects, to read each in light of the other can prove nevertheless illuminating for both the theological and the philosophical reader—and perhaps above all for the reader who wants to read in both directions at once, the reader concerned with those points of interplay and undecidability where theology and philosophy inform, provoke, and challenge one another in endlessly complex ways. In order, then, to guide readers back into the theological thinking of *The Idol and Distance,* and in order to extend an ongoing dialogue along the complex and unstable borders between theology and philosophy, I will here frame the book's core concerns in relation to those of Marion's more recent phenomenological writings.

---

[1] Marion's main theological works include *The Idol and Distance* (published in French in 1977; cited in the body of the text, according to the English edition, as ID), *God without Being,* trans. Thomas A. Carlson (Chicago: University of Chicago Press, 1991; published in French in 1982), and *Prolégomènes à la charité* (Paris: Editions de la Différance, 1986). His primary phenomenological works include *Reduction and Givenness,* trans. Thomas A. Carlson (Evanston: Northwestern University Press, 1998; published in French in 1989; hereafter cited as RD), and, most recently, *Etant donné: Essai d'une phénoménologie de la donation* (Paris: Presses Universitaires de France, 1997; cited in the body of the text as ED).

One can quickly sketch that frame as follows. In both his theological and his phenomenological projects, Marion's central effort to free the absolute or unconditional (be it theology's God or phenomenology's phenomenon) from the various limits and preconditions of human thought and language (signaled especially by the thought and language of Being) will imply a thoroughgoing critique of all metaphysics, and above all of the modern metaphysics centered on the active, spontaneous subject who occupies modern philosophy from Descartes through Hegel and Nietzsche. Such a critique of the subject, in both the theological and phenomenological registers, is carried out primarily in terms of some overwhelming or inconceivable "gift" or "givenness" whose presence can be excessive to the point of appearing as absence. It would be just such a gift or givenness that first gives rise to the self of any eventual subjectivity, and it would do so by means of the defining but indeterminate "call" that givenness exercises over the nascent subject, over the "me" that might eventually speak as "I." That call is "received," both phenomenologically and theologically, only through the constitutive response or addiction of an insurmountably passive self who is first given to itself *by* givenness because it is in its very origin given over *to* givenness—in the blindness of a birth into language where the seeing and speaking subject eventually emerges.

Before elaborating these significant structural similarities between Marion's theology and phenomenology, we should note the manner in which he wants clearly to distinguish the two domains, for such a distinction already says much about his phenomenological and theological visions. "Between phenomenology and theology," Marion tells us, in response to the various charges that his phenomenology amounts to a special metaphysics or to a Christian theology of the Father,[2] "the border passes between revelation as possibility and revelation as historicity. There could be no danger of confusion between these domains."[3] By articulat-

---

[2] On this charge, see the polemical essay by Dominique Janicaud, *Le Tournant théologique de la phénoménologie française* (Combas: Editions de l'Eclat, 1991), esp. pp. 44–54, and, at another level, the much discussed remarks by Jacques Derrida in *Given Time: I. Counterfeit Money,* trans. Peggy Kamuf (Chicago: University of Chicago Press, 1992), p. 52, note 10.

[3] "Metaphysics and Phenomenology: A Relief for Theology," trans. Thomas A. Carlson, in *Critical Inquiry* 20, no. 4 (summer 1994), p. 590.

ing the possibility of an irreducible and unconditional—or "saturated"—phenomenon[4] whose unforeseeability, nonrepeatability, and irreducibility to present presence would count it as a "revelation," phenomenology says nothing about the actual historical occurrence or meaning of such a phenomenon, but simply articulates it as possibility;[5] theology, by contrast, does not simply articulate phenomenal possibilities, but rather begins *as* theology only *in* a faithful response to historical actuality, and thus even if it draws on phenomenological method to elucidate such actuality (as Marion himself will, for example, in the phenomenology of the idol and the icon, which shapes his entire theology), it remains in its basic presuppositions—those of an historical Revelation and faith—distinct from the science that, in principle, suspends all presupposition.[6] The faith presupposition that in phenomenology would be a burden or a blockage is in theology the first and necessary blessing—and in his theological writing Marion very clearly assumes and accepts such a faith in "the insurpassable primacy of Christian revelation" (ID, 20).

In his most recent phenomenological work, *Etant donné: Essai*

---

[4] Saturating and thus inverting the four Kantian categories of quantity, quality, relation, and modality (in the event, the idol, the flesh, and the icon, respectively), Marion's "saturated phenomenon" does not obey the conditions of any horizon or the reduction to any I. For his elaboration of the saturated phenomenon in relation to the categories, the horizon, and the I, see "The Saturated Phenomenon," trans. Thomas A. Carlson, *Philosophy Today* (spring 1996), pp. 103–24 (hereafter cited as SP); and, especially, ED, §§ 21–23.

[5] See SP, p. 120: "We will therefore call this appearance that is purely of itself and starting from itself, this phenomenon that does not subject its possibility to any preliminary determination, a revelation. And—we insist on this—here it is purely and simply a matter of the phenomenon taken in its fullest meaning."

[6] As Marion indicates in the issue of *Revue de métaphysique et de morale* dedicated to a discussion of RD (January-March 1991; hereafter cited as RMM), within his theological and historical work "the transgression of the metaphysical point of departure could ensure itself a nonmetaphysical (and nonontological) point of arrival because it relied on external givens, which were admitted by hypothesis, or rather assumed as positions. This privilege, however, remains ambiguous: if it grants a point of arrival, it concedes it only by admitting a fait accompli (of history or belief), without rendering it accessible in principle; thought remains, then, in a situation of heteronymy and subjection, since it must import the results of an evidence that it can nevertheless not secure directly. It is this ambiguity that the [phenomenological] approach rejects: for in phenomenology, the only thing that matters is the 'principle of all principles' " (RMM, p. 67)—which would imply the "principle of the absence of presuppositions [*Prinzip der Voraussetzunglosigkeit*]" (on this, see RD, p. 9).

d'une phénoménologie de la donation, where "revelation" is taken to represent the fullest form of the saturated phenomenon (as a saturation of saturation, which includes in one phenomenon all four modes of possible saturation),[7] Marion elaborates at greater length this distinction between phenomenological and theological approaches to revelation—not only to answer the charge that his phenomenology itself is "really" a poorly disguised theology or metaphysics, but also, equally important, to protect the integrity of theology as Marion understands it:

> Phenomenology describes possibilities and never considers the phenomenon of revelation except as a possibility of phenomenality, which it would formulate thus: if God manifests (or manifested) himself, he will make use of a paradox in the second degree; Revelation (of God by himself, *theo*-logical), if it takes place, will assume the phenomenal figure of the phenomenon of revelation, of the paradox of paradoxes, of saturation in the second degree. To be sure, *R*evelation (as actuality) is never confused with revelation (as a possible phenomenon)—we scrupulously respect this conceptual difference by means of its graphic translation. But phenomenology, which owes it to phenomenality to go this far, does not go any farther, and must never decide on the fact of Revelation, nor on its historicity, nor on its actuality, nor on its meaning. It must not do so, not only out of concern to distinguish knowledges and to delimit their respective regions, but first because it in no way has the means to do so: the fact (if there is one) of Revelation exceeds the scope of all science, including phenomenology; only a theology, and on condition that it lets itself be constructed starting from this fact alone (K. Barth or H. U. von Balthasar, more, no doubt, than R. Bultmann or K. Rahner), could eventually reach it. Even if it had the desire to do so (and, clearly, such was never the case), phenomenology would not have the power to turn to theology. And one must know nothing of theology, of its procedures and its problematics, even simply to envisage this unlikelihood.[8]

Defending himself in this passage against the charge of a theological or metaphysical turn in his phenomenology, Marion helps us to understand what we will find in his theology. First, the theology will presuppose the historical actuality (and the insurpassable

---

[7] See ED, pp. 331–35.
[8] Ibid., p. 329, note 1.

primacy) of a Christian Revelation; it will not treat the mere possibility of revelation in general (which phenomenology can and should rightly attempt). Second, that historically actual Revelation would be rightly understood for Marion, if at all, only by means of a truly *theo*logical thinking such as that of Barth or von Balthasar—that is, a thinking that would claim to start from God's unconditional *self*-revelation, treating it on or in its own terms (and not, as in weaker theologians like Rahner or Bultmann, on or in the terms of humanity's existential capacity to receive or be open to something like Revelation).

Now, while Marion insists on this distinction between phenomenology and theology, as a distinction between the possible and the actual, it is clear already in the passage just quoted that his phenomenological conception of what might count as revelation is itself not theologically neutral. Rather, that conception of revelation is informed by, and consistent with, one possible understanding of revelation to the exclusion of another (that of Barth and von Balthasar as opposed to that of Rahner and Bultmann). Conversely, as the reader of *The Idol and Distance* will see, Marion's reflection on what he takes to be the historically actual Revelation of a Christian Father God, who would give himself only in the withdrawal of "distance," is a reflection that draws in decisive ways already on phenomenological method—above all in the fundamental analysis of idol and icon. If it is true, then, that Marion's phenomenology is not, or does not intend to be, in any straightforward way a theology, it is also true that his theology and phenomenology inform one another more or otherwise than Marion himself might allow, for the former already operates in a quasi-phenomenological manner, and the latter in fact accepts the understanding of revelation set out in the former (to the exclusion of other historically actual, and therefore possible, understandings of revelation).

At the risk, then, of being counted among those who "know nothing of theology, of its procedures and its problematics," I turn now to a brief consideration of the structural similarities between Marion's theological and phenomenological projects.

Marion's theological and phenomenological projects are both situated in response to the "end" of metaphysics, itself understood in terms of its "onto-theological constitution."[9] Seeking to realize and pass beyond that end, seeking to play outside the game of onto-theology, Marion's theology and phenomenology alike will attack above all the characteristically metaphysical subjection of the ab-solute or unconditional—be it the Christian God specifically or the saturated phenomenon more broadly—to the preconditions and limits of human thought and language.

In his theological response to this "end" of metaphysics, Marion focuses on the "death of God" and, correlatively, the cultural and intellectual crisis of nihilism that, consuming French intellectuals in the 1960s and 1970s, comes to be associated with thinkers from Marx, Nietzsche, and Freud to Heidegger, the structuralists, and poststructuralists such as Derrida. This theological response—and this would in principle distinguish it from Marion's phenomenological work—is the response of one who presupposes the insurpassable primacy of the Christian revelation. Having accepted that primacy, *The Idol and Distance* can interpret the modern "death of God" only as a death of the strictly metaphysical *concept* of God, and at this level the core assertion of *The Idol and Distance* is straightforward: the seeming absence or failure of God in modern (or postmodern) thought and culture, the apparent withdrawal or distance of any God from our all too human concerns, is in fact, and must rightly be, the primary figure today of God's eternally faithful presence—for the real presence of God is now, as by right always, a function, precisely, of distance, withdrawal, or absence.

The three figures who occupy the center of *The Idol and Distance*—Nietzsche, Hölderlin, and the Pseudo-Dionysius—would, in Marion's eyes, share just this insight: "In all of these cases, the indisputably apparent absence of the divine becomes the very center of a questioning concerning its manifestation" (ID, 21). While Hölderlin's withdrawal of the divine and Nietzsche's twi-

---

[9] The indispensable text for understanding this starting point of Marion's projects remains Heidegger's essay "The Onto-theological Constitution of Metaphysics," trans. Joan Stambaugh, in *Identity and Difference* (New York: Harper and Row, 1969). Unlike the many broad, global uses of the term, which would count as "onto-theology" most all philosophical and theological thinking prior to Heidegger or Derrida, Marion's use of the term "onto-theology" will be more precise and more restricted, hence allowing for an outside that others will not recognize.

light of the idols would mark distinctively modern aspects of divine manifestation, they can nevertheless prove consistent with a reading of the Dionysian, or already biblical, approach to revelation in terms of distance and its obscurity. In and through his investigations of Nietzsche, Hölderlin, and Dionysius, Marion is thus able to affirm, under the name of "paternal distance," and consistent with biblical and modern thinking alike, that "the withdrawal of the divine would perhaps constitute its ultimate form of revelation" (ID, 80).

Thus, the evidence of God and our ignorance of that evidence in fact merge "for the one who finally conceives withdrawal as the most radical mode of presence for God, and for Him alone" (ID, 89). The God of Marion's Christian revelation is the God whom no one can see without dying, or perhaps more exactly the God whose generous love surpasses all knowledge or understanding. That love is exercised primordially through paternal distance, which, precisely and only as distance, opens the only true space for filial relation; a seeming absence or poverty thus proves to be the most generous plenitude. Gift and abandon, then, remain inseparable according to a truth that is both Christological and trinitarian: "Poverty coincides with overabundance in the divine because God admits—what is shown by the Spirit—the distance of a Son" (ID, 111).

This coincidence of poverty and overabundance, this paternal distance, withdrawal, or absence that constitutes the very movement of love, is precisely what metaphysical *concepts* of God, in their attempt to grasp and make present to comprehension, simply fail to see or to show. In showing too much, in their pretension to equivalence with God himself, the necessarily limited concepts produced by metaphysics would in fact show too little, for God by definition would exceed every concept or definition. The modern collapse or failure of the metaphysical concepts of God, then, would prove theologically promising, for it would reopen the space for a true thought and language of the unthinkable and ineffable love of the Father.

From the perspective informed by paternal distance, therefore, the "death of God" does not mark a disappearance of God himself, who by definition remains indefinable and incomprehensible and so never simply present *or* absent, but rather the failure or destruction of all concepts and language through which we may have sought to define or comprehend a limited and present "God." Within the history of metaphysics defined as "onto-theology," those concepts and language would have assumed numerous forms—from Plato's ἰδέα τοῦ ἀγάθου, Aristotle's νοήσεως νοήσις and the Plotinian One, through the five ways of Aquinas, to Descartes's *causa sui,* Leibniz's principle of sufficient reason, Kant's moral God, and Hegel's absolute subjectivity—but in all cases, the principle remains the same: metaphysics produces a limited concept of "God" that it wrongly wants, in turn, to equate fully or adequately with God himself (ID, 10).

The destruction of such concepts and their language, for Marion, constitutes only a destruction of conceptual and linguistic "idols," for idolatry consists in nothing other than "the subjection of the divine to the human conditions for experience of the divine" (ID, 6). "The distance of God," however, means that "no idol can announce the death or the life of God, because 'he dwells in an inaccessible light' (I Timothy 1:6)" (ID, 76). The destruction of onto-theology's conceptual idols, then, as carried out by the "death of God" itself, would clear a space for the "icon," that is, a space for the "negative theophany" in which we are freed to encounter the visibility of the invisible, which would demand a thought and language of the unconditional that itself eludes thought and language.

This concern to free the unconditional from any and all conditions that human thought might set upon its appearance, a concern central to Marion's theological project overall and to its core treatment of idol and icon specifically, defines also the starting point of his phenomenological work. Indeed, Marion's central phenomenological aim—to free phenomenality from the metaphysical preconditions set either by subjectivity (as with transcendental apperception in Kant) or by God (as with the principle of sufficient reason in Leibniz)[10]—can be taken to mark a generalization of the specifically theological concern to free the appearance of the Christian God from idolatry. A phenomenon whose appearance depends on something other than that phenomenon itself possesses, for Marion, only an "alienated phenomenality,"

---

[10] See ED, pp. 251–57.

and such alienation, which amounts to a form of idolatry, is characteristic of metaphysics, for "[w]ithin the rule of metaphysics, the possibility of appearing never belongs to that which appears, nor its phenomenality to the phenomenon" (ED, 255). Against such metaphysical alienation, Marion will insist that the phenomenon owes its phenomenality neither to any metaphysical God nor to any transcendental ego, but rather constitutes its own, unconditional, and irreducible self-showing. Following Heidegger at this level, Marion's phenomenology insists that the phenomenon "in its fullest sense" is that alone which "appears truly as itself, of itself, and starting from itself, since it alone appears without the limits of a horizon, nor the reduction to an *I* and constitutes itself, to the point of giving *itself* as a *self*" (ED, 304–5).[11]

Just as Marion's theology would pass beyond metaphysics by freeing God's self-revelation in distance from every limiting concept that would seek to render that God present under the idolatrous conditions of thought, so his phenomenology would pass beyond metaphysics by freeing the phenomenon's self-showing from any a priori conditions, whether those of the thinking subject or those of a metaphysical God.

Now, Marion's theological attempt in *The Idol and Distance* to articulate the unconditional self-showing of God implies a critique not only of metaphysics as an "onto-theology" whose concepts of God would seek to determine the indeterminate—when the question of God would rightly be the "question of the indeterminate itself—let us say, of the Ab-solute" (ID, 2)—but also of the Heideggerian thinking that itself defines, elucidates, and seeks to overcome onto-theology. If onto-theology constitutes an idolatry insofar as it subjects the appearance of God to the limits of conceptual thinking, the Heideggerian critique of onto-theology would itself, for Marion, harbor its own idolatry, insofar as it subjects the appearance of God, beyond onto-theology, to its own conditions: the unquestioned priority of Being and, correlatively,

---

[11] See in Heidegger, e.g., *Being and Time,* trans. Macquarrie and Robinson (Oxford: Basil Blackwell, 1962), p. 54: "the showing-itself-in-itself" (*das Sich-an-ihm-selbst-zeigende*); *History of the Concept of Time,* trans. Theodore Kisiel (Bloomington: Indiana University Press, 1985), p. 85: "letting the manifest in itself be seen from itself" (*das an ihm selbst Offenbare von ihm selbst her sehen lassen*).

the primacy of that being for whom alone Being is an issue—
Dasein. Already in the period of *Being and Time,* Marion emphasizes, Heidegger insists that "the analytic of *Dasein* precedes and
determines the condition of the being that affects the Christian
event—'christianness.' In a word, the analytic of *Dasein* indicates,
ontologically, a pre-Christian content and datum whose 'christianness' marks only an ontic corrective" (ID, 208). According to
this framework (which, one might note, depends on Heidegger's
important but problematic distinction between "founding" and
"founded" domains of discourse),[12] "God will never be able to
appear within the field of questioning thought except under the
mediating conditions first of 'christianness' and then of *Dasein*"
(ID, 209). Since God here can play only an ontic role in modifying the ontologically prior *Dasein,* God is reduced to a "supreme"
being who is not in fact supreme—since in order to operate at all
he must first operate within the conditions set, precisely, by *Dasein.* A similar logic remains operative in the later Heidegger,
where the appearance of God is subjected either to the "worlding" of the world (in the fourfold of earth and sky, mortals and
divinities) or to the "truth of Being," within which alone there
would open, first, "the essence of the sacred" and, then, "the
essence of divinity" in whose light alone can it be thought and
said what the name "God" must name (Heidegger, quoted in ID,
209–10). Even in these later contexts, the subjection of God to
the primacy of worldhood or to the truth of Being implies still a
subjection to *Dasein,* insofar as *Dasein* remains that being alone
for whom Being and world are ever an issue.

On Marion's reading, this persistent primacy of *Dasein* marks
the trace even in Heidegger of modern metaphysics' preoccupa-
tion with "the subject," and Marion's theology and phenomenology alike will involve a thoroughgoing critique of that subject.

---

[12] Derrida and John Caputo, among others, have addressed the instability of
this distinction. See, e.g., Derrida's *Aporias,* trans. Thomas Dutoit (Stanford:
Stanford University Press, 1993); *The Gift of Death,* trans. David Wills (Chicago:
University of Chicago Press, 1995); and *Specters of Marx,* trans. Peggy Kamuf (New
York: Routledge, 1994); and Caputo's treatment of these and other texts in *The
Prayers and Tears of Jacques Derrida: Religion without Religion* (Bloomington: Indi-
ana University Press, 1997). For my own approach to the issue, see "The Binds
that Tie the Ethical and the Religious: Philosophy of Religion after Derrida," in
Svensk Teologisk Kvartalskrift, Årg. 74 (1998), pp. 132–41.

The phenomenological critique aims to articulate what (historically) comes "after" the active, spontaneous subject of modern metaphysics[13] by thinking that which (logically) "precedes" such subjectivity: namely, the radically passive, nascent self, the *me* that precedes the *I*, which, "before" being a subject in the mode of consciousness or language, is *called* to be by the unconditional givenness of phenomenality, a givenness that reaches its summit in the "saturated phenomenon." Echoing or answering the theological God without Being, phenomenology offers explicitly an "I without Being"[14] that Marion names first the "*interloqué*" (the one fundamentally taken aback or surprised in its birth-through-response to an undefined call) and later the "*adonné*" (the one given over in its very genesis as a devoted witness or addict to the givenness of the originary call). Echoing the theological treatment of an inconceivably generous God beyond Being, the phenomenological subject as *interloqué* or *adonné* emerges solely as a function of givenness: "a subjecti[vi]ty entirely in keeping with givenness—one that receives itself entirely from what it receives, given by the given, given to the given" (ED, 373). Prior to the transcendental reduction of objective phenomena to a constituting ego (as in Husserl), and prior to any existential reduction of ontic phenomena to the ontological structures of *Dasein* (as in Heidegger), Marion's phenomenology insists on the necessity of a third reduction to pure "givenness" or "donation" itself[15]— which appears first in the *response* through which alone the *interloqué* or *adonné* receives both that givenness and, through givenness, itself: a self given by and to the given.

This will imply, among other things, that the phenomenological model of subjectivity, founded on the dynamic of generous

---

[13] The task of thinking what comes after the subject is one Marion shares with numerous post-Heideggerian thinkers, especially in France. A volume of essays by these thinkers takes the very title *Who Comes after the Subject?* and it is in that volume that Marion's phenomenological model of subjectivity first appears in English. See "L'Interloqué" in Eduardo Cadava, Peter Connors, and Jean-Luc Nancy, eds., *Who Comes after the Subject?* (New York: Routledge, 1991).

[14] See RMM, p. 66.

[15] Marion intends his French *donation* primarily to translate Husserl's *Gegebenheit,* which is fairly well rendered in English as "givenness." Such an English translation, however, which I often use (notably in *Reduction and Givenness*), loses something of the ambiguity held in both French and English by "donation"— which can indicate giving, the given, and givenness all at once.

call and receptive response, is a model tied essentially to the question of language. The facticity of birth, according to which I am constitutively delayed in my response to the call that first gives birth to me, is signaled by the linguistic givenness whose facticity appears clearly in the dis-appropriating "proper" name: "The 'proper' name results above all else from a call: it was given to *me* before I choose it, know it and even hear it: it was given to *me* because in fact *I* have been given [*interloqué*] as and to *me* [literally: *I* has been given as and to *me*] by the fact of this name" (RMM, 94; see also ED, 401–4). Just as I am always already called by a "proper" name that signals my originary "dispossession" or self-difference and delay, so that call returns over and again in the ever renewed response through which I would "name" but never comprehend the call: "The *adonné* has neither language nor *logos* as its properties, but rather finds itself endowed with them—as gifts, which show themselves only if the *adonné* gives them back [*redonne*] to their unknown origin.—Thus, only the response performs the call, and the *adonné* renders visible and audible what is given to it only by corresponding to it in the act of responding 'here I am!' [*me voici!*]" (ED, 397). Just as I am never present in any presence to receive the call that first gives birth to me, so my constitutive response will never reduce the call to the present presence in which I might comprehend and state it fully; my language, therefore, ever responsive, remains irreducibly open, which means that my endless naming of the call appeals finally to its anonymity.

For Marion, it is this endless naming of the anonymous that signals the temporalization of my historicity as *adonné*: "The respons [*le répons*][16] can annul its originary delay in relation to the call no more than that which shows itself can claim to exhaust that which gives itself. Hence the respons remains always to be completed, it is open to its historicity, which is therefore temporalized radically starting from the already given that is not yet shown" (ED, 418). Phenomenologically, the constitutive and ever delayed response of the *adonné*, wherein alone the given becomes

---

[16] Marion coins the term *répons* to indicate "a response" (*réponse*) that "opens visibility and gives voice to the call," that "makes it into a phenomenon instead of refuting and degrading it" (ED, p. 397).

the shown, "does not cease to rename," precisely, "the anonymity of the call" (ED, 418), which can never be overcome thanks to the insurmountable delay through which I "receive" the call.[17] Thus, on the basis of a temporalization that opens futurally in order ceaselessly to name and rename an always already given and therefore unnameable past, "the history of the *adonné* consists in nothing other than the uninterrupted but finally suspended series of its responses [*de ses répons*]" (ED, 418). In sum, the phenomenological model of subjectivity in which givenness (whose two sides are call and response) functions originarily is a model in which language, with its temporalization of delay, both gives me to myself and at the same time "dispossesses" me—for thanks to my natal delay I never master that language through which I am first called to be and in which, by responding, I come to be. The polyonymy in and through which I would respond endlessly to the sheer givenness marked by the facticity of language constitutes the reverse side of the radical anonymity out of which I will never fully draw that givenness.[18] The movement here between kataphatic and apophatic language, whose interplay issues from the fact that phenomenological givenness can, in its excess, appear as absence,[19] follows the core logic of the theological language that defines subjectivity already in *The Idol and Distance*.

---

[17] At this level I do believe that one can maintain the anonymity of the call in Marion's phenomenology against charges or suspicions such as Derrida's that the phenomenological call is really that of the Father. On Derrida's suspicion, see the much discussed note on p. 52 of *Given Time: I. Counterfeit Money*, trans. Peggy Kamuf (Chicago: University of Chicago Press, 1992). For my treatment of this question in Derrida and Marion, see "The Naming of God and the Possibility of Impossibility: Marion and Derrida between the Theology and Phenomenology of the Gift," chapter 6 of *Indiscretion: Finitude and the Naming of God* (Chicago: University of Chicago Press, 1999).

[18] In Marion's phenomenology, a (or perhaps the) paradigmatic instance of this dynamic can by seen in the Christ as doubly saturated phenomenon: "The fact that the Christ might receive a plurality of names, of which none state his essence, limits itself to reproducing the property of God himself of admitting all names and of rejecting them all (πολύωνυμον καὶ ἀνώνυμον)—the property of convoking an infinity of horizons of nomination in order to de-nominate the one who saturates not only each horizon but the incommensurable sum of horizons" (ED, p. 333).

[19] Of the numerous passages in *Etant donné* where Marion argues quite powerfully that intuitive saturation and intuitive poverty can prove indistinguishable, hence yielding an endless interplay between kataphasis and apophasis (esp. pp. 335–42), see, e.g., p. 340: "The paradox of paradoxes does not have to choose

Just as the *interloqué* or *adonné* comes to birth in—or more precisely as—an irreducibly delayed response to a call that, for this very reason, can never be defined or identified within the fullness or fixity of a name, even as it will provoke the infinite polyonymy of an endless response to that which remains forever anonymous, so already Marion's theological subject—which is modeled on the Christic subject himself—comes to birth in response to the inconceivable goodness, charity, or love of a God whom the subject can never identify or define in a name, but whom for this very reason the subject will name over and again ad infinitum. Just as, phenomenologically, givenness has always already given itself in a call to which my response is always belated, and just as the play of call and response would appear exemplarily in the facticity of language, so theologically, "the unthinkable speaks even before we think we hear it, anterior distance holds out to us a language that precedes and inverts our predication. More essential than the predication that we can (not) employ concerning the unthinkable, there occurs the donation of the Name" (ID, 143)—that is, the unnameable Name of Exodus 3:14 that is given to us ultimately through the Christ in whom, as Dionysius says in his third letter, the transcendent God "is hidden even amidst the revelation." As interpreted Christologically, the unnameable Name, the revelation of the hidden, "comes to us as unthinkable within the thinkable, because the unthinkable *in person* delivers it to us" (ID, 143).

This Christological approach to the giving of the Name in *The Idol and Distance* goes hand in hand with a Christological model of subjectivity. Out of a fundamental passivity, the human subject in Marion's theology receives language—and above all the Name—as a gift, and, emerging in response to that gift, the subject lives in a "Christic mode" (ID, 144) of humanity that involves a "linguistic model of the dispossession of meaning" (ID, 144). That is, the subject who receives language fundamentally as gift never masters in language the fact of such givenness itself. The impossibility of such mastery implies the necessity of a nonpredi-

---

between kataphasis and apophasis any more than between the saturation and the poverty of intuition—it uses them all in order to push to its limits the phenomenality of that which shows itself only inasmuch as it gives itself." For my reading of this important issue, see chapter 6 of *Indiscretion*, esp. pp. 229–36.

cative discourse, such as the hymnic discourse of praise in Dionysius, which would attempt to speak that which remains ineffable.
Hence, just as the Word receives his Name from the Father in
distance and submits his will to the will of the Father even unto
death, so does the theological subject receive its language in such
a way that any possession of meaning through predication is lost,
and predicative discourse "dies" through negation and silence.
But just as Christic death gives way to Resurrection, so does the
silence of the theological subject give way to infinite proclama-
tions of praise (ID, 144). The gift of the unnameable Name
through distance implies the Christological truth that God withdraws in his approach and approaches through withdrawal; correlatively, the subjectivity born in relation to that gift undergoes
linguistically the Christological trial of a dispossession, death, and
silence that open to a resurrection in the nonpredicative discourse of praise or prayer.[20]

It is in just this prayerful response to the unnameable gift of
language, a response that remains ever open in the futural movement of language itself, that theological subjectivity itself first
comes to birth as the recipient of distance. In receiving the distance signaled by language, the theological subject receives nothing less than itself: "Anterior distance escapes every conception.
But precisely, must distance be conceived? Anterior distance conceives us because it engenders us. Distance is given only in order
to be received. Anterior distance demands to be received because
it more fundamentally gives us [the chance] to receive ourselves
in it (ID, 153)." In distance, where causal Goodness kenotically
gives itself in the call that calls us to be, we receive ourselves—we
are given to ourselves by the giving of divine generosity. And just
as the phenomenological subject would be opened to its temporalization and historicity thanks to the originary delay of a response that would endlessly name and rename the call that
provokes it, so the theological subject will live according to the

---

[20] In a debate that is now fairly well known, Derrida challenges Marion's interpretation of praise as nonpredicative in his essay on negative theology "How to
Avoid Speaking: Denials," in Harold Coward and Toby Foshay, eds., *Derrida and
Negative Theology* (Albany: State University of New York Press, 1992) (see esp.
note 16, pp. 136–38). I summarize and enter this debate in chapter 6 of *Indiscretion.*

temporality of that distance which "gives rise to an indefinite series of definitions . . . without any closure ever being able to exhaust the subject. Neither a subject of discourse, nor an object of
science, distance withdraws itself from definition by definition"
(ID, 199).

This reception in which we are first given to ourselves, according
both to the phenomenology of donation and to the theology of
distance, where language and its temporality are opened futurally
and irreducibly thanks to the gift or givenness in response to
which we are always already late, implies, furthermore, the constitutive repetition or redundancy (*redondance*) of the originary giving itself. Just as the givenness of the call in phenomenology
shows itself only in the response where the call is received and
becomes phenomenal, so already in Marion's theology, the paternal gift is received only to the degree that the recipient immediately gives that gift anew.

Phenomenologically, the call through which givenness exerts
itself appears only to the degree that it is received in a response
given to the call—the gift appears, in other words, only in being
regiven. As just indicated, in relation to the gift of language, "only
the response performs the call, and the *adonné* renders visible and
audible what is given to it only by corresponding to it in the act
of responding 'here I am'! [*me voici!*]" (ED, 397). I receive the
call that gives me to myself only to the degree that I am given over
responsively (or responsibly) to that call.[21] Reception of the gift,
then, occurs only in, or even coincides with, its regiving or redundancy—and such redundancy goes to the very heart of phenomenal givenness, "for that which gives itself shows itself only
inasmuch as it finds itself received by the *adonné*, whose proper
function consists in giving in return to the given [the chance]
to show itself; and such a conversion of the given into a shown

_____

[21] Here, as throughout Marion's thinking, Emmanuel Levinas is very much
present. Marion's phenomenology of the call, indeed, depends fundamentally
on the reversal of intentionality developed first by Levinas. For Marion, however,
that reversal of intentionality concerns not only or primarily the ethical accusation that first awakens me (as in Levinas) but rather the more general givenness
of phenomenality as such, which calls or constitutes me before I could ever
intend or constitute it.

phenomenon can therefore be realized only within the obviously finite field where the *adonné* receives and stages" (ED, 426). The given is shown, it becomes apparent in its givenness, only to the degree that a giving responds or corresponds to it, which means that the given cannot be kept without annulling it as given.

Likewise theologically, regiving or redundancy is essential to the paternal gift—an insight that Marion develops especially on the basis of Dionysius's hierarchical vision. There, in a reasoning that Marion takes as his own, Dionysius situates the redundant interplay between the generosity of giving and the responsiveness or responsibility of receiving within the hierarchical framework of emanation and return: "The gift that issues from the origin reaches the hierarchical terms only by giving itself, but the latter receive it only by giving themselves to that which they receive thus. The essential is perhaps this: each member receives the gift only in order to give it, such that this gift, in the same gesture, regives the gift in redundancy ('emanation') and, giving, sends the original gift back into its foundation ('return')" (ID, 165). The defining redundancy of the gift, central to Marion's phenomenology, is first articulated here in *The Idol and Distance* as a fundamentally theological truth that accounts for "everything": "To receive the gift amounts to receiving the giving act, for God gives nothing except the movement of the infinite kenosis of charity, that is, everything. Man therefore does not receive the gift as such except in welcoming the act of giving, that is, through repetition by giving himself" (ID, 166).[22] To a theological vision, "everything" is given by God through the infinite kenosis of charity, just as to phenomenological vision, "everything" without exception must obey the law of givenness (including nothing), since the given "such as it gives itself" is finally "without limit or reserve" (ED, 425). The reception of that gift, then, both theologically and phenomenologically, is a question of repetition and responsibility.

No repetition of the gift, however, no response or responsibility, is perfect, for every recipient of givenness is finite and there-

---

[22] It is a passage like this, of course, that allows one to understand Derrida's suspicion that, even in his phenomenological account of givenness, what Marion really wants to say is that everything is finally a gift from God.

fore repeats giving, or responds to giving, by regiving only in limited measure. This insight, which I will show to be decisive in Marion's most advanced phenomenology, first comes to light in the theological treatment of "participation" that we find in *The Idol and Distance*. The transcendently causal, unthinkable distance of Marion's theology manifests itself, in Dionysian terms, as Goodness, and "the unthinkable, as the distance of Goodness, gives itself—not to be comprehended but to be received" (ID, 155). —That is, the incomprehensible gift of Goodness in or as distance requires the response of reception, not the mastery of comprehension—which means for Marion that the unthinkable becomes thinkable only "for the one who knows how to receive it" (ID, 155). The incomprehensible Goodness to which we can respond only "unknowingly" demands at the same time that we "know" how to receive it (in our ultimate ignorance). The limits of such knowing, the limits of our very capacity to receive, will determine the degree to which an unlimited giving actually appears to us, for as Marion indicates, "the traverse through distance is measured solely according to the measure of the welcome that each participant can or cannot offer" (ID, 158). Divine generosity itself, then, knows no limits, and thus the limitations of its appearance are inherent not to that generosity itself but to our finite reception of it. "If distance delivers the unthinkable without measure," Marion insists, "the measure of the imparticipable participation will be fixed by each participant" (ID, 158).

The kind of logic articulated here in terms of the imparticipable participation operative in Dionysian contexts proves also decisive, although perhaps not highlighted, in Marion's phenomenology, where the limits of my ability to receive givenness (i.e., my absolute finitude) will need somehow to be reconciled with the still intact principle that "what gives itself shows itself" (ED, 426). According to Marion's core phenomenological position, givenness remains without limit or reserve, and what gives itself does necessarily show itself—but I do not always receive that self-showing, or it does not always appear for me. The apparent non-appearance of an over-full phenomenal givenness must therefore be my responsibility and not a defect or lack of givenness itself: "since its finitude determines the *adonné* essentially, it cannot by definition receive adequately the given *such as it gives itself—*

namely, without limit or reserve" (ED, 425; emphasis added). Just
as Marion insists theologically that the infinite self-giving of kenotic Goodness is met by my inevitably partial participation, so he
argues phenomenologically that the unrestricted givenness of
phenomenality appears to me only in part and according to the
limits of my finitude.

But what, phenomenologically, makes the difference between
what gives itself without restriction and what actually appears *for
me*? Marion attempts to reconcile the limits of my ability to receive
givenness with the foundational principle that what gives itself
shows itself by appealing, finally, to a pre-phenomenological obscurity or blindness and, therein, to a pre-phenomenological or
pre-rational choice or decision out of which alone any given phenomenon could ever become phenomenal: "At the birth of the
visible (at the conversion of that which gives itself into that which
shows itself), there comes into play, in a pre-phenomenological
and pre-rational obscurity, the choice or refusal of 'the great reason'—of unconditional givenness" (ED, 422). One must be careful to understand this choice correctly: if I move by choice or
decision from pre-phenomenological obscurity to the light of
phenomenal givenness, that choice or decision itself must not become an a priori condition of such givenness, for this would contradict Marion's entire project to free the unconditional from
subjection to any subject or first principle; the choice, then, to *see*
givenness must itself already be a function or gift *of* givenness
itself: "Nothing of what gives itself can show itself except to the
adonné and through it. Not through constitution, anticipatory decision, or exposure to the other,[23] but through the will to indeed
see, [which is] originally derived from givenness itself" (ED,
422). In other words, if I am able to convert the given into the
seen only through an act of decision wherein, from out of pre-
phenomenological blindness, I will to see, that decision and will
must themselves be given to me solely by the givenness that is to
be seen.[24] Phenomenological vision, then, is founded originally

---

[23] That is, not in Husserl, not in Heidegger, nor even in Levinas.

[24] Here establishing the phenomenological priority of will over understanding, Marion inverts the metaphysical scheme (seen, for example, in Descartes):
"What metaphysics stigmatizes as error defines, on the contrary, in phenomenological terms, the fundamental exercise of the respons [*répons*] such as it con-

in a pre-phenomenological act that looks something like the faith for which the Christ's divinity appears "evidently"—but only 'to those who have eyes to see' (ID, 172), that is, those who have been given to see. The logic of a faith that sees only to the degree that it receives the necessary will to see is a logic equally decisive to Marion's phenomenology and theology—even if the latter has an actual content while the former articulates only possibility.[25]

As I have noted, and as will be evident to the reader, Marion assumes in *The Idol and Distance* a faith in the insurpassable primacy of the Christian God's *self*-revelation. The properly *theo*-logical thinking that would answer such revelation, Marion's theology of distance, would be a theology of Goodness, generosity, charity, kenosis, or self-giving—and of all the other infinitely possible names for the inconceivable gift in response to which we would most fundamentally receive ourselves. Marion's theology would be, in short, if this were not redundant, a theology of love. And love, in the form of the ab-solute that "dissolves the tie that ties it to our thought" (ID, 141), would under no condition be subject to conditions. "The kenosis sets no condition for revealing itself," Marion's core assertion goes, "because in that revelation it gives itself and reveals nothing other than this unconditional gift. Our lack of respect, in a word, our 'unsuitability,' even grounded in ontological destiny, cannot set any condition upon this gift without precondition. For the mystery consists precisely in this: God loves those who do not love him, manifests himself to those who turn away, and all the *more* that they turn away" (ID, 215).

Just as the phenomenon "in its fullest sense" shows itself of itself and starting from itself, without precondition, even to the one who does not yet see it, so here in Marion's theology, God loves even those who do not love him, shows himself even to those

---

verts that which gives itself into that which shows itself. For in order to phenomenalize the given, it is necessary first to admit it ('to will' indeed to see it) and to receive oneself from it as being given over to it, in order thus to see (eventually to comprehend through 'understanding') what it shows. The decision to respond, and hence to receive, precedes the possibility of seeing, and hence of conceiving" (ED, p. 420).

[25] At this point one might question anew Marion's insistence in 1991 that, "as soon as it is no longer a question of theology or history, but of phenomenology, the givenness of what is at issue requires replacing (or confirming) an indirect faith or tradition with an immediate intuition" (RMM, p. 67).

who do not yet see him. And just as my will to see phenomenal givenness would itself be a function of that givenness itself, so here my eventual capacity to love and to see God would be given first and only by God's love for me. At this level the structure of Marion's phenomenological vision and the structure of his theological vision are strikingly similar, if not isomorphic: if I see the givenness of the phenomenon, which means if I give myself to it by repeating the act of giving, this is only because that givenness first gave me to myself and moved me to receive givenness in my very being; if I love God, which means if I give myself to him in the love that gives me to others, this is only because God first loved me even when I was not, and moved me to love in my very being.

Such an isomorphism would not mean, as many argue or assume, that Marion's phenomenology is "really" or "only" an indirect means to advance his theology. It could mean, however, that Marion's theology and phenomenology inform one another in more subtle and complex ways than Marion himself sometimes wants to allow. This would stand to reason if Marion's distinction between the historically actual (Revelation, the domain of revealed theology) and the phenomenologically possible (the saturated phenomenon, revelation treated phenomenologically, apart from faith or tradition) finally proves itself unstable. As suggested by the structural similarities I have outlined in this introduction, it could well be the case that one's conception of the possible is substantially and inevitably shaped by what one already takes to be actual—just as one's understanding of the actual would always already be framed by what one imagines to be possible. As Derrida argues of the founding and the founded in Heidegger, so here, perhaps, one could never be sure whether the possible is indebted to the actual or the actual to the possible; one would remain undecided as to which constitutes an example of which.

Perhaps it would be in the light (or obscurity) of such undecidability that we should read the fact that Marion's most developed phenomenological work, *Etant donné*, ends by pointing toward a possible treatment of love—which is precisely where, as indicated by *The Idol and Distance*, his theology actually begins.

THOMAS A. CARLSON

ENGLISH EDITIONS USED

The following English editions have served as references for the translation of quotations in *The Idol and Distance*. When I rely wholly or mainly on the published English translation, I indicate such by citing the translator and page number (following references to the original text and/or its French translation). When I have modified the published English translation, I indicate such by "mod."

Dionysius the Areopagite

While they do not usually appear here word for word, I have nevertheless relied considerably on the translations of the Dionysian writings by Colm Luibheid in *Pseudo-Dionysius: The Complete Works* (New York: Paulist Press, 1987).

Martin Heidegger

"The Onto-theological Constitution of Metaphysics," in *Identity and Difference*. Trans. Joan Stambaugh. New York: Harper and Row, 1969.

Friedrich Hölderlin

For translations of the following poems, I have relied on *Friedrich Hölderlin: Selected Poems and Fragments,* trans. Michael Hamburger (London: Penguin Books, 1994):
  "Bread and Wine"
  "Celebration of Peace"
  "Greece"

"Homecoming"
"Menon's Lament for Diotima"
"The Only One"
"Patmos"
"The Rhine"
"What Is God?"

For translations of the following poems, I have relied on *Hymns and Fragments by Friedrich Hölderlin,* trans. Richard Sieburth (Princeton: Princeton University Press, 1984):
"In Lovely Blue"
"Mnemosyne"
"The Nearest the Best"
"The Vatican"
"We Set Out from the Abyss"

FRIEDRICH NIETZSCHE

Antichrist, trans. Walter Kaufmann, in *The Portable Nietzsche.* New York: Penguin Books, 1982.

Beyond Good and Evil, trans. Walter Kaufmann. New York: Random House, 1966.

Daybreak, trans. R. J. Hollingdale. Cambridge: Cambridge University Press, 1997.

Ecce Homo, trans. Walter Kaufmann. New York: Random House, 1967.

The Gay Science, trans. Walter Kaufmann. New York: Random House, 1974.

On the Genealogy of Morals, trans. Walter Kaufmann. New York: Random House, 1967.

Human, All Too Human, trans. R. J. Hollingdale. Cambridge: Cambridge University Press, 1996.

Thus Spoke Zarathustra, trans. Walter Kaufmann, in *The Portable Nietzsche.* New York:Penguin Books, 1982.

Twilight of the Idols, trans. Walter Kaufmann, in *The Portable Nietzsche.* New York: Penguin Books, 1982.

The Will to Power, trans. Walter Kaufmann and R. J. Hollingdale. New York: Random House, 1967.

OPENING

What you are about to read results, for me, from an evidence and an urgency. I have yielded to the one as to the other, not without misgivings and anxieties, but now also without regrets.

First the evidence: what the last (or next-to-last) metaphysical word calls the "death of God" does not signify that God passes out of play, but indicates the *modern* face of his insistent and eternal fidelity. Furthermore, that absence—when its place is directly delimited by a concept—pertains to what God says of Himself in his revelation through the Christ: namely, that it is from him that all paternity, in heaven and on earth, receives its name. In this sense, no "death of God" goes as far as the desertion of Christ by the Father on Good Friday; and from the bottom of the infernal abyss that opened at the very heart of our history, once and for all, there issues the insurpassable filiation that eternally confesses the paternity of the Father. Revealing himself as Father, God advances in his very withdrawal. For this reason, since Christ was son in the measure of such a *distance,* any "death of God," any "flight of the gods," finds both its truth and its overcoming in a desert that grows only in the measure that the Son traverses it toward the Father. The only thing I will try to say here is this: that the trinitarian play repeats in advance all of our desolations, including that of metaphysics, in a seriousness that is all the more serene, and in a danger that is all the more serious, insofar as they issue from love, from its patience, from its labor, and from its humility. In order to make possible the trinitarian repetition of the "death of God," I have turned to the theology of divine names. Here one is dealing with a theme so profoundly biblical and patristic that we cannot attribute to chance the fact that its quasi disappearance after (or with) Suarez coincided with the decline of dogmatic theology. Denys's enterprise obviously does not aim to reject all discourse concerning God, in favor of some dubious apophasis, but rather to work language deeply enough that it not enter into a methodological contradiction with that which it dares claim to express: a discourse of praise—which we should now risk. In this way *distance* is outlined.

It remained to follow as closely as possible the conceptual rigor to which the distance that we came to see in his works seemed susceptible. Within the contemporary horizon, distance refers immediately, with another—quite problematic—evidence, to difference. And primarily to the ontological difference of which, by hard-fought struggle, Heidegger conquered the site where it becomes thinkable—at the price and with the goal of a step back out of metaphysics. But then wouldn't the development with which one credited distance simply transpose—as a simple, arbitrary, and vain copy—the opening up of the Fold? Undoubtedly not, as soon as one recognizes more exactly the stakes of the dispute: what is the status of the commerce that God (such as the discourse of praise now aims at Him) maintains with Being—and Being such as metaphysics presents it, *or even* such as a "new beginning" would free it for another divine dwelling? If one holds that distance remains radically other than the question of Being (by an alterity itself still unthought), then it stands, for a moment, in alliance with the double critical authority that E. Levinas (in the name of the Other) and J. Derrida (by difference) graft upon the ontological difference. But it stands in such alliance only for a moment, since distance requires even more than the inversion or generalization of ontological difference. It remains then to take seriously the reprise to which Heidegger himself also submitted difference (in *Zeit und Sein*), by understanding it on the basis of the (anonymous?) donation of the gift. In this case, and in the breakthrough signaled by H. Urs von Balthasar, it becomes possible not, to be sure, to liken the gift where Being is sheltered to the gift where the Father (for-)gives us in the Son, but to sense that between them there plays a sort of redoubling of distance: distance places the gift of Being at a distance from itself, as its icon. And there also, there especially, "without change or confusion, without division or separation."

An urgency also: it led me, I have to admit, to omit some undoubtedly indispensable precautions and preliminaries. I mobilize here a precise conceptual pair, idol/icon, without giving it a sufficient phenomenological and cultural description: I freely admit this. And not without a certain violence, I transpose this pair from the properly cultural domain into the conceptual domain. With regard to the *idol,* this transposition can nevertheless be authorized by, for example, Second Isaiah (40:18, "According to what can you imagine God? And what idol (*demût*) of Him can you offer?"), and by Saint Athanasius. As for the *icon,* its theological semantics always went beyond the aesthetic meaning, which is founded only on the former, as was shown *a contrario* by iconoclasm. I invoke several authors (mainly Nietzsche, Hölderlin, Denys the Areopagite, M. Heidegger, E. Levinas, J. Derrida, and H. Urs von Balthasar). Why these references, and why such an assorted choice? Wouldn't I have gained much—and to begin with in readability—by moving forward openly toward an immediate declaration? Perhaps, but it could be that philosophy and theology come together in this (which opposes them to literature)—that they cannot advance a single step without a tradition that sustains them; that the relation to tradition should become a critical one in no way changes the dependency—on the contrary. Therefore, if I have advanced one step, then I owe that advancement to those who have given me something to think. I should specify further that I have attempted neither to cover myself with authorities (for the reading of an author doubles the risk rather than diminishing it) nor to critique supposedly heterodox thought (for their greatness never founders in simple heterodoxy), nor above all to impose on them a forced baptism (which, the indecency aside, would betray the officiant's little faith). I wanted to let myself be taught about distance by those who render it thinkable. To be sure, the revelation of the paternity of God does not await the confirmation or refutation of any thinkers, Christian or not; but it could be that we can reach the site that distance and modernity point out to us only if certain thinkers permit us to do so. Finally, I do not think that we need to enter into the false debate that would ask whether the authors invoked here indeed had the "intentions" that my interpretation would have lent to them: thinkers have no intentions, or, when they do, those intentions rarely stand up to the height of their thinking; the history of philosophy shows this sufficiently. The sole criterion for an interpretation is its fecundity. Anything that gives to think honors the one who gives it—on condition, of course, that the one who receives does think. I leave it up to the reader to judge whether the consequence confirms the principle.

This urgency and this evidence led me to privilege the marches of metaphysics. These marches, however, are not margins. They do not so much pass outside a territory as defend it. With this particularity: that the marches defend metaphysics not from external invaders but indeed from itself. Therefore, only the marches and their marquis maintain the possibility of taking onto-theological idolatry into view, and therefore of surpassing it, because they remain on the flank of metaphysics, without, however, deserting it in the decisive test. In order to raise a doubt— would we be dealing here with one of those posthumous and unsuitable prize givings where terroristic ridicule gives the dunce's cap to one and the cross to the other?—let me specify one point. In its greatest actors philosophy offers this interest and this charm: the more a thinker proceeds toward onto-theology, the more, by making it play clearly, he exceeds it. In such thinkers metaphysics assumes its onto-theological face only in being surpassed, at a certain point, by the thought of the icon. There is no doubt, for example, that Saint Thomas (provided one envisage him starting from the theory of analogy, itself seen according to the divine names), Descartes (reading him according to the idea of infinity), Kant (understood according to the transcendental imagination, but also the "appearance of reason"), Schelling (according to the stakes of subjecti-vi-ty), and a few others would allow one to advance quite far in the direction of what *distance* indicates. I have not, moreover, given up the pursuit elsewhere, in other forms, of what I outline here.

That I remain the only one responsible for what follows does not exclude (on the contrary) that nothing would have been possible without a good deal of help. To H. Urs von Balthasar my approach owes much, save the weaknesses in its implementation; the proportions of what is involved here nevertheless forbid me from transforming a dependency into an affiliation. I owe much to the remarks and criticisms of those who read part or all of the text—F. Alquié, J. Beaufret, J.-F. Courtine—or who assisted me with their advice—R. Roques, F. Fédier, G. Kalinowski, H. Birault. As for R. Brague, M. Costantini, and E. Martineau—they know what these pages owe to their own efforts and to our common encounters. Finally, I want to say that without the recent initiatives of P. Nemo and the oldest trust of Maxime Charles, I would have neither undertaken nor completed this collection. I hope that all will here accept my gratitude.

J.-L. MARION
Paris, 22 November 1976

The Idol and Distance

The Marches of Metaphysics

Remain the celestial, the one killed . . .

René Char

§ 1. THE IDOL

IT REMAINS, THEN, to question. To question a statement before debating its validity, before invalidating or affirming it. More than deciding whether or not "God is dead," I will ask, perhaps with greater reason and profit, under what conditions the statement "God is dead" becomes, or remains, thinkable. If what one names "God" passes into the emptiness of a death at a given point in the history of thought, let us say, to be simple, when a "madman" proclaims it to a public who hears nothing (and laughs), in the second half of a century that is numbered the nineteenth since the life, death, and (for some) resurrection of Jesus, the Christ, then that "God," from the very first, was not one. For a "God" who can die harbors already, even when he is not yet dying, such a weakness that from the outset he falls short of the idea that we cannot not form of a "God." And is it not the least of courtesies that he should satisfy a propaedeutic concept, even if it is only our own? A "God" who decides to die dies from the beginning, since he undoubtedly needs a beginning—which means that the "death of God" sets forth a contradiction: that which dies does not have any right to claim, even when it is alive, to be "God." What is it that dies in the "death of God" if not that which could not in any case merit the name of "God"? And therefore the "death of God" expresses, beyond the death of "God," the death of that which announces it: the death of the "death of God" itself. The contradiction of the terms of the proposition comes to completion in the self-erasure of the proposition: it renders null and void that which it states by annulling the object of the statement. Nevertheless, the statement still has meaning and pertinence, and we are not done meditating on it. Might not the argumentation that here denounces a sophism be itself, par excellence, sophistic, avoiding the true and fundamental question with a formal remark? Let us start again then. In order to establish an atheism in the modern sense of the term, that is, a doctrine that denies existence to any "supreme Being" (or the like), one requires a demonstration, and a rigorous one. One requires, therefore, a conceptual thinking that is compelling. And thus a concept of "God" is necessary here, a concept that would enter into the demonstration to provide the ultimate point on which it rests. It does not matter whether that concept is negative or positive, whether it issues from this or that cultural sphere, provided that it ensure a rigorous—that is, a defined—object for the demonstration. In its conclusion of exclusion, that demonstration is worth as much as the concept of "God" that sustains it. The reasoning of a conceptual atheism, which is the only compelling one, proceeds hypothetically: if "God" is x, while x is y (contradictory, illusory, dangerous, unhealthy, alienating, etc.), then "God" is y; therefore, if y suffices to disqualify that which it connotes (and we admit this), "God is dead." This calls for two remarks. First, that atheism, conceptual of course, is only ever valid as far as the concept of "God" that it mobilizes extends. For the demonstration that refutes "God" demands from him one last service: to furnish the object that supports and nourishes the refutation. If, then, "God" covers a particular semantic terrain, the refutation will not eliminate God absolutely but only the meaning of God that its initial "God" offers to be disputed. In order to refute the Absolute absolutely, it would be necessary, as it would be, moreover, to demonstrate a nonexistence in general, to enumerate exhaustively all the possible concepts of "God," in order to rely on them to the point of rejecting them all. Conceptual atheism becomes rigorous only by remaining regional. Thus can it ceaselessly reproduce itself and find new faces for itself. Thus can it progress without ever extinguishing, even for the one who practices it, even the hint of a question of God, as a question of the indeterminate itself—let us say, of the Ab-solute. Thus, finally, can the "believer" practice conceptual atheism just as well as the unbeliever: as a rigorous atheist with respect to a particular idea of God, the one who pronounces that atheism does not claim to decide on the Ab-solute. Atheism remains demonstrative by recognizing it-

self to be circumscribed. It is an atheism that is indefinitely dupli-
cated because rigorously finite.

Next, one notices the unevenness of conceptual atheism, or
rather the metamorphosis of the concept that sustains it. Before
the demonstration, the concept "God" neither permits nor mobilizes a refutation unless it attains, in one way or another, God,
whether the true God or the supposedly such. It is necessary that
the concept merit the attention of a polemic—in a word, that
"God" be God. But at its end, the completed demonstration takes
away from the initial concept of "God" any usefulness ("God is
dead"); consequently, the final disqualification springs back ret-
roactively upon the original point on which it rests; if one has
demonstrated that "God" does not hold, in what way has one
touched God? In fact, in order to conclude, the reasoning must
destroy the point on which it rests; but then it concludes nothing,
unless that the initial point of support in fact ensured no support
at all for the demonstration. The rigor of the conclusion is paid
for by the rigor of the condition: "God" is dead only if "God"
can die, that is, if in the first place it was not a question, in the
demonstration, of God. This reasoning highlights the contradiction of its object only by showing the emptiness of its success: only
the shadow of God, "God," remains prey to it. The prey rewards
it only with a skin. The demonstration locates, enumerates, and
authenticates shadows, which in return disqualify it: the more the
demonstration triumphs over so many indefinitely pursued
"Gods," the more it betrays the emptiness of the self-critical procedure that both qualifies and disqualifies it. Conceptual atheism
remains rigorous only by remaining not only regional but irrelevant. The collapse through self-critique projects it, moreover, into
the repetition of the critique. The path of regional critiques ensues, quite logically, from the unavoidable self-critique that concludes each of them. Atheism progresses with each of the
concepts of "God" that its self-falsification aims at, invests, and
rejects. Progress belongs to conceptual atheism as intimately as
suicidal humility characterizes it. Hence its indispensable theological function, as we shall see, and the respect that it is suitable to
show it.

But there remains, or there appears, an objection. Why suppose
there to be a contradiction in the sentence "God is dead"? Fur-

ther, why would the contradiction not be the sign of another rigor, that of the tautological and abstract identity "God is God"? Answer: there is no answer; the objection holds completely. But precisely, it holds only on certain conditions, among which are the following: that one renounce conceptual atheism in order to think death and contradiction on the basis of "God," that is, that one renounce the defined security of the quotation marks: that instead of forming a concept-object of "God," upon which to operate a refutation without any risk other than suicidal, one admit that God, by undefinable definition, remains problematic enough that no concept, not even those of death, contradiction, and "God," is sufficient to reform him as incapable of supporting or reinvesting them. In this case God becomes the center of a discourse that orders itself in relation to him, and that understands itself, modifies itself, even overcomes itself, so as to put itself in a position to overcome this last atheistic presupposition: that "God" is defined as one who does not resist death. Would it not be the case that conceptual atheism becomes rigorously conclusive only by ceasing to operate on "God" in order to begin asking itself about God? Would it not manage to do this only by undertaking to confront openly, without the ghostly and finite intermediaries that it domesticates so easily, God as a question? Perhaps. And all the more so insofar as those who meditated on the "death of God" most decisively—Hegel, Hölderlin, Nietzsche, Heidegger, and a few others (among whom Feuerbach is not)—read in that pronouncement something completely other than a refutation of (the existence of) God. They recognized in it the paradoxical but radical manifestation of the divine. We will be able to follow them "from afar" (Luke 22:54) only on condition, first, that we not confuse the death of "God" with the question of God, or more exactly, the "death of God" with the "twilight of the idols."

From God (*Gott*) to the idol (*Götze*), barely one letter is substituted, the last one. The gap that it manifests should become questionable for us: z/x, so to speak. Why the idol here? In order to perceive it, and to specify that upon which a crepuscular light today falls, it is necessary to outline the function, or rather the functioning, of the idol. This presupposes to begin with a certain reservation concerning not the idol but indeed the overly easy

critique that one commonly gives of it. The idol does not person-
ify the god, and consequently it does not deceive the worshipper
who does not see the god in person in it. Quite to the contrary,
the worshipper knows himself to be the artisan who has worked
with metal, wood, or stones to the point of offering the god an
image to be seen (εἴδολων) so that the god should consent to
take on a face in it. The divine does not produce the idol and
does not show up as an idol. The worshipper is perfectly aware
that the god does not coincide with the idol. What, then, does the
worshipper worship in the idol? The face that the god, or rather
the divine, wants to find in it. More exactly, perhaps, what man,
in the city or community, experiences as divine, as the divinity
that precedes any face and any image. Man becomes religious by
preparing a face for the divine: he takes it upon himself to fashion
the face, and then to ask the divine to invest it, as radically as
possible, so as to become his god. Who can decide on the authenticity of the divine that is thus envisaged in the idol? Who can
disqualify the form wherein humanity archaically outlines its silhouette in order, like the κοῦρος, to give to the divine the principal form of Apollo? Who can deny that the chosen divinity
remains in what is delimited by the columns, pediments, and
spacings of a Doric temple? Iconoclastic crudeness sometimes
overturns idols because it does not understand them, or more,
does not see them. Is it necessary, however, to receive the idol as
a correct face of the divinity? Without any doubt, but on condition that the nature of such a divinity be evaluated. It falls to man
to experience and establish it. In the idol the human experience
of the divine precedes the face that that divinity assumes in it. We
experience ourselves at our best in the divine. We fashion a face
in order to ask the divine to open up in it, to look at us in it, to
smile and to threaten. The idol must fix the distant and diffuse
divinity and assure us of its presence, of its power, of its availability. Just as our experience precedes the face of the divine, so our
vital interest proceeds from it: the idol fixes the divine for us permanently, for a commerce where the human hems in the divine
from all angles. What is peculiar to the idol, therefore, has to do
with this: the divine is fixed in it on the basis of the experience of
the divine that is had by man, who, by relying on the idol's mediation, attempts to attract the benevolence and the protection of

what appears in it as a god. The idol presupposes neither the trickery of the priest nor the stupidity of the crowd (as certain biblical authors repeatedly agree, as well as do, beyond the Fathers, including Augustine, Bayle, Fontenelle, and Voltaire). It is characterized solely by the subjection of the divine to the human conditions for experience of the divine, concerning which nothing proves that it is not authentic. The human experience of the divine precedes the idolatrous face. The idolatrous face elaborated by man precedes its investiture by the god. In the idol the divine undoubtedly assumes the actual face of a god. But that god takes its form from the features that we have fashioned for it, in conformity with what we actually experience concerning the divine. In the cases of life and death, of peace and war, of love and drunkenness, of spirit and beauty, we indisputably experience the irrepressible and panic capital of the divine, and we decipher or divine therein faces that we model in order that we might fix so many gods in them. These gods, therefore, conform first to us, or, less summarily, to the modalities of our multiform perception of the divine. The idol reflects back to us, in the face of a god, our own experience of the divine. The idol does not resemble us, but it resembles the divinity that we experience, and it gathers it in a god in order that we might see it. The idol does not deceive; it apprehends the divinity. It apprehends the divinity, and, even when it terrorizes, it reassures by identifying the divinity in the face of a god. Hence its prodigious political effectiveness: it renders close, protective, and faithfully sworn the god who, identifying himself with the city, maintains an identity for it. This is indeed why politics always gives rise to idols, even after paganism; "Big Brother," the "Great Helmsman," the *Führer,* or the "Man we love best" must be divinized: made into gods, they conjure the divine or, more vulgarly, destiny. Idolatry gives the cult of personality its true dignity—that of a familiar, tamed (and therefore undangerously terroristic) figure of the divine. Idolatrous temptation for ancient Israel always depended on political necessities. Conversely, it is to politics first that our time owes the fact that we are not lacking for new idols.

The idol therefore delivers us the divine, wherefore it neither deceives nor disappoints. It delivers the divine to us to the point of enslaving it to us, just as much as it enslaves us to it. The contract that the idol draws up subsidizes the absence of the gods. It is to that very familiarity that one must attribute the disappearance of the sacred and of polytheism, which the late seventeenth century definitively censures: twilight of the divine. Perhaps more surely than any rationalist and/or Christian critique, an overabundant and polymorphous deification annihilated the play of the idol, of the divine, and of the gods. In fact, what the idol works to reabsorb is, precisely, the distance and the withdrawal of the divine: but by establishing such an availability of the divine within the fixed, if not frozen, face of the god, does one not deceitfully but radically eliminate the lofty irruption and the undeniable alterity that properly attest the divine? Subsidizing the absence of the divine, the idol makes the divine available, secures it, and in the end distorts it. Its culmination mortally finishes the divine. The idol attempts to bring us close to the divine and to appropriate it to us: because he fears atheism (in the original sense: being deserted by the gods),[1] the worshipper puts his hand on the divine in the form of a god; but that handling loses what it seizes: there remains to it but an amulet that is too well known, too manipulable, too secure. Everything is set up to allow a Feuerbachian reappropriation of the divine: since, like a mirror, the god reflects back to me my experience of the divine, why not reappropriate for myself what I attribute to the reflection of my own activity? The inversion of the attribution of attributes (a reversed exchange of properties) presupposes that the latter are taken in the same way for both the god and the worshiper. Such a univocity presupposes in its turn that no distance keeps the idol outside of my reach. I attribute to myself the properties of the divine only if properties can be common both to me and to the divine—that is, only if the divine always already belongs to my sphere, as an idol that is close and, for that very reason, vain. Considering the divine as "prey to be captured" (Paul, Philippians 2:6), the idol lacks the distance that identifies and authenti-

---

[1] In this sense, see Saint Paul: "Remember that at that time you were without Christ, excluded from the city of Israel, foreign to the covenants of the promise, without hope, atheists without God in this world!" (Ephesians 2:12). On ἄθεος, see G. Kittel, *Theologisches Wörterbuch zum neuen Testament*, the θέος article, s.v., by Stauffer, vol. III, pp. 120–22; French trans., *Dictionnaire biblique*, G. Kittel, "Dieu" (Geneva: Labor et fides, 1968), pp. 120–24.

cates the divine as such—as what does not belong to us but befalls us. To the idol, by counterpoint, answers the icon. Whose face does the icon offer? "Icon of the invisible God" (Colossians 1:15), says Saint Paul of Christ. It is the figure not of a God who in that figure would lose its invisibility in order to become known to us to the point of familiarity, but of a Father who radiates with a definitive and irreducible transcendence all the more insofar as he unreservedly gives that transcendence to be seen in his Son. The depth of the visible face of the Son delivers to the gaze the invisibility of the Father as such. The icon manifests neither the human face nor the divine nature that no one could envisage but, as the theologians of the icon said, the relation of the one to the other in the hypostasis, the person.[2] The icon conceals and reveals that upon which it rests: the separation in it between the divine and its face. Visibility of the invisible, a visibility where the invisible gives itself to be seen as such, the icon reinforces the one through the other. The separation that joins them in their very irreducibility finally constitutes the ground of the icon. *Distance,* which it is above all no longer a question of abolishing, but of recognizing, becomes the motif of vision, in the double sense of motif: a motivation and a figurative theme. The topology of the mirror, where the idol reflected back to us the authentic but closed image of *our* experience of the divine, is replaced by the typology of the prism: a multiplicity of colors breaks down, or rather orchestrates, that which a prism multiplies according to our power to see—light called white (which it is not) since it remains invisible at the very moment that it renders all things visible. We should remark that in the art of the icon, the codified colors (gold, red, blue, yellow, etc.) do not resemble any "thing" that is supposed to be intrinsically colored thus; their significance is affirmed within a purely semiotic (in this case liturgical) field, where they announce eternity, divinity, glory, humanity, etc. The colors serve in no way as signs of visible things that one would have to give to be seen, because they already are so (to re-produce). They signal from the visible to the irreducible invisibility

---

[2] See L. Oupensky, *Essai sur la théologie de l'icône* (Paris: 1960); P. Evdokimov, *L'Art de l'icône* (Paris: D.D.B., 1970); and especially C. von Schönborn, o.p., *L'Icône du Christ: Fondements théologiques élaborés entre le 1er et le 2e concile de Nicée* (Fribourg, Switzerland: Editions Universitaires, 1976).

that it is a question of producing, of making advance into the visible inasmuch as invisible. The icon properly manifests the nuptial distance that weds, without confusing, the visible and the invisible—that is, the human and the divine. The idol tries to abolish that distance through the availability of the god who is placed permanently within the fixity of a face. The icon preserves and highlights that distance in the invisible depth of an insurpassable and open figure. For the point of view of desire, and therefore of the idolatrous object, as opposed to a god whose insistence one both fears and hopes for at the same time, a god that makes itself a little too pressing and that one can thus lead in one's own way, the icon substitutes a sort of negative theophany: the figure remains authentically insurpassable (norm, self-reference) only in that it opens in its depths upon an invisibility whose distance it does not abolish but reveals.

Hence a question: can the dialectic of atheism, and of the concept that supports but disqualifies it, have any decisive relation with the idol? As idol, the concept arranges a presence of the divine without distance, in a god who reflects back to us our experience or thought, with enough familiarity that we always master its play. It is always a question of keeping the foreignness of the divine out of play through the idolatrous filter of the concept or through the facelike conception of an idol. It is just such a function of the concept of "God" that we must now clarify. From there another question could arise: could not the concept function, also and first, as icon, in the sense that, just as the icon offers the figure of the invisible, "words are not the translation of something else that was there before them"[3] (L. Wittgenstein) but the very pronouncement of what remains at the same time forever ineffable?

§ 2. THE "GOD" OF ONTO-THEOLOGY

Thus, one could interpret the concept, or rather concepts, of "God" as idols, or rather as agents of what the idol, for its part, also brings about—the making available of the divine in a face,

---

[3] Wittgenstein, *Zettel*, § 191; French trans., *Fiches* (Paris: Gallimard, 1970).

which one names the god. Therefore, the philosopher or, better, the metaphysician names the divine: he fixes it as ἰδεα τοῦ ἀγάθου (Plato), as νοήσεως νόησις (Aristotle), as the One (Plotinus). He introduces between the divine, or later the God of Jesus Christ, and naming a simple, banal—and formidable—equals sign; he will speak, like Kant, for example, of the "existence of a moral founder of the world, *that is to say* of God."[4] There is no difficulty in the fact that such a concept might be established by the philosopher as playing the role of a foundation or of a principle of the divine; or, if there is a difficulty, it concerns only the philosopher and his own effort at thinking. That at the end of the demonstration, once the divine has been rigorously identified in a particular concept (once the "proof for the existence of God" has been completed, as one says, or used to say), the philosopher should surreptitiously identify, as if obviously and easily, *this* concept of the divine with something or someone indicated by *God*— this would find confirmation only if God himself confirmed the identification. In short, the question of the existence of God is posed less before the proof than at its end, when it is no longer a question simply of establishing that some concept can be called *God,* nor even that a certain being puts that name into operation, but more radically that that concept or that being coincides with God himself. Thus the five ways that Saint Thomas traces out do not lead absolutely to God; the first leads to the first mover and, once the demonstration has ended, must add innocently, in passing, "and everyone understands this to be God"; the second leads to the first efficient cause, of which it is still necessary to specify that "everyone names it God"; the third leads to the cause of a necessity, which it is still necessary to identify as "what everyone says to be God"; the fourth recognizes a cause of perfection but must also admit that "we say that it is God"; the fifth, finally, indeed locates a final end but must also underline that "we say that it is God."[5] Question: who states the equivalence between the ultimate term at which the demonstration—and therefore rational discourse—ends and the God whom "all" recognize? "All,"

---

[4] Kant, *Critique of Judgement,* § 87.

[5] Saint Thomas, *Summa Theologica,* Ia, q. 2, a. 3. See also *Summa contra Gentiles,* I, 13, and Duns Scotus, *Opus Oxoniense* I, d. 3, q. 2, a. 4, n. 10.

no doubt, but by what right? Who are these "all," and why can they establish an equivalence that neither the theologian nor the philosopher grounds, but upon which they ground themselves? Upon what foundation does the discourse here rest so as to assimilate to a God outside of all discourse the concepts of first, unmoved mover, efficient cause, necessity, perfection, and end? One might respond, perhaps, that with Thomas Aquinas the saint also speaks, that the religious man mobilizes authorities that are other than conceptual, that the philosopher finally appeals to theology (and here, precisely, to the doctrine of divine names that Question XIII will examine). These correct remarks support the Thomistic procedure only by rendering it even more questionable: one therefore needs an authority external to the proof in order that the proof become a "way" that leads to the referent that remains outside of all discourse and properly other (divine). The conceptual discourse admits that it does not produce that authority, since it reaches its ultimate result only through the ungrounded parenthetical phrase of a "that is to say" that is all the less evident insofar as is given as such. When other recourses disappear (such as the *sensus Ecclesiae,* theology as such, holiness), when the consensus of "all" is replaced by the idiomatic phrase "by this I mean . . . ," who will still be able to guarantee the well-foundedness of the equivalence between a probing discourse and its beyond? When Malebranche posits that "By divinity we mean Infinity, Being without restriction, infinitely perfect Being,"[6] he hardly says more, and perhaps even less, than Descartes—"By the name of God, I mean a certain infinite, independent, supremely intelligent, supremely powerful substance"[7]—and than Spinoza—"By God, I mean an absolutely infinite being, that is, a substance made up of infinite attributes."[8] The coincidence of a consensus is now replaced by a perhaps simply nominal definition that attempts to hem in the irreducible Other with a verbal infinity. Properly speaking, what affinity remains between the already

---

[6] Malebranche, *Entretiens sur la Métaphysique et sur la Religion,* VIII, § 1, in *Oeuvres complètes* (Paris: Vrin, 1965), vol. XII–XIII, p. 174. See also *Recherche de la Vérité,* II, II, VIII, § 1, in ibid., vol. I, p. 456 (Paris, 1962).

[7] Descartes, *Meditatio III,* in *Oeuvres,* ed. Adam-Tannery, vol. VII, p. 45, lines 11–13.

[8] Spinoza, *Ethics,* I, definition 6.

supreme being and the phantom-like silhouette that is woven by infinities that are redoubled infinitely in a perhaps meaningless inflation? The closer the concept comes that holds the place of the divine, the more its claim to take its place becomes suspect. When, crowning this labor, Hegel finally states what thought had been aiming at since the ruin of the theories of analogy, and postulates that revealed religion is identical with manifest religion, because "the divine nature is the same (*dasselbe*) as human nature, and that very unity is what needs to be taken into view,"[9] he perhaps indicates the supreme proximity of the divine only by carrying to its highest point the suspicion that the divine, here, coincided with the human only inasmuch as it was never distinguished from it, and never offered anything other than its image reflected by infinity. Feuerbach will do nothing other than formulate this suspicion. The irreducible gap between the final concept and the first approach of God never shone forth as much as with the identification of "God" with the discourse of proof. It does not suffice arbitrarily to baptize that last concept, at the price of a play on words (*Geist*, for example), or a falsely evident equivalence ("that is"), in order for thought to reach, in addition to its proof, what that proof aims at—the divine, or even God himself. Everything happens as if thought led easily, rigorously, and demonstratively to a final concept so as to grasp in it that which takes the place of God: a conceptual Tantalus. The proximity of the idol masks and marks the flight of the divine, and of the separation that authenticates it. By excessively appropriating "God" to itself through proof, thought separates itself from separation, misses distance, and finds itself one morning surrounded by idols, by concepts, and by proofs, but abandoned by the divine— atheistic. Hence, in this sense, the radically atheistic pronouncement of metaphysics, that of Leibniz: "Thus it is necessary that sufficient Reason, which has no need of another Reason, be outside this succession of contingent things, and be found in a substance, which is a cause, or which is a necessary Being, carrying within itself the reason for its existence; otherwise one would not yet have a sufficient reason in which one might finish. And it is

---

[9] *Phänomenologie des Geistes,* ed. Hoffmeister, p. 529. See also the *Encyclopedia of the Philosophical Sciences,* § 593.

this final reason for things that is called God."[10] In what way can sufficient reason, as final reason (*ultima ratio*) made substance, in a word, as the hypostasis of the principle of reason, that is, of the principle of our comprehension of all beings, claim, as little as that might be, to identify itself with God? If it does claim to do this, in what way does that claim avoid interposing an idolatrous face between the divine separation and the human gaze? If it does claim to do so, as it seems to, in the name of what rigor does it produce such a conceptual idol?

It would be necessary to think here, as much as a summary thought can claim to, of what Heidegger renders comprehensible under the title of the onto-theological constitution of metaphysics. Where until now I have written "philosopher," it was in fact necessary to understand "thinker of metaphysics." The production of a concept that makes a claim to equivalence with God indeed pertains to metaphysics. For the question of knowing how God enters into philosophy is decided, in the sense that Heidegger proceeds, only on the basis of philosophy itself, on condition, however, that we understand philosophy in its essence, namely, in its historial face as metaphysics. Metaphysics thinks Being, but in its own way. It does not cease to think it, but only on the basis of the beings that Being sets forth or in which Being puts itself into play.[11] Thus Being, which coincides with no being (ontological difference), nevertheless gives itself to be thought only in the case of a being. Indeed, being declines in a substantive manner a neuter participle (ὄν) that is governed, if one is vigilant to it, by the verbality that thus undertakes to be, that is, to let be. The same ὄν wavers between a being (a "thing") and an undertaking to be, only in that first and more fundamentally ὄν conjoins, composes, and unfolds these two operations, or, if one will, these two interpretations, as one and the same. What Heidegger thus designates

---

[10] *Principes de la Nature et de la Grâce*, § 8, *Philosophischen Schriften*, ed. Gerhardt, vol. VI, 602. See also "Est illud Ens sicut ultima ratio Rerum, et uno vocabulo solet appelari Deus," in *Opuscules et Fragments inédits*, ed. Couturat (Paris, 1903, and Hildesheim, 1966), p. 534.

[11] Here, as throughout the translation, the distinction between the capitalized "Being" and the lowercase "being" corresponds to the distinction between the substantive use of the infinitival *être* and the participial *étant*, which itself corresponds to the distinction in Heidegger's German between *Sein* and *Seiendes*. [Trans.]

as unfolding, refolding, and fold, metaphysics ends up understanding in its own way, which means not understanding it as
such; thus, it privileges beings in their Being, more than Being,
which no being reifies and which, nevertheless, promotes each
being. Metaphysics deploys this privilege of beings in and over
their Being in two ways. First, by thinking, in the mode of the
question that opens Book Z of Aristotle's *Metaphysics,* ὄν as οὐσία
essence, or, if one will, even substance,[12] but especially the privilege of presence over the other temporalizations of time (which
"past" and "future" no longer give, since they are ordered on
the basis of the present). This privilege delivers Being in presence, and in the beings that spring from it, but it also annuls
Being in it. Thus, since a being, inasmuch as present, presents the
achievement of Being, Being manifests itself all the more (verbally) insofar as a being presently (substantially) remains the
place of presence. Hence, second, the movement to the supreme
being. The supreme being in its turn delivers the most present
figure of presence, which alone permits each—nonsupreme—
being to remain already. The supreme being in this sense, exemplarily, grounds each being in its Being, since Being plays fully in
it as presence. But conversely, that supreme being itself finds its
ground only in the present beingness in which Being is bound up
and expressed. If Being did not announce itself in presence, the
supreme being would exercise no foundational decision concerning other beings. This reciprocal play between the Being of beings
in general (ontology, general metaphysics) and the supreme
being (special metaphysics, theology) does not define the onto-
theological constitution of metaphysics but results from it and, in
a sense, marks its profound conciliation (*Austrag,* as Heidegger
says): "The onto-theological constitution of metaphysics proceeds
from the superior power of Difference, which holds separated
one from another, and related one to another (*aus- und zueinan-
derhält*), Being as ground and beings as what is rationally grounded

---

[12] On this point, we should note that the equation of οὐσία and "subject,"
and therefore also its comprehension as "substance," denotes the properly
metaphysical turn that occurs at the very heart of Aristotle's thought. See R.
Boehm, *La Métaphysique d'Aristote: Le fondamental et l'essential,* translated from the
German and presented by E. Martineau (Paris: Gallimard, 1976).

and grounding (*als gegründet-begründendes*)."[13] The reciprocity of beings in their Being and of the supreme being is constituted in their relation of mutual grounding. The supreme being gives the reason for beings in their Being, but thereby shows Being at work, including and first in itself. In this play—engendered characteristically by metaphysics—the supreme being is called upon only to ensure the foundation; making the theology of onto-theology culminate on this point, Leibniz will say in order to "give reason" in "carrying the reason for its existence within itself." It can give the reason for beings in an absolutely satisfactory (sufficient) manner only by giving the reason for itself by itself. Thereby, it does not so much attain ontic independence as manifest its radical dependence with regard to onto-theology, which gives rise to and finds in it the *ultima ratio* that it needs in order to give the reason for (in the sense that one gives up one's arms) other beings infinitely multiplied by their finitude. Thus, "The Being of beings, in the sense of ground, can be represented fundamentally only as *causa sui*. But that is to name the metaphysical concept of God. Metaphysics must think far ahead in the direction of God, because Being is the business of thought, but Being taken in the multiple ways of foundation: as λόγος, as ὑποκείμενον, as substance, as subject," "Conciliation puts Being forward to us and confers it upon us as the ground that brings and presents, a ground that itself needs a rational grounding (*Begründung*) appropriate to it on the basis of what it itself rationally grounds, that is, on the basis of a causation (*Verursachung*) by the most primordial thing (*ursprünglichste Sache*). Which is the cause (*Ursache*) as *causa sui*. Thus sounds, in the measure of that which is in question, the name that God has in philosophy."[14] Descartes's thinking, which is the first to think God as *causa sui* on the basis of the exuberance

---

[13] Heidegger, *Identität und Differenz* (Pfullingen: G. Neske, 1957), p. 63 = French trans. in *Questions* I (Paris: Gallimard, 1968), p. 305. See also, in addition to the whole of this text, *Wegmarken*, particularly "Einleitung zu 'Was ist Metaphysik?'" (Frankfurt a/M: V. Klostermann, 1967), p. 208 = French trans. in *Questions* I, p. 41. The translation of *Austrag* by "conciliation" renders almost nothing of the German, except the most common sense (arrangement, organization, etc.), thus concealing the self-withdrawal (*aus*) through which Being sustains beings (*trag*), all the while abandoning visibility to them. For the sake of convenience, I nevertheless keep the usual translation, despite this insufficiency.

[14] Heidegger, *Identität*, p. 51, then p. 64 = French trans., pp. 294, 306.

of his power, finds in Leibniz its authentic metaphysical status.
The supreme being, provoked by the onto-theological constitution of metaphysics, completes its grounding-in-reason, which is
its sole raison d'être (the supreme being), only by becoming an
absolute ground, a ground that grounds itself. Metaphysics does
not attain and does not conceive the divine, the gods, and still
less God, for themselves, but it meets them as if by accident, along
the detour (sometimes experienced brutally by the two parties)
of a process that goes from the ἀκρότατον ὄν to the *causa sui*—
which means that "the theological character of ontology does not
have to do with the fact that Greek metaphysics was later taken
up and transformed by the ecclesial theology of Christianity. It
has much rather to do with the manner in which being, from the
beginning, is un-concealed (*entborgen*) as being"; "God can enter
into philosophy only in the measure that the latter, of itself and
in conformity with its essence, demands that, and specifies how,
God enters into it."[15] The supreme being of metaphysics, which
culminates in the figure of the *causa sui*, depends fundamentally
on the very essence of metaphysics and, finally, on nothing other.
Moreover, this is why the supreme being, and with it an onto-
theological constitution, remains the same where God, as Christian, disappears. One could show this easily for Feuerbach (M.
Stirner did it, in the case of B. Bauer); one has already tried to
show it for Marx; as for Nietzsche, Heidegger himself indicated it
in a central manner (§§ 4–6). This, moreover, is why Plato, Aristotle, and Plotinus did not await Christianity in order to put the
onto-theological constitution into operation. The supreme being,
whatever it may be, belongs to metaphysics and finds in it alone
its rigor, its scope, and its limits.

Hence a directive for thought that is absolutely decisive for my
argument. The *causa sui* is theologically valid only in onto-theology, where it masters the divine function and uses it at the very
moment that it reveres it. The characteristics of the idol are
equally suitable for a "God" who serves as ground, but himself
receives a ground; a God who expresses supremely the Being of

---

[15] Heidegger, *Wegmarken*, p. 208 = p. 40, and *Identität*, p. 47 = p. 290. See also
Questions IV (Paris, Gallimard, 1976), p. 64; *Vorträge und Aufsätze* I, p. 42 =
French trans. in *Essais et Conférences* (Paris: Gallimard, 1958), p. 56; *Wegmarken*,
p. 180 = French trans. in *Questions* II (Paris: Gallimard, 1966), p. 131.

beings in general and, in this sense, reflects back to them a faithful image of that whereby they are and of that which they are supremely; a God who remains distant from common ontology only within a Conciliation (*Austrag*) that preserves a fundamental familiarity. Produced by and for onto-theology, this "God" is ordained by it like the idol by the city (unless the political game of the idol refers back, conversely, to onto-theology)—with this slight difference that the idol here remains conceptual: not only does it not refer back, like the icon, to the invisible, but it does not even any longer offer any face where the divine looks at us and gives itself to be stared at: "To this God man cannot pray or offer anything, nor can he fall before him in respect, nor play music or dance. Consistent with this, a-theistic thought [*gott-lose* in the Pauline sense], which must abandon the God of the philosophers, God as *causa sui,* is perhaps closer to the divine God. Which means only this: the latter is more freely open than onto-theology would like to believe."[16] It would perhaps be necessary to admit that another path remains open—that which would attempt to envisage, as concerns the divine, another figure than the onto-theological "God." And it would perhaps be necessary to admit therefore that the death of such a "God" does not close that other path or affect the possibility of keeping oneself open for the divine *Wesen* (as Heidegger says, we shall see, in the case of Nietzsche, in § 4). How should we proceed in order to reach that opening? It would be a little too visibly facile to oppose a "true" God to the "God" of onto-theology since, in fact, for us, the one and the other are historially imbricated. Perhaps it would be necessary first to keep silent: "Whoever has any experience of theology taken in its developed completion, whether it be the theology of Christian faith or, just as well, that of philosophy, prefers today to keep silent, as soon as he approaches the domain of the thought of God."[17] But in order to keep silent, it is not enough no longer to be able to say anything, nor even no longer to speak at all. To keep silent is first to reach the site where the speech that states and discourses is no longer acceptable. Onto-

---

[16] Heidegger, *Identität,* pp. 64–65 = p. 306.

[17] Ibid., p. 45 = p. 289. That same experience is alluded to in the text of *Unterwegs zur Sprache* (Pfullingen: G. Neske, 1959), p. 96, which recognizes in the experience, moreover, as well as an "origin," a "future."

theology, precisely, does not allow us to reach that site, since it does not cease, even and especially in the time of triumphant atheism, to force-feed us with ever more supreme beings (and grammar must then suffer much worse than the reduplication of the superlative). When it is a question of God, one must deserve even one's silence. That is why Heidegger elaborates elsewhere what he here calls "keeping silent." He elaborates it in relation to Saint Paul and Paul's effort to designate another discourse (and therefore a silence) than that of the Greeks, and therefore of philosophy. It is

> this uncovering of beings that first made it possible for Christian theology to grab hold of Greek philosophy—to its profit or to its loss is up to the theologians to decide—on the basis of the experience of Christianness (*des Christlichen*), inasmuch as they meditate on what is written in Saint Paul's first letter to the Corinthians: οὐχὶ ἐμώρασεν ὁ θεὸς τὴν σοφίαν τοῦ κόσμου, Has not God convicted the wisdom of the world of folly? (I Corinthians 1:20). Now, the σοφία τοῦ κόσμου is that which, according to 1:22, the ἕλληνες ζητοῦσιν, what the Greeks seek. Aristotle very explicitly calls the πρώτη φιλοσοφία (philosophy properly speaking) ζητουμένη— sought after. Will Christian theology decide yet again to take seriously the word of the Apostle, and, consistently with this, to take seriously that philosophy is folly?[18]

To take seriously that philosophy is a folly means, for us, first (although not exclusively) taking seriously that the "God" of onto-theology is rigorously equivalent to an idol, that which is presented by the Being of beings thought metaphysically; and therefore it means that the seriousness of God cannot begin to appear and grab hold of us unless, through a radical reversal, we claim to advance outside of onto-theology. One should give us credit for being fully aware that this undertaking is a folly and a danger, pretension, and vanity. It is not a question, as with everyone, of "overcoming metaphysics," but of at least posing the question correctly: does the onto-theological idol, triumphant or ruined (it does not matter here), close all access to the icon of God as "icon of the *invisible* God"? According to a well-grounded appearance, Heidegger does not here indicate how to accomplish the step

---

[18] Heidegger, *Wegmarken*, p. 208 = pp. 40–41.

back outside of the idol toward the icon. The text from the apostle Paul, which he cites against a theology that is too accommodating toward onto-theological σοφία, says, however, one word more: to the folly that one must take seriously there corresponds a λόγος that is foreign to onto-theologic, the λόγος τοῦ σταυροῦ (1:18), that of the cross—of the cross where the Word was crucified. On the cross the Word kept silent, but in that way another paradoxical light manifested itself, an *other* discourse. Perhaps it would be necessary to attempt with this discourse to take onto-theology up again from the place where we are. We undoubtedly cannot get out of it, as if one could pass through the idolatrous mirror, nor can we recede back toward a conceptual state of nature that no history would have marked irremediably. There remains, therefore, only one path: to travel through onto-theology itself all along its limits—its marches. The marches do not only delimit a territory, like borders. They defend it, like a glacis, a line of fortifications. They also surround it, an already foreign territory, exposed to danger, half unknown. To take onto-theology tangentially, from the angle of its lines of defense, and thus to expose oneself to what already no longer belongs to it: this will be our way of entering conceptually into the seriousness of a folly, of the folly that aims at the icon and rejects the idol.

§ 3. DISCOURSE TO THE ATHENIANS

To recognize onto-theology as having marches presupposes to begin with—this will be our first presupposition—that onto-theology is admitted as the constitution of metaphysics. In fact, it could perfectly well not be. But this first assumption is not enough. Several indications of exteriority can be envisaged that pass beyond onto-theology. First, the "overcomings" that, in effect, rid themselves (or so they think) of the very terms of the question; I shall attempt not to founder in any such triviality. Next, the properly philosophical meditation on the metaphysical primacy of presence in temporalization, and therefore also of the onto-theological constitution; that meditation, which Heidegger pursued from *Sein und Zeit* all the way to *Zeit und Sein,* remains within the field of philosophy, or it seems to. I shall come back to this below

(§ 17). There remains a final way of proceeding, which questions onto-theology not starting from its interior limit but, as they say, starting from the outside edge of the limit, that which opens immediately upon the foreign: with a view to a non-onto-theological theology. Let us clarify the ultimate presupposition: must one exclude that the λόγος τοῦ σταυροῦ still functions as a λόγος even though, or because it pertains to the Cross, whose folly convicts the wisdom that the Greeks seek of folly? Can this logic be approached by a discourse and offer the support for it? Does this discourse put into play a fundamental position other than onto-theology and the idol of "God" as supreme being? I will try to see how, in fact, other constellations rise in other skies: thus distance, the Father, withdrawal, filial abandon, the traverse of distance. It goes without saying that this elucidation cannot be sketched out polemically. Whoever claims to jump outside of onto-theology in one leap is exposed to the danger of repeating it, by a slight, naively critical inversion. Distance shall become inchoatively intelligible to us only if we discover it starting from onto-theology itself and from its most identifiable state. Distance plays within onto-theology from the beginning, like air, water, and time make the best-tuned woodwinds play: in order to make them explode and/or adapt themselves to daily use. It is therefore necessary to take onto-theology obliquely, not head-on: because no thought can or wants to absorb it, distance remains present to onto-theology, concealed, superimposed. Any metaphysician, if he is among the greatest, maintains, within onto-theology, an oblique relation to it. Distance works him as unbeknownst to him. I shall not be ridiculous enough to "critique" Nietzsche (a ridiculousness almost as great as the claim to "explain" him) on the basis, for example, of the theology revealed by the New Testament. I shall attempt— which appears to me infinitely more risky, decisive, and respectful—to take Nietzsche into view starting from distance. It will therefore be a question, for anyone who admits, like I do, the insurpassable primacy of Christian revelation, to take Nietzsche, the last metaphysician, into view starting from distance, in order no longer to find a Nietzschean position of Christianity, but, following Heidegger's injunction, in order to assign onto-theology to a position of "folly" starting from Christ and Christianity, as the "folly/discourse of the Cross." Can one take onto-theology into view starting from what, in Christianity, might escape it? Once again, it is not a question of critique, nor of recuperation, nor of an inversion of the terms of our reading. It is not a matter of questioning Christianity starting from onto-theology, but of sketching out a perspective on onto-theology—in its Nietzschean culmination—starting from the Christianity made manifest by the apocalypse of Christ. Nietzsche deserves more and, ironically, expected more from his readers than a hagiography that is steeped in piety or packed with polemic and that undoubtedly obscures profoundly the true stakes of what he had to say. Just as one (Heidegger) uncovered a relation between Nietzsche and metaphysics that is more decisive and intimate than the simple critique of "Platonism," so it remains (because of Heidegger's work) to glimpse that his relation to the question of the divine and of Christ is more decisive and intimate than a banal declaration of "atheism." Far from blunting onto-theology and the height to which he carries it, to read Nietzsche starting from Christianity— its march—would perhaps be one of the least unworthy homages.

By way of the Nietzschean threshold, I shall enter into commerce with other border territories of onto-theology: Hölderlin and Denys the Areopagite. This calls for three remarks. This choice reflects an inexcusable, irremediable, but undoubtedly unavoidable arbitrariness. I shall therefore not remedy that arbitrariness by adding some motif to the sequence: the same question seemed to me to traverse these figures—that which is formulated here, according to the naming that I brought it, by *distance:* a distance outside of onto-theology for Nietzsche, a filially received distance of the presence of a God who is paternally in withdrawal for Hölderlin, and a distance traversed liturgically toward the Requisite by the discourse of praise of requestants for Denys. In all of these cases, the indisputably apparent absence of the divine becomes the very center of a questioning concerning its manifestation. Each in his own way, they all recognize that absence, or that withdrawal, as the task of thinking that properly falls to them. My undertaking therefore aims at nothing other than to allow them to speak symphonically, without summoning them in a police-like fashion to a question that would remain foreign to them. Or rather, the distance of God was born for me as from their successive, diverse, unexpected—and harmonically fortuitous—

insistences. It is they who summoned my attention and gave rise to the unique question that now, apparently, summons them. —My path shall often seem arbitrary. The cavalier alacrity of certain "interpretations" (the quotation marks indicating, by understatement, the mistranslations or the misinterpretations) shall seem violent, and even not very serious or objective, to the specialists of Nietzsche, Hölderlin, and Denys. One might even be surprised by the little attention paid to the very important secondary literature dedicated to these authors. To this there are several responses. Having myself the role, elsewhere and sometimes here, of the specialist, I share in advance certain indignations, and I can only accept them, since elsewhere I permit myself similar ones. That said, one must not confuse the silences that a fragmentary essay can or must allow itself with the massive ignorances that I have attempted to sweep away, and that others have helped me to make up for. One must also ask whether objectivity would be in place here: the very particular and precise point of view that guides me here—distance—often takes the finest and most exhaustive studies by surprise; above all, the thinkers gathered here could not be taken as the objects of a technical examination since they obviously command the questioning to which they gave rise. Perhaps the most direct possible approach to them—I do not mean the most naive—alone allows me not to lower them to the level of a text to be explicated or of a thesis to be decided. It is a matter here of nothing other than following as clearly as possible what Nietzsche, Hölderlin, and Denys can still give us to think with regard to distance.[19] My means had to comply with that urgency and that authority. This is the only excuse for their weaknesses. Finally, and conversely, why have I chosen these texts and not others? And moreover why texts? It is not so much a matter of explicating authors as it is of asking them to explicate the situation in which we find ourselves. All are in tune (like the strings of an instrument: in order to allow different sounds but with regu-

---

[19] The right that one can claim to have to submit certain thinkers to a theological approach escapes the danger of a trivial recuperation only if it goes hand in hand with the conviction that a theological contribution can come to us from those same thinkers. That these two movements are not contradictory is certainly what I have learned from H. Urs von Balthasar (particularly *Herrlichkeit*, III/1, *Im Raum der Metaphysik* [Einsiedeln: Johannes Verlag, 1965]).

lated differences) in helping us to think the idea that the "death of God," far from implying the disqualification of the question of God or of the divine, urgently restores the question of their panic, immediate and open confrontation. The disappearance of the onto-theological idol provokes, in concert, the frenetic search for a *corps à corps*, which one hopes to be sometimes nuptial, with the divine, in the disinherited madness of a sadistic insignificance. The unavoidable and mutely urgent task then becomes to learn that only separation can define approach, and withdrawal advent. What we here name distance attempts to apply itself to this. It therefore is not a matter, for me, of explicating authors, but of allowing them to instruct us about distance. The rupture of texts shall therefore be the sign of a doubly suitable incompleteness. This is so, first, because the arbitrariness of our choices and the insufficiency of our readings reflect, and issue from, the urgency of our task: "Some days, one should not be afraid of calling things impossible to describe" (R. Char).[20] I believed that those days had come. Next, this is so because distance presupposes the insufficiency of discourse: an ideological framework, a merely coherent group of theses, even a program of studies would definitively close access to distance, since distance implies withdrawal as a mode of advent, and it requires nonfulfillment as a decency with respect to discourse; would this not be the most elementary propriety, as well as the greatest audacity?

Hence the discourse to the Athenians. My own discourse does not in fact remain solitary, unheard of, or even original (originality, so recent an invention, claims to attest an author, while it relieves itself of an origin): it reproduces, I mean to say, it must try to rediscover, if it wants only to remain, the theological situation, the tactical disposition, and the crucial reversal of the discourse that the apostle Paul held on the areopagus before the Athenians (Acts of the Apostles 17:16–34). First, the theological situation: Paul enters into a city (and therefore into a politics) that he (and he alone) sees to be "devoted to idols" (17:17). What idols? The discourse will later speak of idols "of gold, silver, stone, sculpture of art and of the human conception" (17:29)—

---

[20] René Char, *Recherche de la Base et du Sommet* (Paris: Gallimard, coll. "Poésie," 1971), p. 8.

thus, idols in the monumental sense of the term. But curiously, the mention of general idolatry is followed first by the enumeration of "those who find themselves passing by" (17:17), that is, beside the Jews and pagan worshippers, "some Epicurian and Stoic philosophers" (17:18). Everything happens as if the philosophers also came under the jurisdiction of idolatry—only having purified it, that is, having conceptualized it. Their "God" receives—as a supreme honor, but also as the price of its idolatrous compromise—a definition. The fact that here the "atheism" of the Epicurians is assimilated with the logical and physical "God" of the Stoics further confirms the conceptual idolatry. The Epicurians would benefit, in this sense, from a favorable prejudice—theologically speaking. Visible idolatry is no more refuted by substituting one image for another, than conceptual idolatry collapses before another concept of "God." It is effaced only before the absence of a concept, an absence that is definitive and that initiates another approach to God as the "unknown God" (17:23). Using the "unknown god" whose idol appeared among the mass of others—of the known gods, Paul does not undertake to reveal their until-then concealed identity. For if he declares that "I announce to you the one whom you worship without knowing him" and if he indeed announces the "God who made the world, and all that is in it" (17:24), this latter retrocedes not only from the world, but also from the understanding that measures the world and is finally measured by the world: the Ab-sol-ute. He is the Unthinkable, insofar as He reveals the distance of Goodness in the encounter of creation, as Denys will say (§§ 13–14). The relation to God escapes the conceptualization in which we comprehend idols, in order to comprehend us, as incomprehensible. Hence the tactical disposition that one would have to be able to borrow from Paul. The incomprehensible comprehends us because "In Him we live, we move, and we are": the Being of beings itself, like (Nietzschean?) "life" or (dialectical?) movement, which also name it in their own way, results from the incomprehensible; far from our attaining it, it comes to us, as one of the gifts of the Unthinkable. This means that the idols no longer mediate our relation to the "God," but we ourselves are immediately summoned to mediate the deformed relation of the idols to God. The place of the debate is displaced: naked, with unveiled

face before the faceless God, we no longer look at him in an idolatrously privileged face, but He first looks at us and looks after us
under his invisible look. The invisible look of God summons us to
see his very invisibility. In this sense "we are God's offspring"
(17:29). The resemblance henceforth becomes the exposed place
that mobilizes us for a mutual look: could God not annihilate us,
in favor of an idol of man, as we missed him in the case of those
idols that we indefinitely rejected? The confrontation with the
"living" God, a terrible thing except for the one who happily
ignores it, follows the collapse of the idols. "Who shall be able to
stand it?" The *dies irae* terrorizes, first and fundamentally, because
he uncovers to us the invisible face that looks at us and that no
one can envisage. Thus Paul evokes the only imaginable face of
the invisible, the risen Christ (17:31–32), "icon of the invisible
God." It is at this precise moment—the essential moment—that
the crowd draws aside and laughs (as it also laughs when the
Nietzschean madman announces the inaudible and unheard of,
that "God is dead"; see § 4). The tactics fail here, as do all tactics,
rhetorics, or pragmatics as soon as it is a question of the essential.
In the first letter to the Corinthians, Paul will replace the impossibility of making the invisible seen with the crucial reversal. That
crucial reversal consists in beginning with the λόγος of the Cross,
against the wisdom of the world, with the "folly of the kerygma"
that "scandalizes," with the "crucified Christ" (see §2). Hence
the direct passage to the icon, which the collapse of the idols
does not suffice to receive or even to glimpse. Hence the direct
contemplation of the "paradox of this face,"[21] of the envisigeable
face of the Invisible, a paradox in the sense that "glory," and to
begin with the "glory of God," gives itself to be seen at an angle,
sideways, askew—in a word inverted (παρά-δοξον). For us, this
means first that the journey through the idols, their collapse and
the unthinkable that they deliver from another "great closing,"
could be completed only in the iconic face of Christ. It means,

---

[21] Here René Char (*Fureur et Mystère* [Paris: Gallimard, coll. "Poésie," 1962],
"L'Absent"), who says in his own way what the Fathers contemplate in the paradoxical face of Christ: the "paradox of God"; thus Athanasius, *Against the Pa-
gans*, § 42; Cyril of Alexandria, *That Christ Is One* (P.G. 75, 753 a = *Deux Dialogues
christologiques,* coll. "Sources chrétiennes" [Paris: Cerf, 1964], p. 430, and 759 b
= p. 452).

next, that the attention that will perhaps be paid to the beginning of my essay would then have to undergo, as the discourse to the Athenians requires, ironic or disdainful resistance when and each time that, paradoxically, the Christ will arise therein as the figure of revelation and as the only norm. The correctness of my argument will be verified, in a sense, only by its failure—provided that this be theological and not literary. Failure speaks, in its own way, as an adman and therefore with little importance, the crucial logic, or rather it inscribes discourse in that logic. But in this status failure remains as provisional as it is serious: for some nevertheless listened to Paul. Among them was a certain Denys, called the Areopagite, the very one whom the tradition wants to recognize, despite the gap of several centuries, in the author of the Dionysian corpus, and in whom that author wants one to recognize him.

Hence nothing could be more rigorous than to complete, with a reading of Denys, a text that the recollection of the discourse to the Athenians inaugurates—the one issues, as certainly as paradoxically, from the other. Thus I write for Denys, and those like him.

The Collapse of the Idols and Confrontation with the Divine: Nietzsche

"All the gods are dead: now, we want the overman to live!" In thinking crudely, one could be of the opinion that this word says that mastery over beings passes from God to man, or, even more crudely, that Nietzsche puts man in the place of God. Those who have such an opinion do not think divinely enough of God. Man can never put himself in the place of God, because the essence of man never reaches the domain of the essence of God. On the contrary, compared to this impossibility, something much more disquieting can come about—something whose essence we have hardly begun to think.

M. Heidegger, *Holzwege*

§ 4. The Idol and Metaphysics

WHO DOES NOT KNOW that Nietzsche announced the death of God? But we also know to what triviality of argument and design that announcement falls when thought abandons itself to evading the immense event expressed in the announcement. The "death of God" can seem to reveal the disappearance of the divine, of the gods, even of God, only by referring back first to an otherwise more rigorous event of thought—that whose trial Nietzsche underwent and that his life consigned in a text where the whiteness of the last pages pays for the obscurity of a spiritual night. What is this event of thought—or, more modestly: what can we perceive of it in the shock wave through which it does not cease to shake us? Whether we classify ourselves among the "believers" or among the "atheists" does not spare us from meditating on our shared atheism, which is evident through a banal objectivity and a rigorous metaphysics. We find ourselves with the faces of ἄθεοι, as Saint Paul says (Ephesians 2:12), of the god-less, deserted by the god(s) in a world emptied of the divine—*Gottlosen,* says Nietzsche (*Gay Science,* § 280).[1] For before postulating the disappearance of something like the unthinkable, we must, as far as our reach allows, conceive or admit that the "death of God" concerns first the life of man, precisely because it rises therefrom. It is not so much a matter of the debased and unseemly connection between the "death of God" and that of man. It is a matter of opening up the situation in which man must be found as *Dasein* in order that the "death of God" might befall him. That situation does not depend in any way on individual convictions or on psychological predispositions—not that those of Nietzsche remain indifferent; but they become significant only when understood within an otherwise rigorous, and in a sense inevitable, site. It is precisely that site that we must here seek out. Which is the man who states the word of Zarathustra, "God is dead"?

To this question at least one man could respond: the very one who announces the news. In § 125 of the *Gay Science,* the madman proclaims that "God is dead," but—and this is the center of the text—without himself understanding how the murder happened or how men were sufficient for such a scandal: "We have killed him, *you and I.* It is we all who are his murderers. But how were we able to do that? How were we able to empty the sea?" All murders have a place, a time, and in the end a corpse—except the death of God. And this must indeed be called a murder, since there are murderers—us. But precisely, this murder does not have a time: already committed, no one has noticed it, and the herald arrives "too early." As in tragedy, the messenger comes to

---

[1] I cite the texts according to title and paragraph. In certain cases, I give the pagination from the French translation of the Colli-Montinari edition (Friedrich Nietzsche, *Oeuvres philosophiques complètes,* vol. III, *Le Cas de Wagner, Crépuscule des idoles, l'Antéchrist, Ecce Homo, Nietzsche contra Wagner,* trans. J.-Cl. Hemery [Paris: Gallimard, 1974]). For the fragments I give the reference to *Nietzsche Werke, Kritische Gesamtausgabe,* ed. G. Colli and M. Montinari (Berlin: W. de Gruyter, 1967 ff.) and, for the sake of convenience, to the paragraph of the collection titled *Der Wille zur Macht,* ed. P. Gast and E. Förster-Nietzsche, reprinted by Kröner (Stuttgart, 1964). Finally, the *Dionysian Dithyrambs* are cited according to the bilingual edition of J. Cl. Hemery, following Colli-Montinari, vol. VI/3 (Gallimard: Paris, 1974). The name "Zarathustra" indicates the character, whereas *Zarathustra* abbreviates the title of *Also sprach Zarathustra* (cited according to part and title of the fragment).

declare the catastrophe in the fourth act; but here no tragedy has begun, no chorus is upset over the death of the hero or frightened by the monster. The comedy continues, a comedy whose actors continue to laugh only in order, at best, to "look with astonishment." The announcement is astonishing in that it is not heard: no place echoes it, not even the mountain where the saint lives (*Zarathustra,* Foreword, § 2). Above all, the corpse itself is missing: the churches where the madman sings the *Requiem* of the divine as if in a forensic chorus offer nothing but mausoleums— tombs empty of the body (*Grabmäler*). There is no body from the crime at all. Crime and criminals everywhere. Would the murder have taken place without anyone having noticed it, but in such a way that all might, with the passing of time, take part in it?

But in fact, what gesture does the madman make? "I seek God! I seek God!" he screams (as opposed to the fool of Anselm and the Psalmist who denies *in corde suo*). What does he want if not to *see* God? But precisely, is not that a death? In Nietzschean terms, no one can see God without God dying. For the God presents his effigy in the ναός of the Temple only by concealing it in the halfobscurity of a doubt, of an imagination, and of a dream. "The religious imagination for a long time *refuses* absolutely to believe in the identity of the god and an image: the image is supposed to be the visible evidence that the *numen* of the divinity is, in some mysterious, not fully comprehensible way, active in this place and bound to it. The oldest image of the god is supposed to *reveal and at the same time conceal* the god—to intimate his presence but not expose it to view" (*Human All Too Human*, II, I, § 22; Hollingdale, 267, mod.).

The idol of the temple dies from being seen in full light, since then it appears as what it is (or at least as what it becomes under *such* a light): warped wood, forged metal, sculpted stone. The god remains visible in the idol only if the gaze is made chaste enough not to seek to possess the god in flesh and bone—in and as an idol. One must leave it to the god not to be restrained by the idol, in order that the idol might show us how to divine the wavering of the divine, like a half-smile, over it. The idol ceases to fulfill its role—half-presence of the semidivine—as soon as the worshipper takes it into view face on. For the invisible in it, that is, the sole visibility of the divine, disappears immediately. In a sense, the idol does not have to be seen in order to remain an idol—despite the etymology. As seen, it rends the shadows that invested it with the invisible. It refutes itself by the *index* of its own vanity. In the light of his lantern, which like the sun lights up that which remains to be thought, that which remains to be lived, what did the madman see? He saw, like the most hideous man (*Zarathustra,* IV) seen by God, God. The most hideous man killed God because God, who saw him with an eye that sees all, killed him with a glance. To return that glance, to see the God as such, is to kill him. For one then sees nothing but an idol. Or rather, what one sees gives rise in turn to this suspicion: "and what if God were *not* truth and it were precisely this which is proved? if he were vanity, the lust for power, the impatience, the terror, the enraptured and fearful illusion (*Wahn*) of men?" (*Daybreak,* I, § 93; Hollingdale, 93, mod.). In seeing God one immediately discovers his nature, his revocation, in a word, the quotation marks that, from this point on, must frame him in our text—"God." For illusion must be understood precisely as an idol seen too close. The madman, and therefore Zarathustra, has one eye too many, provisionally. "Oh! My brothers, this God that I created was the work of human hands and a human illusion (*Wahnsinn*)!" (*Zarathustra,* I, "On the After-wordly"). Thus Nietzsche does not only name "God": he points out his idolatrous status through the addition of an intermediary: some *concept* or other. Because "God is a conjecture (*Muttmass-ung*)" (*Zarathustra,* II, "Upon the Blessed Isles"), he can be approached, that is, attacked and sunk, only as a "concept of God." Man rejects only what he attains. Hence the rigor of vocabulary to which the Nietzschean language restrains itself: "How? Is man only a mistake (*Fehlgriff*) of God? Or is God a mistake of man?" (*Twilight of the Idols,* "Maxims and Arrows"); "the concept of 'God' invented as the counter-concept of life" (*Ecce Homo,* "Why I Am a Destiny"). "The concept 'God' represents a retreat from life, a criticism of and even a disdain for life."[2] It is evident that the "critique of the Christian concept of God" (*Antichrist,* §16; see also §18) maintains its pertinence only in being exerted on "God," the idol that it sees—otherwise it would lose all pertinence by not recognizing that the "concept of God" can neither permit nor promise anything concerning God, since it is "a divine

---

[2] *Will to Power,* § 141 = VIII, 3, 230, 15 [42] [Kaufmann, 91, mod.].

privilege to be conceptually inconceivable (*unbegreiflich*)" (*Day-break,* V, § 544). The properly idolatrous status of the "God" thus approached could be confirmed by the other reservations that, like *Begriff,* mark its separation from something like God. One of the most decisive remains the *Gottbildung:* to forge an image of the "God." Thus, "one hypostasizes a state in a person, and affirms that that state, when it befalls us, is the effect produced by a person. In other words, in the psychological fabrication of God (*Gottbildung*), a state, in order to be an effect, is personified as a cause."[3] Here the "religious instinct, that is the god-making instinct (*gottbildende*)" is openly and fully at play: not only does it fall to that instinct to produce "God," but above all that instinct attests, by bringing its own play to light, that the "God" thus encountered, since it is produced, remains an idol—a thought that, even if "it makes everything menacing," remains a thought that it belongs to man to "create," as much as his world, as much as his own divinity (*Zarathustra,* II, "Upon the Blessed Isles"). The emergence of the idolatrous process between "God" and man alone offers the terrain where a genealogical inquiry might unfold. The critical autopsy of the conceptual or imaginative corpse of the Christian "God" offers the occasion for bringing out more radically the idolatrous power in general—which forges "gods" in the image of men: "This will suffice, once and for all, concerning the origin of the 'holy God'." But, "*in itself,* the conception of the gods does not necessarily entail this debasement of the imagination which we have been briefly reconstructing. There are ways of using the fiction (*Erdichtung*) of gods more noble than this self-crucifixion and this degradation of man which have been the masterpiece of humanity during the past millennia" (*Genealogy of Morals,* II, § 23). The genealogies of the "God" through *ressentiment,* or through the priest, or through whatever, offer only particular cases, but the most visible, of the human process of *Erdichtung* of the "gods," of *Gottbildung,* that traverses history as a whole. On this point the aberrant production of Christianity is no exception; its "God," even if it translates an infinitely perverse state of the will to power (see § 6 below) does not illustrate any

---

[3] Ibid., §135 = VIII, 3, 98, 14 [124] [Kaufmann, 86, mod.] and § 1038 = VIII, 3, 323, 17 [4] § 5.

less—and perhaps illustrates even more than the others—its idolatrous process. One can judge "God" only on appearances, which
reveal him to be an idol. Thus degraded to his status as—
symptomatic—epiphenomenon of the will to power, he supports
the idol factory.

The "Christian God" is an idol, to be sure, but of what? Of
itself, of course; idol of itself [*de soi*]—of a self [*un moi*] that marks
and advances itself therein. What self—or, if one will, what state
of the self is at issue? "[T]hat Christian belief, which was Plato's
belief, that God is the truth, that the truth is divine" (*Gay Science*,
V, § 344). Idol: a production of the "god/God" (Plato/Christian-
ity) starting from the truth, from the will to truth as a figure of
the will to power. The search for the truth, which here constitutes
an idol, an epoch, and a screen, admits of another name for
Nietzsche: morals. Truth and knowledge are reciprocal in the
same reactive will. This comes down to saying that the proclamation of the "death of God," in order to be rigorously articulated,
as is precisely the case, must attack, that is, rest upon, a precise
idol—the idol forged by the will to truth and morals. Hence a
paradoxical consequence that is at least sensed beforehand: the
"death of God" remains a seriously thinkable event only by sur-
rounding the "God" who dies with quotation marks. It maintains
its power only over a vain idol of that which God, if he "is," is not.
Twilight falls irremediably only on an idol. There is nothing more
foreign to the "death of God" than common atheism; it is a matter both of much less (an idol) and of much more—of an event
that is reached by convictions no more than it is provoked by
unbelief.

What idol dies, then? The idol that morals (as a face of the will
to power) produced: "Question: with morals was the pantheistic
Yes to all things also rendered impossible? At bottom, it is only the
moral God that has been overcome/abandoned."[4] That only this
"God" was eliminated does not prevent the fact that it is indeed
him who was: "The 'Father' in God is fundamentally refuted; as
well as the 'judge,' the 'rewarder' " (*Beyond Good and Evil*, II, §
53). When it is a question of the "God" not yet "thought as the

---

[4] Ibid., § 55 = VIII, 1, 217, 5 [71], n. 7 [Kaufmann, 36].

Being-become-free against morality,"[5] one should not be surprised that morality maintains complete power over him, as the
idol that it produced. As this "God" attracts the gazes of men
toward the demi-obscurity where he becomes concrete—gazes
whose *ressentiment* is assured and becomes more marked only by
using him—those same gazes reflect back to him their scrupulous
cruelty and their fearless exactitude. The speech of *ressentiment*
called God that which weakens, that which teaches weakness, that
which induces weakness. An idolatrous dependence of "God"
with regard to his origin—*ressentiment*. This is indeed why the genealogy demonstrates nothing less than his genesis, his suicide.
Or, if one wishes, the *ressentiment* that produces the moral idol
"God" can also proclaim his futility, that is, his uselessness. "You
see what it was that really triumphed over the Christian god:
Christian morality itself, the concept of truthfulness that was understood ever more rigorously, the refinement of the Christian
conscience obtained in the confessional, translated and sublimated into scientific conscience, into intellectual probity at any
price" (*Gay Science*, V, § 357; Kaufmann, 307, mod. = *Genealogy of
Morals*, III, § 27). The overcoming of the idol of morality remains
a self-overcoming of morality (*Beyond Good and Evil*, § 2); this is
indeed why it does not suffice to announce the "death of God"
in order to overcome nihilism. On the contrary, such an announcement inaugurates it and renders it possible, by leaving morality robbed of its murdered idol. It belongs therefore to the very
definition of the idol that the morality that invests it in the very
same movement deposes it; in a sense, from one moment to the
next, there is only the time of a wink—that of the gaze that in
seeing the idol kills it. "They have created their God on the basis

---

[5] Ibid., § 1035 = VIII, 2, 247, 10 [203]. See "For those who do not think, a
philosophy and a morality in brief is needed: God" (V, 2, 484, 12 [53]), and
more explicitly: "Religions are destroyed by belief in morality. The Christian
moral God is not tenable: hence 'atheism'—as if there could be no other kinds
of god" (§ 151 = VIII, 1, 112, 2 [107] [Kaufmann, 95]); and "You call that the
self-destruction of God: but it is only its slough: —he sheds his moral skin! And
you will immediately find him, beyond good and evil," *Böse Weisheit*, § 89, a
collection of aphorisms from the years 1882–83 published by Koegel, in *Friedrich
Nietzsche Werke*, vol. XII, § 375 (Leipzig, 1897) = *Nietzsches Werke* (Leipzig, 1901),
vol. XII (*Unveröffentliches aus Zeit der frölichen Wissenschaft und der Zarathustra*,
1881–1886), p. 389, § 532 = *Friedrich Nietzsche Gesammelte Werke* (Munich: Musa-
rion Verlag, 1925), vol. XIV, p. 80.

of nothingness: what is so surprising if it has now become nothingness to them?" (*Dithyrambs of Dionysus,* autumn 88, 194; see
Beyond Good and Evil, § 55). Morality disqualifies its idol precisely
because it alone qualified it and, in that movement, mortally saw
it. This brings out, once again, the same paradox: the "death of
God" carries as far as morality carries. But are we not insidiously
and in a revisionist manner deadening Nietzsche's case by reducing its impact to morality, by limiting the meditation to a collection of ethical aphorisms? Perhaps—unless, on the contrary, the
"God" of morality concentrates in himself more, or something
other, than what one imagines. (a) *God* functions as an idol, and
Nietzsche explicitly specifies that Christian belief is identical, in
his genealogical meditation, with that of Plato (*Gay Science,* V, §
344). Heidegger says in this sense that "in the word 'God is dead'
the name God, thought essentially, is posited as the suprasensible
world of ideals, which contain the goal established beyond earthly
life for that very life, which determines it from above and therefore in a certain manner from the outside"; or again, "God is the
name for the domain of ideas and ideals."[6] Just as "God" can no
longer be explained except by morality, the latter likewise refers
to something like "Plato," or what Nietzsche understands by that.
(b) Metaphysics in its very history, which morality punctuates in
its beginnings (Plato) and its end (Schopenhauer). What is at
stake in the "death of God" escapes triviality only by returning
from an irrelevant caricature to metaphysics, through an interposed morality. Why metaphysics? Because in it "God" still idolatrously maintains his role and finds his place: "the place that
thought metaphysically returns to God is the place of causal ef-
fecting and the conservation of beings as creatures."[7] Over the
"God" who is an idolatrous mirror of morality is superimposed
the idolatrous function that metaphysics imposed, or wanted to
impose, on the Christian God—after having managed to do so for
the other gods: "God and the gods in the sense of metaphysical
experience . . . are dead" (ibid.). They are dead in their idolatrous function: less in morality than in what morality covers and

---

[6] *Holzwege,* pp. 203 and 199 = French trans. *Chemins,* pp. 181 and 178. For
our future development on Nietzsche's metaphysics, we refer to M. Heidegger,
Nietzsche, I and II (Pfullingen: G. Neske, 1961).

[7] *Holzwege,* p. 235 = p. 210.

mobilizes, what Nietzsche names "Platonism" but which one can perhaps understand as the onto-theological structure of metaphysics. "God" is there summoned—and not only invoked—as the supreme being who, within the field of a discourse on the Being of beings (*ontologia, metaphysica generalis*), fulfills the function of concentrating its exemplary perfection (*ens realissimum, causa sui, ipsum esse,* etc.) and of causally ensuring the coherence of a world. Caught within such a *metaphysica specialis* (*theologia,* if one will), the "God" simply answers to the name that one gives him: "id quod omnes nominant Deum," "Man hat Gott genannt, was . . ."[8] Between the conclusion of the proofs or definitions of the supreme being and its baptism as "God" the *hiatus,* which no demonstrative rigor narrows but indeed underlines all the more, remains gaping. And in the measure that the metaphysical (and then moral) "God" is substituted for it, there steals away what could have allowed thought to test itself according to the divinity of God even in concepts. But then would the "death of God" liberate the *metaphysical* horizon? Undoubtedly so—even if Nietzsche effects that liberation within the onto-theological structure of metaphysics. For by playing therein, he makes it ineffably stand out, and he shows its idolatrous functioning, without effect one might say—without effect because the onto-theological structure of metaphysics survives the "death of God" enough to demonstrate its idolatrous stature. —For our argument, it is enough to point out the idol's double framework: morality and metaphysics, a double machine, a machinery or machination that assumes the title of "God" without any other right than fact.

If morality and metaphysics produce idols, and if the "death of God" revokes them, must one conclude that the space is freed up for an overcoming of metaphysics, or, more vulgarly, for a new morality? It is not up to us to decide this, since, in any case, many others are occupied with doing so. Would not what is at least liberated thus be, rather, the divine without the mask of any idol? For as Nietzsche perhaps finally shows, atheism itself remains idolatrous—it presupposes an idol upon which to exert its negation, an "idea of 'God' " that is subject to rejection. The "death of God" offers only an inverted face of certain cults of "God": noth-

---

[8] *Will to Power,* § 54 = VIII, 3, 206, 15 [13]. See § 2, and notes 4–10.

ing has changed except the violent lighting that freezes the "God" in the stone of its image. The idol remains precisely when the "God" dies, since this very death consecrates that other facticity. Because at the point of "the death of God" there silently persists the phantom-idol of the divine, it is still necessary to overcome the half-living idols of the already dead "gods." Metaphysical idolatry is not yet surpassed with atheism—which is still pegged to the warning of idols; it must proceed all the way to the expectation of a nonidolatrous face of the divine, transgress nihilisms to the point of appealing to the "new gods."

It would be time to ask whether Nietzsche, far from having advocated any militant atheism, as some imbecilic ideologues insist on maintaining through prudence and for the sake of recovery, was not in fact, with the madman, the one "who seeks God inasmuch as he cries toward God," or even more singularly, "the last German philosopher who sought God with passion and pain" (Heidegger).[9] "Not having overturned the idol, but having broken the idolater in *yourself*—that was your courage" (*Dithyrambs*, 202). To break the idolater in oneself is to inhabit a nonidolatrous space in order there to confront insolently, head on, the divinity that mysteriously haunts those fields.

§ 5. The Darkness of Noon

The death of the idols frees up a space—an empty space. The trial is henceforth joined with the emptiness of a desertion, in expectation of a new presence. For, precisely because of its opening up through evacuation, the place of the divine becomes gaping—gaping, fascinating in that degree, and all the more demanding. Unlike others that opened up only in the last resort, the question of an occupation of the divine does not at all have to mature for long in order to appear. It does not even result from the "death of God," through the space of a consequence, or the arrangement of an implication. It strictly coincides with it.

---

[9] See, respectively, *Holzwege*, p. 247 = p. 219, and the *Discours du Rectorat*, p. 12.

This is why Nietzsche brings together the two elements in a single sequence: "Is not the greatness of this deed too great for us? Must we ourselves not become gods simply to appear worthy of it?" (*Gay Science*, § 125; Kaufmann, 181). How are we to understand this? Is it not simply moving backward to install new terms by way of a dead "God"? Is this not to perpetuate the objection that he exercised against the world? (*Ecce Homo*, "Why I Am a Destiny," § 8, II, p. 341; see also *Antichrist*, § 18, etc.). Perhaps—unless the place held by the God who is murderous because he is creator of the world does not exhaust the topic of the divine. Unless the divine can play its part in a manner other than that whose meaninglessness his death makes evident. It is necessary to admit that one can at least listen to that other way of experiencing the divine. On this condition one thread guides our reflection. How is one to determine the new way of the divine without being regretful in the reactive manner of conceiving, or of receiving the idol that has just died? By defining the situation in which the man who saw the old god dead finds himself. To that man falls the position of "God," not like an inheritance after the death of the legator, but like a power falls to the one who takes possession of a territory that he does not know, but that he alone knew how to recognize, identify, and already invest. "God is dead," the gods are still lacking, and man experiences himself in a superlative that is still to be shouldered.

Nietzsche names the trial that summons man to his superlative and to the divine *nihilism:* there "where the highest values devaluate themselves," where "the goal is lacking" and "the answer to the *why?*" finds no answer, *Dasein* itself becomes "untenable."[10] The "death of God," as it assigns the fable of the other world to its end, and therefore provokes—and coronates—the end of the supposed "highest values," leaves the world of beings not to collapse but to falter. To say and to see that the world collapses is the role of simple pessimism, or the cold rage of passive nihilism. That the world falters should be understood "*seinsgeschichtlich,*" as Heidegger said—at the level of the history of Being. This means that the history of Being (Being as destiny and therefore as his-

---

[10] Respectively, *Will to Power*, § 2 = VIII, 2, 14, 9 [35] and § 39 = VIII, 2, 237, 10 [92].

tory) here reaches the historial moment where being no longer enjoys the guarantee—as exemplary as inexhaustible—of a supreme being who, through reference, comparison, and resumption, includes being in the status of the *ens commune*. Beings do not disappear in their beingness: there is no end of the world, no devastating collapse that would annihilate beings in their ontic assurance but, more disquieting, a suspicion concerning the Being of beings. Beings remain, but their right to be falters, the instance is veiled that attests their beingness by the ontic splendor of its own completion. The highest values disappear—and with them disappears the value of the world. Or, less summarily— because the other-world no longer exercises the comparison that oppresses this world here, the liberation of intraworldly beings uncovers them as "free": free, like those free variables that remain incalculable and without an assignable value (numerical or otherwise) when they are not comprehended by bound variables. The disappearance of the oppressive highest values cleanses the horizon of any moral suspicion—only to uncover another, infinitely deeper one: because the world is finally the only world, the world finds itself alone with itself. By abolishing the other world, it is not this world here that exercises, in its turn, the oppression of morality. "*With the true world we have also abolished the apparent world!*" Then the hour of the briefest shadow appears: the hour when no form other than that of the world is imposed on it. Nietzsche follows the announcement of a single world, moreover, with this sequence: "Noon: the hour of the briefest shadow; end of the longest erring; high point of humanity; INCIPIT ZARATHUSTRA" (*Twilight of the Idols,* "How the 'True World' Finally Became a Fable," p. 81; Kaufmann, 486, mod.). Under a noon sun, the shadow becomes the briefest. Each thing loses its shadow, which is reabsorbed within the thing itself. Absolute noon brings everything to light: never has the world abandoned so little of itself to the darkness. A light falls on every thing; at each thing's noon, a vertical sun weighs down on it that does not darken it with any shadow from elsewhere; the thing appears in the full light where not even the least shadow obscures it from a complete evidence. The light of evidence enshrines the thing. Torn away from any darkness, does the thing live on in itself? Never so little. What the briefest shadow procures, in its very concern to mask nothing, is not the thing but its phantom, without form because without relief, without a site because without any distances, without color because saturated with whiteness. Overwhelmed by light, the thing is accordingly obscured. Not because it disappears from sight—but because no world welcomes it, and because it procures no world. Light without shadow allows the world to freeze, or to dissolve—it doesn't matter which, precisely because a world demands a perspective. Only shadow establishes relief, delimits forms, puts things in place. The true world, now rejected, will project that shadow further along the bias of its grim and low-angled light. The world disappears. Or rather, its "worldhood" disappears, since the "highest values" are followed not—alas—by collapse but by the lunatic and solar platitude of infinite equiva-lences. Would it be necessary to say that the world disappears with the "highest values"? Not at all. Would it perhaps be necessary to ask whether the world remains with only one perspective that will ensure it? A pointless question, since the whole world knows that Nietzsche set forth "the perspectival character of being (*Dasein*)" (*Gay Science*, V, § 374). But precisely, in what way is *Dasein* itself found to depend on perspective? The thing must have a perspective precisely because perspective subsists, as the "essentially *explanatory* [status] of Dasein" (ibid.), after the evacuation of the divine, that is, the idolatrous, projective. The idol exercised a perspectivism and thus was finally able to appear backward as the gaze's simple vanishing point outside of the world—in its turn as an effect of perspective. The thing remains to be taken into perspective, even if it does waste away in the luminous platitude that, in this sense, would reduce it to an idol of itself: a mask without depth. Only the vision (and therefore the infinity of competing or harmonious visions, like monads) of the world in perspective saves its appearances. *Dasein,* as will to power, must, in all of its forms (above all in the capacity of an organism), receive a perspective from a gaze. Who can thus see, if "God is dead," to the point of making a world? "We who think and feel, we are the ones who actually and ceaselessly *make* something which is not yet: this world which grows eternally, as a whole, a world of valuations, colors, accents, perspectives, degrees, affirmations and negations" (ibid., V, § 301). To give perspective is to make a world. But then who are we, if we are, who are—"we"? What must one become in order to state that our perspective orders, lays out, appraises, constructs, organizes a world—in short, sees it by bringing it under its gaze? "Around heroes, everything becomes tragedy, around demi-gods, satire; and around God everything becomes—what? Perhaps 'world'?" (*Beyond Good and Evil*, § 150). Would one have to become a god in order that, at the heart of nihilism, things should again become a "world"? The madman had expressed it with more rigor than one—than we believed. The "death of God" requires, in order for beings to be evaluated and placed perspectivally in the world, that a "we" take it up again in its will to power. To evaluate the world is the very act of a god; or better—to evaluate is the act in which man and world assume a finally divine face. It is not necessary to be, or to replace, the idolatrous "God" in order to play this game—on the contrary. For this game renders divine only those who play it with uncovered face—not idolatrously. But who can risk this game? "The death of God" and the briefest shadow summon one to it. Who enters into it? The very one who announces that shadow and goes on immediately to this: *incipit Zarathustra*. Not *tragoedia* but *incipit Zarathustra—et fit mundus*.

Zarathustra, who is followed by his shadow. For he does not leap beyond it but uses it in order to place himself within a perspective—within a world. What role does Zarathustra give to himself? To establish beings in their Being, that is, to evaluate. To evaluate: to place beings in perspective with respect to one another, to establish them in themselves according to their common Being, to maintain them outside of faltering nihilism.

> Values—man first puts them in things, in order to preserve himself—, he first created the meaning of things, a human meaning! Therefore he calls himself "man," which means: the esteemer.
>
> To esteem is to create: hear this, you creators! Esteeming (*schätzen*) itself is of all esteemed things the most estimable treasure (*Schatz*). Through esteeming alone is there value: and without esteeming, the voice of *Dasein* would be empty. Hear this, you creators! (*Zarathustra*, I, "On the Thousand and One Goals," Kaufmann, 171, mod.)

To accomplish the valuation that puts in the world the things that are put in perspective falls to man—to Zarathustra. It is called esteeming, evaluating. Man "defines himself as the being-who-essentially (*Wesen*) measures values, evaluates and measures as the 'valuating animal as such' (*abschätzende*)" (*Genealogy of Morals,* II, § 8; Kaufmann, 70, mod.). To valuate therefore defines at one and the same time the valuating man and the valuated world. The two unfold in concert because the essence of the one constitutes the condition of possibility of the essence of the other. The scale of the valuated world presupposes the rigorous depth—even if it is still a matter of a surface effect—of the valuation. What is it to valuate? It is to measure a thing according to one's will to power.[11] It is to valuate the thing according to the will to power that organizes and constructs itself in that thing in order there to affirm itself. But the thing can exercise that affirmation through an active or reactive will to power, according to whether it can itself freely affirm itself, or, not without constraints, come to terms with others that it negates—secretly, because it cannot do so actually. Each thing testifies to a will to power limited to its essence—or rather, a will to power whose limitation offers something like a chart of its essence. To say of man that, of all things esteemed, he himself constitutes the treasure (*Schatz*) inasmuch as he harbors the secret of value—the right to esteem (*schätzen*)—therefore signifies that in place of a limited will to power, which appraises only its *Umwelt* without that environment ever becoming a world for it, man measures those other wills to power, in that through his intervention is exercised the *schätzen* itself, the will to power itself, life itself—for "life itself forces us to posit values; life itself values through us *when* we posit values" (*Twilight of the Idols,* "Morality as Anti-Nature," § 5, Kaufmann, 490, mod.). Evaluation itself traverses the evaluations of man, who no longer evaluates only with the blind or limited evaluation of other figures of the will to power, but offers the final appeal through which everything in the world receives its evaluation. Or finally, with the evaluation of man, the value of every being is at issue: in him alone a perspective takes on the dimensions of a world. It falls to man to establish the value of every being without exception: this is no arbitrarily idealist subjectivism but the establishment of man as the place of the production of beings in their Being. In order to reach their

---

[11] *Will to Power,* § 675 = VIII, 2, 287, 11 [96] [Kaufmann, 356, mod.].

Being, beings must pass through valuation itself, through man. In man lies valuation itself, "but this appraisal (*das Abschätzen*) itself is still Being."[12] Consequently, it is as world that the valuation of man must be understood for "this world is the will to power—and nothing besides"[13]—as world? Zarathustra will experience this condition with the "abyssal thought": that of the Eternal Return. To valuate to the point that a world is established presupposes that the perspective does not rely on a will to power that, after having made its own the *Umwelt* that lies at the furthest remove from its affirmation, retracts into a negation that excludes from its world what it can no longer see in perspective. A perspective is discovered as world only by avoiding *no* valuation, that is, by deploying a will to power that takes exception to no being. Therefore, whatever the being might be that provokes the will to power to valuation, that will must never revoke that being. This means never experiencing in the will to power a term that would be irreducible to its affirmation, never being forced into a reactive behavior that negates, denies, or prevaricates before the being that escapes it. Man must therefore let himself at this point be governed by valuating, which the will to power in him allows, in the infinity of its perspective, every state of the will to power that presents itself—without excepting the worst, that is, the mediocre. More essential than all of its valuations, valuating accepts the condition that makes those valuations possible: to support with the gaze what the gaze has to put in perspective. To support does not indicate only that one endures, but that one sustains and provides. To provide—to reject no being that falters in its value, as nihilism would encourage one to do, not to negate the beings that a will to power cannot actively approach, but to meet beings in the value through which they reach Being. The eternal return: that nothing that is be excluded from one's perspective, such that nothing that occurs be subject to erasure or censure. The future has nothing better to do than to give again what passes, because nothing passes that the will to power cannot read in its Being as a being to be valued. Perspective becomes world only if the will to power wills every being without having to reject or deny any of

---

[12] Ibid.
[13] Ibid., § 1067 = VII, 3, 339, 38 [12] [Kaufmann, 550].

them because of reactive fear: "To will the Dionysian, to say Yes (*Ja-sagen*) to the world as it is, without subtraction, exception or selection," strictly amounts to "willing the eternal circulation." The very formula "absolute yea-saying to the world"[14] must be understood as something like a production: before the *yes,* no world. Only the *yes,* because it neither rejects nor omits anything that befalls the will to power, makes possible an infinite-world perspective. The "men who say-yes-absolutely-to-the-world (*Weltbejahendsten*)" (*Beyond Good and Evil,* § 56) could not say *yes* to anything other than a world, since saying *no* amounts to limiting one's perspective in order to cut it off from a world. Man reaches the world only by welcoming it with a yes. And again: the *yes* can only be absolute, without the limits of the vulgar (tripartite) concept of time managing to restrict it. Past and future offer no refuge to a shifty denial. They are absorbed again in the *yes,* which summons their two caverns without exception or end: they engulf nothing, but reserve a flat and ever more vast surplus for affirmation, which will be able to recognize in them, in the following round, the chronicle of its hesitations in an endless convocation. And, without exception, the present: all the way to the indecision that my pen here—in an instant that the printer will present to the hypothetical reader—betrays. —*Yes,* world, eternal return: the Being of each being (the valuation of value) calls for the completion of a totality, where the being is absorbed in its completeness: the ultimate accumulation that capitalizes nothing but, if one wishes to recognize in it the other dimension of onto-theology, announces something like being in its supreme figure. This is perhaps why Nietzsche surrounds that theological figure with rejected adjectives: the yes is Dionysian, which allows one to "stand in a Dionysian relation to *Dasein.*"[15] That Dionysus, ever more insistent, should come to brush against the thinker of the "abyssal thought" is in itself nothing strange: the very situation of the thinker becomes divine, since he gathers in himself the estimation of the world. It is not that he establishes himself as the supreme being. But the supreme sum of beings—where the world

---

[14] Respectively, ibid., § 1041 = VIII, 3, 288, 16 [32], and § 1019 = VIII, 2, 134, 10 [21] [Kaufmann, 536, 527, mod.].

[15] Ibid., § 1041 = VIII, 3, 288, 16 [32] [Kaufmann, 536].

alone becomes the supreme being—is stated only in a *yes,* which the thinker alone can say. And which he must say divinely, like Dionysus. But who will be able to bear the weight of the "abyssal thought" that lightens the world to the point of making it its own supreme being?

The trial of thinking the "abyssal thought"—of being "hunted by you, thought! Unnameable! Hidden! Atrocious!" ("Ariadne's Lament," in *Dithyrambs,* 56)—reaches Zarathustra first and thus honors him. If, however, by slow approaches, Zarathustra touches the unthinkable thought, he does not manage in the end to make it his own, that is, to make himself according to it, to make himself his own: when he spontaneously evokes it and, standing himself for the "prophet of the circle," gives unreserved expression to his own *Abgrund,* he finds himself submerged by it—annihilated with disgust and pain (*Zarathustra,* III, "The Convalescent," 1). Thus he collapses—like Nietzsche himself one day—"as one dead" (ibid., 2); Zarathustra must still learn from his faithful animals, in order to become accustomed to a thought that exceeds him. He himself will go in search of higher men who, perhaps more than he, or at least as much, will bear the unbearable. The fourth part of *Zarathustra* is tragic in that the "higher men," who must complete what Zarathustra begins, endlessly collapse and, far from surpassing him, prove incapable even of accompanying him. The perpetual "ass festival" that disqualifies them springs back upon Zarathustra, whose reported and rejected announcement betrays immediate impotence. The incompletion of *Zarathustra* betrays the incompletion in Zarathustra of the man—of the Overman— whom he prefigures without being able to embody him. In the "dangerous going over" (*gefährliches Hinüber*) that he undertakes, because "man is something that must be overcome (*überwunden*)" (*Zarathustra,* Preface, §§ 3 and 4), Zarathustra himself remains on the path, a tightrope walker frozen by a bottomless vestige before attaining the second pole. In a letter to Carl Fuchs (29 July 1888), Nietzsche diagnoses, with the extreme lucidity that runs through him regarding the essential, the profound reason for the insufficiency of the man and of the work: "The fourth part of *Zarathustra,* treated by me with that reserve before the 'Publico,' which, precisely, did *not* have to be maintained in relation to the first three, gives me bitter regret. . . . More precisely, it is a question of

an interlude (*Zwischenakt*) between Zarathustra and the one who
follows ('I will not give you any name . . .'). The precise title, which
would seem more characteristic: *The Temptation of Zarathustra*/An
Interlude (*Zwischenspiel*)."[16] The between (*Zwischen* . . .) where
Zarathustra is immobilized, where trial becomes to him a temptation, is situated in the fourth part. The latter recounts Zarathustra's inability to meet "what *I* am looking for: the higher man"
(*Zarathustra*, IV, "Conversation with the Kings"). Or rather, there
is nothing easier, finally, than to meet them; but one finds nothing that Zarathustra has not, in person and in his person, conquered. The higher men succeed only in regressing to the "ass
festival," to just short of nihilism. Zarathustra remains in the form
of the lion even if, in the end, "my children are close." The inflation of the fourth part and the accumulation of plans for parts
that were supposed to be joined to it only better betray the evidence: after the third part (which thinks the eternal return) Zarathustra as a character is no longer up to the task of thought that
he opened. He no longer plants his feet with the somnambulistic
soundness of one whom an event commands (it being understood that "the greatest thoughts are the greatest events"; *Beyond
Good and Evil*, § 285), on the invisible path of thought. This is why
Beyond Good and Evil (1886), which immediately follows *Zarathustra* (private edition of the fourth part, 1885), is exasperated by
waiting for the one or for those who will complete what Zarathustra left hanging. The book for all and none, where all finally await
the arrival of the one who sneaks away—or who never finishes
arriving, Zarathustra—is followed by the "Prelude to a philosophy
of the future": the *Zwischenspiel* now looks toward an overture that
the *Vorspiel* restlessly seeks. Perhaps it would be necessary to understand all of *Jenseits* on the basis of the concluding poem,
"From High Mountains": old friends (the first pole of the tightrope, higher men) turn away from "me"; it is therefore necessary
to wait for new friends: "My *new* friends! Come, it is time, it is
time!" The friend who comes is again, in the final verse, "Zarathustra, . . . the friend, the guest of guests." But which is he here?
Does he coincide with the earlier Zarathustra, or, on the contrary,

---

[16] Letter to C. Fuchs, 29 July 1888, in K. Schlechta, *Friedrich Nietzsche, Werke in
drei Bände* (Munich, 1966), vol. III, 1306–7.

does he come after him, as called by him? Whom must we recognize in the *I* that the poem expresses and whose arrival the poem announces? In a word, the binary structure of waiting (Zarathustra—the higher men) is replaced by a ternary play of arrival: old friends—I—Zarathustra, as the new friend. This new Zarathustra no longer waits, no longer seeks nor speaks: these traits characterize, on the contrary, the *I:* he is only awaited and, in the end, arrives furtively, closer in this way to the figure of Zarathustra in the so precious poem "Sils Maria" (the final elaboration of which is completed with its insertion in Book IV of the *Gay Science,* thus, in 1887):

> It was there that, seated, I waited, I waited—
> but for nothing,
> Beyond good and evil, enjoying now the
> light,
> now the darkness, having wholly become pure play,
> wholly sea, wholly noon, wholly
> time without end.
> When suddenly, friends! The one became two.
> And Zarathustra came over me, passing by my
> side.[17]

Within the ternary play that is established with *Jenseits* one must include the "new philosophers": this name is only half suitable for them since they will want to remain riddles (§§ 42–43). Their role will consist in "revaluating and inverting the 'eternal val-

---

[17] The quoted text from 1887 is not the only one to announce this other Zarathustra whom it is necessary to await, and who does not speak at length. We should remark at least two others. In *Ecce Homo* the presentation of *Thus Spoke Zarathustra* concludes its paragraph 1 in the following way: "I was in this coastal region again in the fall of 1886 when he visited this small forgotten world of bliss for the last time. It was on these two walks that the whole of *Zarathustra I* occurred to me, and especially Zarathustra himself as a type: rather he *overtook me*" (pp. 307–8; Kaufmann, 297–98). In the *Genealogy of Morals,* II, § 25: "But what am I saying? Enough! Enough! At this point it behooves me only to be silent; or I shall usurp that to which only one younger, 'heavier with future,' and stronger than I has a right—that to which only *Zarathustra* has a right, *Zarathustra the godless.*" Invoked here as "*he [who] must come one day*" (ibid., § 24), Zarathustra remains problematic, ahead of our nihilistic impotence, and therefore could not speak to us: We could not bear the discourse that he would deliver, supposing that he should ever say anything other than *yes.* The abundance—even carried by a remarkable poetry—of discourses of *Zarathustra* seems strictly incompatible with the one who is announced here elliptically.

ues'," and therefore in "bearing the weight of such a responsibility"—that of carrying out the universal evaluation of values in a "humanity" (§ 23), to the point of allowing a world to open up. But it is on the basis of that role and of the demands of the will to power as the creation of a world that they can be glimpsed and thus awaited. It remains that no one can ensure their coming: "Are there today such philosophers? Is it not *necessary* that there already be such philosophers?" (§ 211). Postulated only in the name of a lapse in the exercise of the will to power as the affirmation of a world, must these philosophers only be dreamed or indeed confidently awaited? But in that case, is not awaiting them of a piece with awaiting a new Zarathustra?

Not at all, for the "new philosophers" are distinguished from the old ones in that, instead of vulgarizing or censuring the divine, they welcome it. Or rather, ceasing to master the play of the divine, they are welcomed in it: it is not the philosophers who reach the divine but indeed the divine that plays at philosophizing. "Even that Dionysus is a philosopher, and that gods, too, thus do philosophy, seems to me to be a novelty that is far from innocuous and might arouse suspicion precisely among philosophers" (*Beyond Good and Evil,* § 295; Kaufmann, 235).[18] The philosophers quite simply could not understand (it is not even a question of admitting) that the divine grabs hold of philosophy, so that the "new philosopher" no longer serves but as a mask, among other names (of which the second is Zarathustra) for Dionysus. Why can, or must, this god philosophize? Perhaps because no one can bear the weight of the "abyssal thought" if not a god—a god who knows how to dance, there indeed where the will to power of the old man fails to bear the eternal return. That this god might one day place itself in our school signifies perhaps nothing other than his coming among us, in order to speak in a human manner the great *Amen.* This is to say here that Dionysus, in place of the old figure of Zarathustra, returns to establish, again, the ternary play: the old philosophers—*I*—Dionysus. *I* enters as the middle term (if not the mediator) between the god

---

[18] *Beyond Good and Evil,* § 295. On the permanence of the gap that at one and the same time unites and separates Zarathustra and the Overman (and thus Dionysus), see *Vorträge* I, p. 99 = "Qui est le Zarathoustra de Nietzsche," in *Essais et Conférences* (Paris: Gallimard, 1958), p. 124 and passim.

and the others, among whom would be the reader. Curiously, however, the sequence, which thus qualifies the *I* in its role ("he would say to me . . . it is thus that he said to me one day"), reveals another character, parallel with the *I* but distinct from it: "It happens that I love humans—he was alluding to Ariadne, who was there." What is the relation between Dionysus, Ariadne, and *I*? Why would Zarathustra disappear from this play?

Zarathustra's insufficiency is marked out from the moment of his collapse before the "abyssal thought." That thought can be clearly explained as "a *Dionysian Yes* to the world as it is . . . it wants the eternal circle."[19] The thought of the Eternal Return is Dionysian. But "Zarathustra himself is quite simply an old atheist: He believes neither in old nor in new gods. Zarathustra says that he would become, but he does not become—Do not misunderstand him. A type of god after the type of the creative spirit, of the 'great man'."[20] The affirmation of the great man, that, in a word, of the Zarathustra who speaks and succumbs in *Zarathustra*, remains that of "*his* type of man, a relatively superhuman type, [which] is superhuman precisely in its relation to the *good*" (*Ecce Homo*, "Why I Am a Destiny," § 5; Kaufmann, 331), superhuman only relatively, relative to its point of departure, the man who is inhumanly called good. But precisely, in reversing values, eyes fixed upon the original adversary, Zarathustra remains tied to him like a lion; the *yes* that he should say to beings in general ceaselessly takes the polemical form of a *no*. Between the tactical *no* and the strategically aimed *yes* creeps in the contraction, the narrowness, and the failure that distinguish Zarathustra from Dionysus.[21] An old atheist, Zarathustra does not know the Dionysian

---

[19] *Will to Power,* § 1041 = VIII, 3; 288, 16 [32].

[20] Ibid., § 1038 = VIII, 3, 324, 17 [4], § 5 [Kaufmann, 535, mod.].

[21] One should note in this regard a relatively strange text in *Ecce Homo*, "Why I Write Such Good Books," *Thus Spoke Zarathustra*, § 7 [Kaufmann, 306–8], where there appears—but only as a "psychological problem"—a question that in fact runs throughout all of *Ecce Homo* (see, in the same collection, *Beyond Good and Evil*, § 1, and "Why I Am a Destiny," §§ 1 and 4): how are we to understand the fact that the refusal of denial might offer a face of the *Yes/Amen*? Curiously, whereas in the other passages the question finds an answer, in the one where it is applied to Zarathustra, the answer is not explicitly formulated. On the contrary, Nietzsche repeats and deepens the paradox in order, all of a sudden, to move on to Dionysus: "But it is the concept of Dionysus once again." Must we understand this to mean that to the question that Zarathustra poses, the question that

ease that is in harmonious accord with the fullness of the world freed by the absolute *Yes*. Before the enormity and the deformity of the beings that ask for their reaffirmation by the Eternal Return, Zarathustra breaks down: his knowledge of beings turns against him to torture him, instead of arranging a return of the world upon its own affirmation:

> A corpse
> Crushed under a thousand weights heaped up
> Crushed under its own weight,
> *A Man who knows!*
> *Who knows himself!*
> The *wise* Zarathustra! . . .
> You sought the heaviest burden:
> You found *yourself,*
> You will not be able to reject yourself by yourself . . .
> Zarathustra! . . .
> Self-knower (*Selbstkenner*)!
> Self-torturer (*Selbsthenker*)! . . .
>
>   (*Dithyrambs*, "Among Birds of Prey," 42, 44)

In a word, Zarathustra again becomes reactive when his will to power, through weakness, deters transforming the knowledge of all beings, the most unbearable of thoughts, into affirmation. According to the rule of *ressentiment*, he turns against himself, in a suicidal negation, what he cannot manage to will positively in the actuality of a world. If he was able to overcome himself, "he was not god enough to announce the 'Dionysian world,' the 'Dionysian philosophy,' or 'Dionysus philosophizing.' Thus his sufferings had to be reinterpreted as those of a 'god' " (K. Reinhardt). What Zarathustra could not accomplish—to arrive, in the suffering inflicted by the "abyssal thought," at the ultimate *Yes* that produces a world by provoking the Eternal Return—only a god will do.

It is indeed necessary to understand that the decisive event of the Nietzschean anabasis consists much less in the announcement

---

he *is*, there answers only another who replaces him—Dionysus? Only *another* can support the unbearable thought that Zarathustra was unable to bear, and which therefore he could present only reactively, and that other characterizes the thought as Dionysian.

of Zarathustra than in Zarathustra's inability to withstand the announcement of Dionysus. Who will withstand the abyssal, Dionysian thought, "the great educative thought"?[22] Only provisional answers are given to this question. Let us enumerate them. From the ternary play between Ariadne, *I*, and Dionysus, Zarathustra (who at best will merge with one of these three figures) is excluded. As for Ariadne, one must already say that she, exclusively, mythically, and even erotically, will receive Dionysus. And therefore one must say that the expectation of the god—that is to say, the approach of the human to the "Dionysian thought"—invests the scene where Ariadne allows herself to be approached by Dionysus. But who is Ariadne, and why does she enter here? "Thus suffers a god, a Dionysus. The answer to such a dithyramb of solar solitude in the light would be Ariadne.—Who besides me knows what Ariadne is!—For all these riddles nobody so far had any solution; I doubt that anybody even saw any riddles here" (*Ecce Homo*, "Why I Write Such Good Books; *Thus Spoke Zarathustra*," § 8, p. 317; Kaufmann, 308, mod.). Ariadne becomes the place for meetings with Dionysus, a place that only *I*, that is, Nietzsche, knows (the sentence is not an interrogative but an exclamatory assertion). Why does Nietzsche not proclaim Ariadne, whom he nonetheless knows? Perhaps because he knows her too well.

In order to clarify Ariadne's identity, let us return to that of the *I*. Why does Nietzsche say *I* instead of letting Zarathustra or someone else speak, for example, Ariadne? First, because the *Yes* can be said only by the one who gives and abandons himself in it, in the sense that Zarathustra, precisely, did not respond to the invocation "*Give first yourself as an offering*, Oh Zarathustra!" (*Dithyrambs*, "On the Poverty of the Richest," 76). The word called for by the "the abyssal thought" cannot be pronounced by an interposed mask, since it is a question of becoming oneself the *Yes*:

> Blazon of necessity!
> Sublime star of Being!
> —which no wish reaches,
> Which no *No* soils.
> Eternal *Yes* of Being,

---

[22] *Will to Power*, § 1056 = VII, 2, 69, 25 [227].

Eternally I am your *Yes:*
For I love you, Oh eternity!
(ibid., "Glory and Eternity," IV, 70),

"*being oneself* the eternal *Yes* to all things" (*Ecce Homo,* "Why I
Write Such Good Books; *Thus Spoke Zarathustra,*" § 6, p. 314; Kaufmann, 306). Being oneself, and not only the saying of a language
where thought remains disengaged and as if at a distance from a
body that speaks for it, without it; this means being corporally:
"*We ourselves,* we free spirits, are nothing less than a 'revaluation
of all values,' an *incarnate* declaration of war and triumph over all
the ancient conceptions of 'true' and 'untrue' " (*Antichrist,* § 13;
Kaufmann, 579). This amounts to saying that the "great reason"
of the body, which not only expresses the *I* but performs it, can
alone preside over the reversal to the *yes* and over the Dionysian
encounter. Consequently, no one can replace the body that says *I*
and names me, in order to pronounce the *yes.* Nietzsche must
give up leaving it to someone else to carry out that task: "In the
end one has to do everything *oneself* in order to know a few things
oneself: that is, one has *a lot* to do" (*Beyond Good and Evil,* § 45;
Kaufmann, 59–60). Only an *I* can say the *Yes* in which Dionysus is
performed and experienced, and only a body can ensure that *I.*
Anybody whom a body does not inscribe in egoism is replaceable.
The only one to become irreplaceable is the one who risks "pos-
sessing the truth in a body" (Rimbaud), more than in a soul. Thus
was it necessary that Nietzsche himself have taken place, there
where Zarathustra, the higher men, and their substitutes failed,
in order to confront the god and to pronounce the Dionysian *yes.*
But that multiple failure acts only as the occasional and quasi-
anecdotal reason for a more radically compelling investiture: the
will to power can give rise to a world around itself only by not
stealing away from "the task of giving a body to knowledge (*ein-
zuverleiben*) and making it instinctive" (*Gay Science,* § 11; Kaufmann, 85, mod.). No proxy frees Friedrich Nietzsche from giving
a body to the "abyssal thought"—from exposing himself to Dionysus face on. Thus might we better understand why and how
Nietzsche attributes to himself an infinity of names—Julius Cae-
sar, the Immoralist, the *Untier,* Phoenix, Cardinal Antonelli, the
Crucified, Dionysus, etc.: he himself dispossesses his body of *an*

identity, "Nietzsche," in order to lend it successively to the encounters and trials of the divine, which he risks receiving in the
Dionysian *Yes:* "What is disagreeable and strongly affects my modesty is the fact that, in the end, I am every name in history."[23]
Anonymity is replaced by an equivalent polyonymy: the body,
where Nietzsche abandons himself to the risk of the divine, runs
through all the figures that are incorporated with it, there to be
carried to their completion in the ultimate dialogue. Perhaps
might one thus understand the final identification of the *I* with
Ariadne: here it is not first a question of the famous note to Cos-
ima Wagner, which, in a sense, has nothing to do with this (it
lets Ariadne fall back into anecdote)—but indeed of "Ariadne's
Lament." In appearance, these simply copy the song of "The Magician," which appears in part IV of *Zarathustra,* to the point that
for a long time *Ariadne's Lament,* along with the other poems from
the same collection, were gathered by Nietzsche with the goal
of a separate edition titled *Songs of Zarathustra.* According to K.
Reinhardt, it is only "at the end, a little before his plunge into
darkness," or else, according to Colli-Montinari, "in the very last
days, when the precursory signs of the collapse were multiplying,"[24] that Nietzsche changed the initial title to *Dithyrambs of Dionysus.* This means that the modifications then made hastily to the
poems correspond to the passage from Zarathustra to Dionysus,
as to the passage of Nietzsche into his collapse or plunge into
darkness (*Umnachtung*) that one vulgarly names madness. On
both points, the corrections made to *Ariadne's Lament* between
the *Songs* and the *Dithyrambs* shed some light—at least if one follows K. Reinhardt's conclusions.

Passage to Dionysus. (a) The partner of the "unknown god"
veers from the masculine ("dein stolzester Gefanger," *Zarathustra,* IV) to the feminine ("deine stolzeste Gefangne," *Lament*),
that is, from a man who derisively imitates the suffering of waiting
for a god, to a woman who suffers from an absent god and confus-

---

[23] Letter to J. Burckhardt, 5/6 January 1889, in K. Schlechta, *Friedrich Nietzsche, Werke,* III, 1351.

[24] First, K. Reinhardt, p. 312, with which K. Schlechta agrees (*Friedrich Nietzsche, Werke,* III, *Philosophischer Nachbericht,* pp. 1389–90), as opposed to E. F. Podach (*Friedrich Nietzsche, Werke der Zusammenbruch* [Heidelberg, 1961], p. 355 ff.), then Colli-Montinari, French trans., *Dithyrambs,* p. 242.

edly desires his coming. (b) Compared to a poem from the same collection, "Among Birds of Prey," one can remark that the *Lament* no longer speaks of a self-affliction (*"Selbstkennster! / Selbsthenker!... /* Was schlichst du *dich* ein / In *dich*—in *dich?"*), but of a veritable alterity in the suffering, which assigns to the god the role of making suffer: "Du Folterer! / Du Henker—Gott!" This is a suffering that henceforth is inscribed in and attests to the trial of an encounter. (c) If the "No: come back!" that introduces the penultimate verse is found already in a poem attached to Book V of the *Gay Science* (*Songs of Prince Vogelfrei,* "Rimus Remedium, or: how poets console themselves") and in the song of "The Magician," there is a crucial difference—here the "unknown god" "becomes visible in a smaragdine beauty." His name is Dionysus. Between the *Songs* and the *Dithyrambs,* masculine tomfoolery becomes feminine desire, a fantastic torture, a pain come from elsewhere, the call to return, the appearance of the god in person. Therefore, if here, at the very moment of his collapse, Nietzsche passes, by a few corrections, from one site to the other, it is because he himself, having become at one and the same time Ariadne and Dionysus, has *in fact* experienced the divine—and pronounced corporally, with neither mask nor proxy, the great *Yes.* The last texts prepared for printing therefore contain these *inedita, inaudita* par excellence—the investment of a poem by the divine (letter to Catulle Mendès, Turin, 1 January 1889).[25] From the passage to Dionysus to the passage into darkness the distance is short. It is still necessary to risk saying something about that darkness. Let us let Nietzsche himself say it:

> While it is constantly suggested to us today that, instead of a grain of salt, a grain of the spice of madness is joined to genius, all earlier people found it much more likely that wherever there is madness there is also a grain of genius and wisdom—something 'divine,' as one whispered to oneself. . . . All superior men who were irresistibly drawn to throw off the yolk of any kind of morality and to frame new laws had, *if they were not actually mad,* no alternative but to make themselves or pretend to be mad. (*Daybreak,* I, § 14; Hollingdale, 14)

---

[25] In *Dithyrambs,* p. 242, and in Podach, *Werke der Zusammenbruch,* p. 356, and facsimile, p. XXIII.

Perhaps what common sense names madness would be first this sense outside the common that produces illusions, opinions, and conceptions (*Wahnsinn*) that are themselves outside common sense. It is not the case, as imagine the modern Bouvard and Pécuchet, that the genius of the "artist" would fail at its elementary tasks in not being stirred up by a little madness; but the very fact of a sudden attack by madness attests to the play of another force—declared or dissimulated: the divine. To whatever nervous disease, physiological decay, or psychological weariness Friedrich Nietzsche, German subject, born in 1844, professor of Greek philology at the University of Basel, placed on leave of absence with pension, may have succumbed one January day in 1889, on the Plaza Carlo Alberto in Turin—it is in the name of the divine that Dionysus whispers in Ariadne's ear: "Sei klug!" and that he succumbs who knew himself previously to be so clever (*klug; Ecce Homo*). To collapse within this plunge into darkness amounts to passing abruptly and definitively, without return, to the nodal point where the will to power valuates all beings without exception, to the point of seeing them in a world—to the point of letting oneself be sucked in by the site of the god, suddenly. The man who, in the nihilist between, did not escape the silent summons to speak the Eternal Return, and thus to think the supreme beingness of worlded beings, that man had to become god: "Dear Professor, in the end I would much rather be a professor at Basel than God; but I did not dare push personal egoism to the point of abandoning for it the creation of the world. You see, one must offer one's sacrifice in one's own way and in the place where one lives."[26] From this sublime sequence there is nothing to remove, nor above all to overestimate as a joke. For here the joke is noth-

---

[26] Letter to J. Burckhardt, 5/6 January 1889 (see note 23). One should note that the antepenultimate fragment (according to Colli-Montinari, VIII, 3, 460 [19] from January 1889) strictly corroborates this indication: "Final reflection . . . after the old God was defeated, I am ready to *rule the world.*" It would be necessary, moreover, to wonder whether the appearance of the "great politics," up to the extraordinary fabrication of the next-to-last letters, does not offer, precisely, one of the figures of the assignment of the thought of the Eternal Return to the person of Nietzsche. P. Klossowski, it seems to me, here works to take seriously the fact that "that of which [Nietzsche] is conscious is precisely the fact that he has stopped being Nietzsche" (*Nietzsche et le cercle vicieux* [Paris: Mercure de France, 1969], pp. 334, 301 ff.).

ing other than the ultimate civility of the one who speaks to us from beyond the grave—not from another world, *but from the middle of this one here*. It was necessary that Nietzsche collapse into the divine in order that he might hear his voice say in concert with Dionysus the *Yes* that creates a world at the very heart of nihilism.

But then, cannot the ultimate *Yes* be pronounced by man, that he collapse also within the plunge into darkness, such that it is never *man* who pronounces it but indeed the divine in whom he must lose himself? And in that case, what form does the divine take, and with what relation to the idols that one has conserved, to the prohibitions that one has set up?

§ 6. THE CHRIST: EVASION OF AN OUTLINE

The darkness of the final delirium (*Wahnsinn*) concludes the destruction of idolatrous illusions (*Wahn*) by exposing, once this veil is torn, an individual, Friedrich Nietzsche, to the unbearable trial of the divine that is immediately (corporally) confronted. The individual pays in cash for the final identification with Dionysus— with the god whose affirmation wills beings even to the point of justifying them in the innocence of a world—by identifying himself also with the Crucified,[27] who shines forth under the ultimate tension of the divine. The radical ambiguity of the relation between Christ and the Nietzschean text (of which the corporally registered plunge into darkness is an integral part)[28] repeats that double designation. To be sure, the Christ is first approached as the "founder of Christianity" and is therefore eliminated along with the idols that it produces, throughout a tireless and tiresome polemic, a rarely fascinating patience. Whether Nietzsche seriously reached the Jesus of history or the Christ of faith (who in the end coincide) matters little, since the material elimination of

---

[27] See the two notes, the one to P. Gast, "To my *maëstro Pietro* / Sing me a new song: the world has cleared and the skies rejoice. / The Crucified" (4 January 1889, in K. Schlechta, *Werke*, III, 1350), the other to Georg Brandes: "To my friend Georg! You have discovered me, it was a game to find me: the difficulty now is to lose me . . . / The Crucified" (4 January 1889, ibid.).

[28] On the equivalence of the texts, both "philosophical" and "nonphilosophical," in another text of which Nietzsche himself is a part, see B. Pautrat, *Versions du soleil: figures et système de Nietzsche* (Paris: Editions du Seuil, 1971), p. 296 ff.

the Christ offers the condition of an otherwise decisive relation to the Christic figure.

Once the (historical, textual, institutional, etc.) material is taken away, what remains of the Christ? Let us not too easily and too quickly accept the nevertheless constant opposition between Christianity and Christ,[29] since it presupposes at least that after the revocation of Christianity one might still evoke, if not invoke, the Christ. The only thing that is worthy of question is whether in fact one must do so. A provisional thesis: Jesus, as the Christ who dies on the cross, perhaps offers the insurpassable figure, even for Nietzsche—especially for him—of the unavoidable trial imposed by man's meeting with the divine. The fact that, for him, the divine is principally and finally called "Dionysus" underlines all the more the fact that a name, a place, and a figure remain to be located in which the one who receives the divine might emerge. Among the names that Nietzsche gives to the divine and to himself, that of the Christ dominates. Let us be clear: it is not the case that, through some contradiction on the part of the thinker or some recuperation on the part of the commentator, what the critique explicitly invalidated is reintroduced; but in fact, once the explicit matter has been gotten rid of, there remains the *figure* of Christ. By this we mean the focal, unavoidable, and unavoided place where he who was supposed to experience the divine ends up. It is the obligatory place because there is no other in history where even those who undertake to substitute themselves for the divine must take up residence—it is an obligatory place inasmuch as there is the obligation of a place. The fact that Nietzsche first preserves and then invests the figure of Christ, a figure emptied by the critique, is what accounts for—without taking it seriously or recuperating it—the multiform, repeated, and half-successful pastiche of the Christ by Nietzsche-the-writer. *Zarathustra* pastiches the Gospels with a talent and an intention that are too visible not to become at times bothersome and out of place: parables, sayings, teachings to the charmed and unintelligent crowd—all of this is taken from the great *logia* of the Synoptics. The fourth part (or already the third) introduces the election

---

[29] See *Antichrist*, § 39, 40, etc., and *Will to Power*, § 159, § 167 = VIII, 2, 350–51, 11 [282], § 168 = VIII, 2, 340, 11 [257], § 195 = VIII, 2, 356, 11 [294].

of the disciples, the private teachings, the deceptions, the trips, etc., echoing the Gospels a second time. The parts outlined were supposed to include a betrayal of the disciples and a death of Zarathustra. And if Zarathustra tends to disappear, would that not be, precisely, because he *is not* dead, because he has not been able to complete his task: to see the "new gods"? The *Antichrist* must be understood, tactically, according to the same eschatological tension that determines his appearance in the New Testament: "Children, the last hour has come. You have heard that an Antichrist had to come, and already now many antichrists have come: by this we know that the last hour is here" (1 John 2:18). In the New Testament the Antichrist precedes and announces the return of Christ only by a counter-will, by an insistent negation. In Nietzschean terms, the reversal of values takes the place of negation: the Antichrist therefore announces directly and in person the parousia of the divine and hastens it by his work of negation. The promulgation of a law against Christianity dated 30 September 1888, according to the "false calendar," that is, the establishment of a today as the first day of a new world, arises from the same situation: eschatology in the form of affirmation achieved in a Dionysian manner.[30] This is indeed why the *Antichrist* maintains a fundamental relation with *Ecce Homo*. "Ecce Homo" or: here is the man who is missing for the last affirmation. The christological pastiche reaches perfection because it plays on several interwoven levels: (a) "*Ecce Homo!*" reprises the Vulgate translation of the ᾽ιδου ὁ ἄνθρωπος from John 19:6. (b) Instead of designating an innocent condemned person, the silent and almost absent term from the triangle that is completed by Pontius Pilate and the crowd, the indication delivers Nietzsche's self-attestation as the one who definitively comes, in place of the idols and even of the

---

[30] This *today* that Nietzsche claims and that inaugurates a new calendar to be counted from the day that Christianity died inverts and pastiches at the same time the *today* that the Christ applies to himself: "and he began to say to them: 'Today this scripture has been fulfilled in your hearing' " (Luke 4:21, see 2:11)—or is made to apply by the Christian: "In many and various ways God spoke of old to our fathers in the prophets; but in these last days he has spoken to us in a Son" (Hebrews 1:1–2, literally, "in this end of the days that are these here . . ."). That one of the days should become the καιρός of a *today*, or that fulfillment should occur in and be identified with a certain moment, pertains to eschatology in the strict sense.

provisional Antichrist. This is a self-investment that condemns the inhabitants of the other-world, and no longer the appointment of a person condemned, by a judge, to the crowd of the world. An assumption of speech and power, *Ecce Homo* indicates the one "who not only grasps the word 'Dionysian,' but grasps *himself* in the word 'Dionysian' " (*Ecce Homo*, "Why I Write Such Good Books," *The Birth of Tragedy*, § 2, p. 287; Kaufmann, 272–73, mod.), echoing the one who not only conceived God but called himself God. (c) Above all, the one who grasps himself as Dionysian must, in conformity with the "concept of Dionysus," "*be himself* the eternal Yes to all things, the monstrous and unlimited *Yes and Amen*" (ibid., *Thus Spoke Zarathustra*, § 6, p. 314; Kaufmann, 306, mod.). It is a question of pronouncing the *Yes* of the Eternal Return, which Nietzsche constantly and consciously equates with that which it translates, the Hebrew *Amen*.[31] It is certainly not by chance if Nietzsche equates them. Ostensibly, he is miming the *Amen* of Christ, his ultimate word to the Father, which expresses the last benediction, the *berakha* that unites God and man from the bottom of the abyss: "In him it is always *Yes*. And the promises of God found in him their *Yes*. Thus it is still through him that the *Amen* passes through us to God, to his glory" (2 Corinthians 1:20). Thus the world is justified—reconciled with itself and with the Father in the *Amen* of Christ. Therefore, and this is the crucial point, the pastiche here becomes conscious imitation. It is not a question of minimizing the fact that the man of the great *Amen* and the Christ are distinct. It is on the contrary a question of understanding how, on the basis of such similarities, the irreducible antagonism remains. The formal comparisons culminate in a unique figure: the world finds justice or innocence, which immortalizes it in the *Yes/Amen* that must be pronounced eschatologi-

---

[31] See *Zarathustra*, III, "Before Sunrise," "the formidable and unlimited pronouncement of the *Yes* and *Amen*," and also "The Seven Seals," which admits of another title, "the song of the *Yes* and *Amen*" (*Zarathustra*, III), etc. Let us recall that the Hebrew *Amen* that ratifies an oath also includes the idea of a confidence given to that which or to the one whom the *Amen* addresses (according to the verb corresponding to *nifal*: to remain, to be reliable, whence, in *hifal*, to believe in, to have confidence in). Crucial point: to think the *Yes* as an *Amen* amounts to presupposing the world to be not only acceptable and bearable, but credible and faithful. It presupposes not only not refusing it, but having complete confidence in it, and abandoning oneself to it at the moment of receiving it.

cally and corporally by a man who risks, in that game, everything of himself, that man who remains to appear. We thus define a doubly empty figure. Empty because one can, at least apparently, pour into it the Nietzschean semantic just as well as the biblical semantic. The correspondences, transcriptions, and displacements remain possible here on condition of a minimum dual erudition. The figure plays the role of a common structure and is valid only as a structure. Why then identify it starting from one of its two possible values and risk the "Christic structure"? No doubt because of the arbitrariness of a reading, which always follows, whatever detours it concedes, its steepest line. But arbitrariness can also be justified after the fact—at least when it is a question of reading. There is a Christic structure in the Nietzschean text because the anteriority of the Christian event thoroughly structures the refutation by imposing on it the terms of the debate. Next, because the Nietzschean text there finds a more comprehensive rigor: that is, the plunge into darkness, like the symptoms that, miming the announcements of the Passion, precede it, becomes rigorously foreseeable and, far from shattering the expression of the thought, attest through the ultimate event to its infallible rigor. Moreover, the "Christic structure" is reinforced by the second vacuity of the figure. It is empty also because to "the One who is coming" (it is known that ὁ ἐρχομενος in John designates Christ) and who actually came there answers in the Nietzschean text only the half-presence of the one who must still come. The half-personal names accumulate on the body and the face of Friedrich Nietzsche, as in order to baptize him and invest him with the will to power that must supremely evaluate the world. Because the "new friends" do not come, because only Friedrich Nietzsche risks taking their place at the last minute, because finally he himself could not do it—he founders in the darkness. If one will, Nietzsche did not have to die from the trial of the divine, like Empedocles or—in a completely different way—Jesus, precisely because he was not up to it. Dying is reserved for the Overman, as dying characterizes only the true prophets. To the true death of Christ, the Nietzschean mime can oppose only a half-death: the plunge into darkness itself. Death of the spirit without death of the body: the spirit therefore did not totally invest his body, which subsists alone. The will to power was therefore not totally embodied. A "Platonism," then, remains, but one that is covered over by the ultimate crisis. That half-death lacks a complete incarnation, which would have totally joined the body with the spirit. The incarnation that was missing from that death was missing also from his life: because no one was coming, Friedrich Nietzsche was obligated, by the rigor of an alluring lucidity, to allow a metaphysical adoptionism play upon his own person.[32] But the history of theology has overabundantly established that adoptionism never delivers any human instrument but to a half-god: hence the final failure—to which the darkness testified for

---

[32] The divine and the enunciation of the unbearable thought must be paid for corporally; the fact that Friedrich Nietzsche consents to this in person, that is, the fact that he disposes of his body for such an arrival, would suffice to recall the application of Psalm 40 to Christ by the Letter to the Hebrews (10:5): "Consequently, when Christ came into the world, he said, 'You desired neither sacrifices nor offerings, but you fashioned me a body.'" This version, due to the Septuagint, mentions "body" where the Masoretic gives: ". . . You opened my ears." It has been remarked that the two versions of the biblical text can in some way be harmonized: Allowing the divine to take on a body presupposes the opening of the senses to its presence; corporality indicates availability (obedience, if one wants) (see R. Brague, "La Prière du Christ," in *Résurrection* 31, no. 3 [Paris, 1969], p. 31, and J. Ratzinger, *Der Gott Jesu Christi* [Munich: Kösel, 1976], pp. 53–55). Now, the correspondence of the two themes could be found in the Nietzschean text. Indeed, the Nietzschean introduction to destiny, or better, the recognition by Nietzsche of the corporal identity between himself and destiny ("I know my fate," in *Ecce Homo*, "Why I Am a Destiny," § 1, p. 332 [Kaufmann, 326]) coincides with this strange consideration: "All of us know, some of us even know from experience, which animal has long ears (*Langohr*). Well then, I dare assert that I have the smallest ears (*die kleinsten Ohren*). This is of no small interest to the little women—it seems to me that they may feel I understand them better" (*Ecce Homo*, "Why I Write Such Good Books," § 2, p. 279 [Kaufmann, 263, mod.]). Why ears and "little women"? What relation is there with something like a "destiny"? These questions are answered by the final verse of "Ariadne's Lament" (*Dithyrambs*, p. 62): "Be wise, Ariadne! . . . / You have little ears (*kleine Ohren*), you have my ears: / welcome in the wise word!" The wise word (*kluger Wort*), which in its way answers *Ecce Homo*'s question "Why am I so wise?" comes to Ariadne (who perhaps replaces the "little woman") only through small ears. Dionysus adds "my ears," just as Nietzsche previously; would they both be identical? Perhaps—unless Friedrich Nietzsche coincides with Ariadne: The advised wisdom comes to him only through a small ear, and thus through fine hearing—that which characterizes the god himself. To have fine hearing is to have the hearing of the god, and to hear in it the word of the god; it is thus to receive it, in the echo of a tympanum, in the labyrinth of an internal ear—"I am your labyrinth," the last word of Dionysus as he penetrates Ariadne—in the ear where a body listens to a body, "smagardine beauty." The god is born corporally through the ear.

ten years. The figure remains doubly empty: an ambivalent "Christic structure" and the failure of an impossible substitution for Christ. In a word, we are dealing with a hollowed out christology (eschatological and reversed). I am not saying that Nietzsche meditated on the mystery of Christ, nor even that he undertook consciously to repeat the mystery of Christ after or at the moment of emptying it, nor above all that he failed with reference to some norm. I am saying that the coherence of the Nietzschean text, including the plunge into darkness, becomes visible in this way, in this way more than otherwise, and perhaps that Christ haunts Nietzschean thought more profoundly than as an adversary or a reference—he remains the typical and ultimate place where that thought lives, whether consciously or unconsciously.

An empty figure of Christ. Why does the "Christic structure" nevertheless not impede the text from letting the one that it mimes escape? The outline of an answer to that question can only come from another question: what does Christ become in the Nietzschean text in order that the "Christic structure" should desert him? Now, precisely, there is nothing stranger than the theological penetration and the respectful intimacy with which Nietzsche approaches Christ. There is nothing stranger since Christ is taken into view positively and at length, such that the "Christic structure" is doubled, but through the simple juxtaposition, without any confrontation, of an obvious and sometimes mediocre critique of the historical Christ. Why then does the rift between the one and the other insinuate itself? Again, there is nothing stranger, since Christ is invested with characteristics that in other texts only the overman can receive, such that the reciprocal inclusion of the overman and the Christ would seem to be avoidable. Why, finally, does it fade in the name of a more radical rigor?

Christ receives, then, certain traits of the overman. First, he is defined by "great love," which wants to be to the dimensions of the world and wants the world to its dimension, the god(s) included. Thus,

> It is possible that underneath the holy fable and disguise of Jesus' life there lies concealed one of the most painful cases of the martyrdom of *knowledge about love:* the martyrdom of the most innocent

and desirous heart, never sated by any human love; *demanding* love, to be loved and nothing else, with hardness, with insanity (*mit Wahnsinn*), with terrible eruptions against those who denied him love; the story of a poor fellow, unsated and insatiable in love, who has to invent hell in order to send to it those who did not *want* to love him—and who finally, having gained knowledge about human love, had to invent a god who is all love, all *ability* to love—who has mercy on human love because it is so utterly wretched and unknowing! (*Beyond Good and Evil*, § 269; Kaufmann, 219–20)[33]

This is a remarkable (quasi-Victorine, except for a few details) reconstruction of Christ according to love alone, which "the most innocent heart" releases from any reactive suspicion. Above all, one must understand that the double abandon of love defined here (according to men, to God) presupposes that Nietzsche penetrates and confirms more fundamentally the mystery of the Cross. The love that demands and that abandons itself to the point of dying requires, in order to justify itself in its own eyes, nothing other than that very abandon. It develops no other discourse of a posteriori justification, nor of compensatory claims: it deploys an absolutely just and justified gesture, without internal fault, *index sui*, and overfilled with itself—without the exteriority of a legal authority, in the immediate assurance of sons. "Jesus said to his Jews: 'the law was made for servants—love God as I love him, as his son! What are morals to us sons of God!' " (*Beyond Good and Evil*, § 164; Kaufmann, 91). In a happy, serene, and, if we might dare to say it, "dancing" practice, Nietzsche recognizes very exactly the assurance of a son upon whom demand no longer weighs from the outside (morality, law), but in whom it plays intimately (love). "Salvation through faith (namely, that there is no

---

[33] A variant of the same text indicates: "and knew how to love even the one whom no one on earth loved sufficiently" (in *Par-delà Bien et Mal, Oeuvres philosophiques complètes*, French trans. of *Nietzsche Werke*, ed. Colli-Montinari [Paris: Gallimard, 1971], p. 386). It is therefore a question, even more clearly here, of a triangle among world-God (Father)-Christ, where only the last one named can, by loving the one whom no one was yet able to love, reach the great *Amen*, and thus an absolutely nonreactive situation with respect to the world. This amounts to saying that the supposed invention of God by Christ reflects the attempt at a universal affirmation, and therefore must be counted to his credit. That this presence of the Father is only invented changes in no way the positivity of the Christic affirmation but simply weakens the relation that Nietzsche has with it.

means of becoming a son of God except by following the *praxis of life* taught by Christ)":[34] Indeed, Christic *praxis* constitutes the absolute norm, without which nothing other must intervene that comments or compensates. "This 'bringer of glad tidings' died as he had lived, as he had taught—*not* to 'redeem men' but to show how one must live. This *practice* is his legacy to mankind . . . his behavior on the cross" (*Antichrist,* § 35; Kaufmann, 608–9). What is this behavior? On the cross, as before each episode of the Passion, Christ neither avoids nor evades the worst but suffers it. Moreover, he does not accuse, does not "ask anyone to account for his acts"; love the wicked, Nietzsche concludes. But what does this "love" here signify? It signifies that one does not seek—as opposed to the disciples—an answer to the enigma of the Cross: it is not necessary to find any culprits, because Christ lodges no complaint. The Jews accuse the innocent one, but the innocent one does not accuse the unjust, nor does he demand their punishment, nor even the recognition of his own innocence.[35] The Christ does not bring any accusation against the world. Even more, he declares it innocent. Before the ignominious death itself, his *Yes/Amen* does not regress into a *no.* Is it necessary to conclude that for Nietzsche himself the Christ expresses the great awaited *Amen* of a Dionysian breakthrough, and that in his own way he bears the unbearable within the innocence of an affirmation that, precisely there, does not recoil, that, in a word, he outlines the Eternal Return? One shouldn't too hastily accuse such

---

[34] *Will to Power,* § 170 = VIII, 2, 357, 11 [295]. See also § 159, and 167 = VIII, 2, 351, 11 [282] [Kaufmann, 102, mod.].

[35] Innocence does not indicate nonculpability so much as it outlines a perfect ignorance of the alternative between culpability and nonculpability. To give innocence to the world is to let it be seen by the one who does not judge it, not even in order to acquit it. Thus the innocence of the world depends on the gaze that strictly accuses neither its contours nor its lines, in the purely optical sense of the term. The question is transported from being in general and its acquittal (Stirner, Feuerbach, and in a sense Marx remain there) to the one who will bring to bear on it a gaze that is offside and outside of judgment. The question therefore becomes that of the innocent one, who alone excuses the world from justice. But *innocent* appears, as if by accident, as a name of Christ (M.-J. Le Guillou, *L'Innocent* [Paris: Fayard, 1971]), as "the one who comes from elsewhere." The innocent one, by renouncing justice, attacks it: He therefore finds himself accused by it of a-justice. He therefore dies and, thereby, records all the better the fact that justice lacks/misses innocence. According to the innocence of becoming also, the parallel with the Christ could be developed.

questions of an indecent inanity, for Nietzsche establishes at least
their common presupposition: that the Christ, by loving on the
Cross, overcomes *ressentiment.* It is precisely this that his disciples
were unable to admit or even glimpse: "Evidently the small community did *not* understand the main point, the exemplary character of this kind of death, the freedom, the superiority over any
feeling of *ressentiment*" (*Antichrist,* § 40; Kaufmann, 615). The
community does not comprehend that *ressentiment* disappears before love, affirmation, and the *Amen.* It therefore undertakes to
exercise its reprisals upon those who and that which the *Amen* of
Christ had declared innocent. Hence the return of a judging and
vengeful God, which mythically transcribes the reactive exteriority
of *ressentiment:* "Precisely the most unevangelical feeling, *revenge,*
came to the fore again" (ibid.), a feeling that created "gods born
of *ressentiment.*" The caesura between Christ and, depending on
the case, "the small community," the Jews, the apostle Paul, etc.,
has to do with this: whereas "Christianity is a naive beginning
toward a Buddhistic *peace movement* in the very middle of and starting from (*mitten aus*) the people of *ressentiment* par excellence, to
the point of issuing therefrom (*heraus*),"[36] and whereas, as such a
praxis, "genuine, original Christianity will be possible at all
times" (*Antichrist,* § 39; Kaufmann, 613), *ressentiment* immediately
reinterpreted it, abolished it, and developed it into a reactive system (law, morals) that organizes history with the aim of accusing
beings (parousia, judgment, hell). Since the Nietzschean event
aims entirely to deconstruct that accusation (vengeance), and
since only the Christ previously managed to pass beyond *ressentiment* equally well, can one put off the question of their confluence
and complicity? One should note at least the first privilege of the
Nietzschean Christ: as opposed to Christians, he overcomes *ressentiment* and, in his own way, pronounces an *Amen* that declares his
world innocent.

   The second characteristic privilege of the Christ is this: just as
he overcomes *ressentiment,* so he passes beyond—and again on the
Cross—the idolatrous relation to the divine. The first privilege
allows the Christ to enter into accord with the *Amen,* which remains to be pronounced, and thus to bear, as one bears a gaze,

---

[36] *Will to Power,* § 167 = VIII, 2, 350, 11 [282].

the necessity of an affirmation free of all *ressentiment* (§ 2). The second privilege, freeing the Christ from the idolatrous relation to the divine, removes him, perhaps, by dint of deepening his relation with the Father, from the "death of God." Two texts allow us to think this. Before the gaze of the suffering man, sickness dissipates the illusions and enchantments with which what Nietzsche later calls the will to power habitually flatters itself: "It is possible that this is what happened to the founder of Christianity on the cross: for the bitterest of all exclamations 'my God, why hast thou forsaken me!' contains, in its ultimate significance, evidence of a general disappointment and enlightenment over the idol (*Wahn*) of his life; at the moment of supreme agony he acquired an insight into himself of the kind told by the poet of the poor dying Don Quixote" (*Daybreak,* II, § 114; Hollingdale, 114). A trivial reading, which would reduce the Christ evoked here to a naïf who is finally disabused at the supreme moment of divine illusion, would miss the essential point. What the cross disqualifies is the idolatrous illusion of the Christ. Or rather that illusion (*Wahn*) here becomes untenable which would imagine itself to be an idol with the title of God. What imposes suffering, but also what allows one to dare to confront it, is that no idolatrous representation (*Wahn*) usurps the name of God with a false guarantee. In a radical sense, the cry of Christ and of Psalm 22 does not only betray the solitude of one who is abandoned; it reveals that those idols collapse that would embrace man within a closed, illusory, and gentle sphere to the point of depriving him of any authentic access to something like the divine—the supreme risk of alterity, separation, and singularity. The Christ cries with the cry of a *foetus* hurling at life: the cry of the one who pierces the idolatrous veil to swim in the ocean of distance. That we are dealing here with a death of the idolatrous representation of the divine, and therefore with a "dangerous" liberation for the approach of the divine in person, Nietzsche himself moreover confirms:

> *Danger in personality.*—The more God has counted as a discrete person, the less faithful one has been to him. Men are far more attached to their mental representations (*Gedankenbilder*) than they are to their most beloved beloved: that is why they sacrifice them-

selves for the state, the church, and also for God—so long as he remains *their own* production (*Erzeugnis*), *their idea* (*Gedanke*), and is not taken all too much for a person. In the latter case they almost always wrangle with him: even the most devout of men gave vent, indeed, to the bitter exclamation: "My God, why hast thou forsaken me!" (*Human All Too Human,* II, "The Wanderer and His Shadow," § 80; Hollingdale, 330)

The decisive progress made here has to do with the opposition between idols (*Gedankenbilder, Erzeugnis,* and *Gedanke*), which play the role of domesticated substitutes for the divine, and the person: the unrepresented and unrepresentable term of an aim whose space is discovered only in an attachment; abandon coincides exactly with the person because "danger" characterizes that person. The danger of the person consists in the fact that the person is never possessed, never fixed, never represented; the person opens only in opening an unlimited field, where she safeguards the separation that preserves her. Her solitude is approached only at the cost of an irrepressible solitude. Only in their mutual abandon do persons appear invisibly to themselves—only thus do they abandon themselves one to the other. This is why the "very bitter word" is not the last: the danger of the person delivers the relation between persons without any idolatrous obstacle. Thus the ultimate word of the Christ, "Father, into your hands I commit my spirit" (Luke 23:46; see also John 19:30: "He says: 'Everything is finished,' and then, bowing his head, he gives (up) his spirit"). Would abandon become the condition of a relation to God as a person and not as an idol? But then one would have to admit that abandon offers one of the faces of communion—perhaps the highest. Remarkably, Nietzsche posits the first equivalence. He no doubt misses the second, by symptomatically omitting the ultimate word of the Christ on the cross. The conjunction of abandon and the person in the same "danger," or better, the conjunction of persons in the unique danger of their mutual abandon, or even the conjunction of the gift and abandon in the play of persons—there is the mystery that Nietzsche just touches upon only then to avoid it.

That light touch then yields, massively, to omission. The question of the person yields before the mystery of the person's danger, thus to be stated without risk, and to be lost, like a battle:

"the oldest and most primitive personal relationship (*Personen-Verhältnis*), that between buyer and seller, creditor and debtor: it was here that one person first encountered another person, that one person first *measured himself* against another" (*Genealogy of Morals*, II, § 8; Kaufmann, 70). The relation between persons slips toward valuation, hence the will to power: a relation where persons, valuating one another with their gazes, again become visible images and defined representations: idols, then. The risks of a battle obfuscate the danger of the person, which is otherwise trying. Questioning disappears before the evidence of a thesis that is already known—"man defines himself as the Being that measures values, evaluates and measures, as the 'valuating animal as such' " (ibid., repeated from *Zarathustra*, I, "The Thousand and One Goals"). The trial of the cross becomes simply a particular case of the play of the will to power, and even of its reactive form—*ressentiment*. Through a stupefying equivocation, it happens in fact that Nietzsche interprets the cross *also* as a phenomenon of *ressentiment*, and a particular, if exceptional, case of the concepts of "debt," "duty," "bad conscience," etc.: " Suddenly we stand before the paradoxical and horrifying expedient that afforded temporary relief for tormented humanity, that stroke of genius on the part of Christianity: God sacrifices himself for the guilt of mankind, God himself makes payment to himself, God as the only being who can redeem man from what has become unredeemable for man himself—the creditor sacrifices himself for his debtor, out of *love* (is this believable?), out of love for his debtor!" (*Genealogy of Morals*, II, § 21; Kaufmann, 92, mod.). This text calls for several remarks. First, the reactive relation here set up between God and God strongly contradicts the "dangerous" relation of the Christ, which passes beyond *ressentiment* and the idol (*Wahn*) to the "person" of God. In fact, making God play only with himself, one attributes to God an idolatrous conception of man: just as previously (§ 4) man masks the divine by elaborating an idol that, before dying, in any case kills the approach of the gods or God, so here, God, seeing only an image of himself in the role and place of the dying/failing man, dreams of a salvation that he plays out vainly and oneirically for himself. Even God eludes the danger of the person, because the other God "who rules" remains an idol of man. Christ, on the contrary, whom the

Nietzschean gaze here radically misses, by assuming human nature absolutely (and by assuring it all the more), becomes rigorously human, man—and not the idol of man. According to the rigor that distinguishes thinkers, even within heretical logic, the docetism of this text goes hand in hand with modalism: God, who misses the nonidolatrous person, misses himself as person. He admits within himself neither the multiplicity nor the danger of the person: the divine other of God is not divinely other, but the simple mark of a private comedy. In view of these consequences, why introduce the explanation of *ressentiment?*—Because, second, the explanation of love is not credible. Or rather, love here remains a derived concept, and as such illusory. Why? The solution of a paradox that we have sketched little by little depends on this decision: the Nietzschean Christ passes beyond *ressentiment* and pronounces in regard to it an *Amen;* he passes beyond the idolatrous conception of God and in advance traverses the "death of God"; he becomes finally one of the privileged names through which the one whom the darkness approaches is named for himself and the world. And yet, "Have I been understood? —Dionysius versus the Crucified . . ." (*Ecce Homo,* "Why I Am a Destiny," § 9). But it is precisely this that remains to be understood.

§ 7. WHY IS NIETZSCHE STILL IDOLATROUS?

If the privileges of the Christ do not spare him an unappealable disqualification, perhaps the reason for this is found less in the Nietzschean interpretation of the Christ than in that of "God." More precisely, Christ is one of the names for the one who experiences the divine. But of what divinity does Christ experience the divinity? Of the "God" to whom Nietzsche attributes Christianity, or rather whom Christianity allows Nietzsche to conceive. The Christ, as privileged as he may be, is worth only as much as the divine thus approached. The "God" of such a divinity claims to be the "God" of love; but precisely, "must one believe" that he is and acts "through love" (*Genealogy of Morals,* II, § 21)? Love suffices neither to define nor to account for a "God" into whom only the analysis of *ressentiment* penetrates. Alone, love is not worthy of faith, because "God" does not reveal himself therein in good faith. Upon the love by which "God" loves, Nietzsche visits two critiques that are distinct and uneven but perhaps not contradictory. First, that "God" loves only in hating, and therefore not suitably, and is therefore not defined by love alone. Next, that love includes hate as one of its components, which Christian love misunderstands.

The love by which God loves is ἔρως that aims at exclusive possession. It first requires strict reciprocity: "A God who loves men, provided only that they believe in him, and who casts an evil eye and threats upon anyone who does not believe in his love! What? A love encapsuled in if-clauses attributed to an almighty God! A love that has not even mastered the feelings of honor and vindictiveness!" (*Gay Science*, § 141; Kaufmann, 190, mod.). Like a sentimental ruse, this reciprocity masks the taking-possession of the other. Self-sacrifice becomes the indirect path of a sacrifice to oneself of the other: "These people believe themselves to be disinterested in love, because they hope for the advantage of another being, often against their own advantage. But in exchange they would like to *possess* that being. . . . Even God, here, constitutes no exception . . . he becomes terrible when one does not love him in return" (*The Case of Wagner*, § 2). The egoistic ruse of love, which in fact does not love the other, but only the pleasure that his possession (voluntary: submission) offers in return. A ruse, but above all the bankruptcy of a love that regresses to the simple level of an armed demand—retaliation. Whence the inversion of the "God of love" into a judge. "God" disqualifies himself by revealing, through the vengeance that he exercises as judge, that his love aims only, in fact, at possession. Only the one who has not yet spotted that ambivalence can invoke him as a "God of love"—or more radically, the one who has not understood the mystery proper to love: "He who loves loves beyond recompense and retaliation." Conclusion: the "God of love" himself "does not have high enough an idea of love"[37] and misses what is essen-

---

[37] See *Gay Science*, § 140, "*Too Jewish.*—If God wished to become an object of love, he should have given up judging and justice first of all; a judge, even a merciful judge, is no object of love. The founder of Christianity was not refined enough in his feelings at this point—being a Jew" (Kaufmann, 191); *Zarathustra*, IV, "Retired," "Did this God not want to be a judge too?" (Kaufmann, 373);

tial about it, which is properly divine. He ignores, that is, that "Love of *one* is a barbarism; for it is exercised at the expense of all others. The love of God, too" (*Beyond Good and Evil*, § 67; Kaufmann, 79): love is shared or disappears; exclusivism amounts to egoism. Would it be that the supreme prostitution is, in matters divine, and according to Baudelaire, the rule?[38] Prostituted pluralism aside, the "God of love" ignores also, and perhaps above all, that love is tied to what fools oppose to it—hate. "Must one not first hate oneself, if one wants to love oneself?" (*Ariadne's Lament, Dithyrambs*, 62): penultimate word of the Dionysus who appears and disappears to Ariadne's eyes, ultimate word on love. Love is not valid inasmuch as it claims to present itself as, and confine itself to—precisely, love. It lacks "the seriousness, the suffering, the patience, and the labor" of hate, which alone, in a sense, saves the separation and the waiting, which is to say the space of encounter. Like Hegel, whom for this reason Nietzsche should have taken into view, Nietzsche admits a beyond of love—an other world, where love yields to something vaster and stronger than it. Is it to hate, or to another love? Is that in relation to which the love of the "God of love" proves insufficient and deficient another love or an other than love?

> He did not love enough: else he would also have loved us who laugh. But he hated and mocked us: howling and gnashing of teeth he promised us.
>
> Does one have to curse right away, where one does not love?

Fragment from 1888, "You say your God / is a God of love? / Is the bite of conscience / then a bite of God / a bite by love?" (*Dithyrambs*, 160); etc.

[38] The alternative seems to be an impasse: Either God does not love all men—judge (Nietzsche: a God who is too "Jewish") or else God loves all men—prostitute (Baudelaire). "Love is the taste for prostitution" (*Fusées*, I, 1, in *Oeuvres complètes*, "Pléiade" [Paris: Gallimard, 1947]). "What is love? / The need to leave oneself. / Man is an adoring animal. / To adore is to sacrifice oneself and to prostitute oneself. / Thus all love is prostitution," "The most prostituted Being is the Being par excellence, it is God, since he is the supreme friend for each individual, since he is the common, inexhaustible reservoir of love" (*Mon coeur à nu*, XXV, 45, and an unnumbered fragment, ibid., 1286–87). This is to say that in both cases there lacks one and the same distance: "God"-the-judge lacks the distance that makes even those who refuse the gift enter into love; "God"-the-prostitute lacks the distance that underlines the unknowable all the more insofar as it designates it infinitely. God neither judges nor prostitutes himself, because distance gives rise to the decision of each, in harboring the unique one that distance delivers to all.

That seems bad taste to me. But thus he acted, being unconditional. He came from the mob. And he himself simply did not love
enough: else he would not have been so wroth that one did not
love him. All great love does not *want* love: it wants more. (*Zarathustra*, IV, "On the Higher Man," § 16; Kaufmann, 405)

From the insufficiency of love, the text leads to a beyond of love.
The "God of love" must be rejected first because of his duplicity
(love is doubled by vengeance), and hence for the narrowness of
his love; but that duplicity again could only dissimulate the relation of hate to love, a cruelty that anticipates that of Dionysus.
Nothing unacceptable here except a hypocrisy. The deficiency in
fact does not reside there. More radically, "the God of love" does
not see that love is not sufficient for saying the divine. The "great
love," that which is willed and pronounced by the great *Amen*,
does not want love. It wants much more: love itself, however accomplished it might be (which the "God" of Christianity does
not, in any case, manage to realize), will never attain the perfection that the world awaits. Before that perfection—the Eternal
Return, the sole face of the divine—even love becomes a mask,
a representation, an idol. Disqualified as love, and not only as
caricatured love, both the "God of love" and the one who experiences, approves, and brings that God—the Christ—become idols
of another face of the divine. Despite his privileges, the Christ
must disappear, because the love that he incarnates does not offer
the highest figure of the divine: love, and not only the one who
loves, must let itself be put to death. For what?

Before what does love appear as the last mask that obliterates
the presence of the divine? This amounts to asking what face the
divine can still assume after the "death of God," and before the
still-to-come advent of Dionysus: "Indeed, there is no other alternative for gods: *either* they are those of the will to power, and they
remain a people's gods, *or* the incapacity for power (*Ohnmacht
zur Macht*), and they necessarily become *good*" (*Antichrist*, § 16;
Kaufmann, 583, mod.). The "goodness" here that determines a
"good God" corresponds fairly precisely to the love that would
be deployed and demanded by the Christian "God." This determination is inscribed within an exclusive disjunction where the
other term is defined: will to power. The God must be thought

exclusively by reference to the will to power, either to agree with it, or else to contradict it, and thus still to refer to it: will to the incapacity for power (the "*nihilistic* will wants power" says § 9). As previously, the "God of love" is disqualified in the name of the will to power; but here the "gods" who evacuate that God arise also from will to power. The divinity of the "new gods"[39] springs from the will to power, which provokes, gives rise to, and revokes the gods. "The sole way of maintaining a meaning for the concept 'God' would be: God *not* as the driving force, but God as a maximal state, as [that which makes] an epoch—a point in the evolution of will to power," " 'God' as the moment of culmination: existence [as] an eternal divinization and dedivinization. But in that not a high point of value, but a high point of power," "the world, even if it is no longer a god, is still supposed to be capable of the divine power of creation, the power of infinite transformations."[40] The same alternative ("the sole possibility . . .") reappears. It constrains "God" even more exactly. It does so first because god corresponds to a state of the will to power, be it of a people, be it of biological energies; the indefinite possibility of new gods presupposes their production by (and their subjection to) the will to power alone. Above all, the latter produces the dedivinization of the world even when no god persists. The divine escapes, precedes, and survives the gods. The gods result from the divine, according to an ebb and flow that it is not theirs to control. Nietzsche attributes the divine, which surpasses and comprehends the gods, to the world. How to understand this? Would the world produce the god, contrary to the preceding thought that the god alone gives rise to a world around him (§ 5, *Beyond Good and Evil,* § 150)? Perhaps—unless it be a question, precisely here, again and especially, of that thought. The world arouses, as a state that the will to power organizes, a god as the center from which an affirmation can come to it. The god returns to the world the will to power that gives rise to it. To the will to power that valuates each being and assigns to it its place, the god returns the global justification of the whole of beings as a world—and hence

---

[39] *Will to Power,* § 1038 = VIII, 3, 323, 17 [4], § 5.

[40] Respectively, ibid., § 639 = VIII, 2, 201, 10 [136]; § 712 = VIII, 2, 7, 9 [8]; and § 1062 = VII, 3, 280, 36 [15] [Kaufmann, respectively, pp. 340, 379, 546, mod.].

as divine. The will to power delivers to each being that which for it is Being-value, reproducing thus the investigation and the difference of the ὅ ᾖ ὄv. The god, affirming as a world the divine that gives rise to it, and therefore pronouncing in it the Eternal Return, there becomes a theological point of view: through it, the world becomes to itself its own supreme being. The god, thought as will to power, uncovers a world as the sole supreme being in affirming beings in their Being (value): "God as will to power— that suffices! Everything follows from it—'the world'!"[41] The god clearly finds its place, therefore, in the onto-theological structure of a metaphysics still at work. It is worth what the divine that gives rise to it is worth; it depends radically on the Nietzchean valuation of Being. Its genealogy does not present any secret, since Nietzsche's whole thought is used to bring it fully to light: the god—a state of the will to power that affirms its world. Therefore, quite obviously, the god, "the new gods," can be awaited after Zarathustra. It is enough to locate and follow "the religious, that is to say god-creating (*gottbildende*) instinct," "the god-creating (*gottbildende*) power."[42] The will to power, divine from the beginning to the Eternal Return, therefore produces gods as images and states of its completion—and therefore as idols.

The idols remain. But they now stem from metaphysics: onto-theologically, the will to power and the god/world of the Eternal Return reinforce their bipolar arrangement of the Being of beings. Twilight of the idols, but not of the characteristically metaphysical idol: once the moral "God" is revoked, the "new gods" themselves also remain tied metaphysically to the will to power, they play and dance like idols. Twilight: originally the word designates equally the half-day of the *dawn*. On the idols, the sun never ceases to fall, and it still dispenses enough light so that the last idol should appear, still standing. Nietzsche remains an idolater because he remains a metaphysician: the "death of God," experienced and brilliantly deconstructed, announces the death of the metaphysical God (the "moral God"). But, as the onto-theological structure of metaphysics remains (will to power/Eternal Return), the divinity, an other divinity, reappears under a form that

---

[41] Ibid., § 1037 = VIII, 2, 173–74, 10 [90].

[42] Respectively, ibid., § 1038 = VIII, 3, 323, 17 [4] § 5, and *Antichrist,* § 19.

is still metaphysical. The entrance of God into absence, therefore, is in a sense masked, missed, and censured, even if, as the text that *Holzwege* dedicates to Nietzsche concludes, the madman who seeks God has nothing in common with those "public scoundrels" who make a profession of unbelief. For what becomes problematic here is the very place where that search might see the arrival of what it aims at: to seek "God" does not yet exclude idolatry. If the "new gods" ever arrive—but for a century have they not ceaselessly arrived catastrophically?—this will be, this is only under the always metaphysical form of the will to power indissolubly coupled with the Eternal Return. Thus "God," or the "new gods," play their role in the partition of the Being of beings, thought as presence. Since the "death of God" remains conjoined with the metaphysical trial of nihilism, that which succeeds it as a completion and overcoming remains a divinity that is metaphysically comprehended and received—an idol governed by the will to power, at will. The absence of God—or rather the miniscule and infinite gap where there remains something like God—is obliterated by this "death of God" that is too metaphysical not to be experienced and set off within the sole field of metaphysics. And therefore "God" is still thought starting from the name of Being, without there breaking out at the surface of the discourse another question: and what if God remained beyond the question of Being itself, however it is stated (including the will to power/ Eternal Return)? The withdrawal of God, in this case, would concern, more than the age of nihilism, metaphysics as a whole. The focusing of the question on the terminal episode of the idolatrous "God" of metaphysics distracts one from considering the abyss that opens up, under the play of metaphysics, where there lies perhaps what we call "God." The gap that this abyss lays out—the distance of God, a distance that identifies and also is identified with God—is masked by the "death of God," through a censure that, like all censures, suggests it at the same time. It is above all not a case of "surpassing" Nietzsche, but of granting him that the question he confronted merits the respect of our double attention: (a) As a question concerning the "death of God," it bears on the nihilistic explosion of metaphysical onto-theology and therefore signals toward "new gods" who are themselves situated in their (onto-) theological function. (b) As a question concern-

ing what the "death of God" betrays (reveals and conceals),
namely, the distance of God, which lives in an infinite separation
from the metaphysical posture of Being, and which, from the clos-
est abyss, haunts us.

The "God" who dies remains still too close, metaphysically, for
his death not to be idolatrous, and for the new face that succeeds
him not to reestablish another, still metaphysical idol—that of the
will to power. The equivalence supposed by the "type of God after
(*nach*) the type of creative spirits, of 'great men' "[43] reproduces,
apart from a "death of God," the rivalry—and therefore the
equivalence—between "God" and *Dasein:* "Our greatest re-
proach against *Dasein* was the existence of God," "a governing
and all-seeing God . . . would be the greatest argument against
Dasein."[44] In both cases the different result should not mask the
similarity of the process: refuted or evoked, the "God" depends
on the divine, and the divine on Being, or rather on its metaphysical face at a particular moment—here, nihilism—of its historical
destiny. Henceforth it becomes impossible not to ask: does not
the strict equality of the relation immediately produce a two-faced
idolatry? Do not both the "proofs" and the "disqualifications" of
something that one takes it upon oneself to name "God" offer
but two versions of one discourse held by the same Janus?
Whether the temple conceals it or renders it manifest, what does
it offer other than an idol? It is necessary that its doors be open,
or closed—so says the polemic, as if the essential were not elsewhere: can a "God" who inhabits the temple, or who dies from
having been chased out, still be called God? Whoever takes this
remark as a vain trick, or as a weak argument, does not even approach the site where the absence of God itself becomes rigorous.
For God to become pertinent for us, it is first necessary that we
experience his radical foreignness. It does not matter that the
concept "God" seems inconceivable to us (poorly constructed,
nonverifiable, reducible, and subject to critique), since only an
idol could be identified with the concept. Those who proclaim or
prepare the "death of God" did not have to admit and could not

[43] *Will to Power,* § 1038 = VIII, 3, 323, 17 [4] § 5 [Kaufmann, 535].

[44] Ibid., § 707 = VIII, 2, 201, 10 [137], and § 708 = 2777, 11, [72] [Kaufmann,
377, mod.]. See also *Twilight of the Idols,* "The Four Great Errors," §§ 7–8, *Daybreak,* § 13, *Genealogy of Morals,* II, § 20, *Antichrist,* § 26, etc.

have admitted any deviation from a straightforward equivalence between *Dasein* and "God." Feuerbach, Stirner, and Marx rely on the supremely idolatrous identification of "God" with the absolute Knowledge that Hegel had constructed for them in order to empty one concept of its content to the benefit of another, in a metaphysical system of communicating vessels.[45] Nietzsche himself did not revoke this equivalence. To pass beyond it, it would have been necessary to admit *the distance of God*. By this one attempts to indicate, not conceptually, unless with a trivial incoherence, that the gap that falls outside of the metaphysical thought of being in its Being can alone free the field where God does not become an idol—an historical figure within onto-theology. That one nevertheless does not necessarily say that God "is beyond Being" has to do with another question. The distance of God: no idol can announce the death or the life of God, because "he dwells in an inaccessible light" (I Timothy 1:6) attained by no light, no access, no dwelling. But the distance preserves as well the most inescapable proximity to what we can no longer idolize. Laying out that proximity would perhaps be, without regard to the disqualified debates, the most difficult task.

Nietzsche remains an idolater because, as the final metaphysician, he does not enter into distance. This undoubtedly has to do with a cleft (*Kluft*) that nothing could fill or even measure, since it determines "the right to create values" (*Genealogy of Morals*, I, § 2). But precisely because of its strict relation to value, which in fact ensures its rigor as a concept, distance plays only between the

---

[45] Marx: "All of these consequences follow from a single fact: the worker finds himself before the product of his labor in the same relation as with a *foreign* object. Given that, it is obvious that the more the worker expends himself in his labor, the more powerful the foreign world, the world of objects that he creates before himself becomes and the more he himself is impoverished, the more his interior world becomes poor, the less he possesses for himself. It is exactly (*ebenso*) as in religion. The more man places in God, the less he possesses in himself/for himself" (*1844 Manuscripts*, XXII, *Karl Marx-Friedrich Engels, Werke, Ergänzungsband*, Erster Teil [Berlin, 1968], p. 512). Likewise Feuerbach: "To enrich God, man must become poor; so that God may be everything, man must be nothing" (*Essence of Christianity*, Introduction [1841], ch. 2 = Ludwig Feuerbach, *Gesammelte Werke* [Berlin: Ak. Verlag, 1973], Bd. 5, p. 65). The equivalence and the self-subsistence of the attributes/predicates alone permit, in Feuerbach, their transfer from "God" to man. The radical absence of negative theology thus becomes the explicit condition of a strictly idolatrous destruction.

terms that evaluation concerns, "between man and man, class and class" (*Twilight of the Idols,* "The Raving of an 'Inactual' One," § 37, p. 132). If ever it is exercised in the intimacy of the valuating will to power, like an "always renewed desire to widen distance within the soul itself," it is with the aim of producing the "aristocracy" that must pronounce the *Amen* (*Beyond Good and Evil,* § 257).

Nietzschean distance maintains, to be sure, a relation with the divine, but within onto-theology, on the basis of equivalence. Thus it reinforces the metaphysical idolatry where "God" is defined as a state of the will to power. Within that grade-related function, the "feeling of distance," far from taking its distance from the metaphysical face of the divine elaborated (and presupposed) by the will to power, radically ignores the distance of God. The Nietzschean distance intervenes only to censure the distance of God, or more, to obliterate it, within the evidence of the text, by substituting itself for it.

And yet, as we have attempted to show, Nietzsche transgressed the idolatrous relation to the divine, since a face-to-face with something finally living within the divine threw him into the ultimate transgression, the plunge into darkness. How to understand the patent contradiction? With regard to the historic acceleration of Nietzsche's destiny, perhaps one could accord some importance to this chronological fact: the texts of the collection called *The Will to Power,* which contain most clearly the onto-theological comprehension of the "gods," do not count among the last fragments. Likewise the texts from *Antichrist,* which are followed by *Ecce Homo, Nietzsche contra Wagner,* and the *Dithyrambs.*[46] It is not impossible that this idolatrous comprehension of the divine issues from a state anterior to, and surpassed by, the unavoidable and progressive convocation of Nietzsche in person to the divine. The plunge into darkness would attest to, and equally conceal, his sole authentic deviation from metaphysics. But concerning that which leaps outside of discourse, we can, here, not yet say anything. We,

---

[46] *Will to Power,* § 1038 = VIII, 3, 323, 17 [4], § 5, date from May–June 1888; § 1037 = VII, 2, 173, 10 [90], from autumn 1887; § 1062 = VII, 3, 280, 36 [15], from June–July 1885; § 638 = VIII, 2, 201, 10 [138], from autumn 1887, etc. None appears, therefore, in the final period. This sign, if fragile, must be remembered.

who remain within the twilight of the idols, can say nothing of the one who has already traveled to the end of night. That we should not be able to say anything is also instructive: Nietzsche believed himself to be advancing beyond or in the place of the idols, in order there to play a metaphysical role. But, as if sucked in through the idols as far as the divine itself, he there succumbed. Dionysus touched him. This is perhaps because, without distance, a distinction can be made between the idols and God no more than the relation to the divine can be supported. Only the infinite separation of distance ensures one of subsisting within the infinite proximity of God. Conceptually idolatrous, too removed from the divine—too close, personally experienced with the divine: a double missing/lacking of distance, which brings together and separates at once, which in a word keeps the divine and man at a good distance—a distance of Goodness. Perhaps this is what Nietzsche teaches, at bottom, that is most precious.

Interlude 1

The terminal situation that we have tried to locate, where Nietzsche, heroic, collapses, fixes him in an unbearable contradiction, where precisely he bears the burden of speaking contraries. The question of the divine arises in a double and inverse, if profoundly coherent, movement. First, the divine presents itself only in its very vanishing—the "death of God," twilight of the idols, passive nihilism, etc.—as a nostalgia and a deliverance. But then, because the metaphysical place of the supreme Being persists, and because the eternal return awaits its affirmation from the one who will bear it, the divine, through a passionate return, demands the immediate assumption of the divine *persona* by man—the Overman, Dionysus, the Crucified, etc. Either absence, where man remains alone, without any other face of the divine than his own twilight idol, or else overabundant investment, where the divine renders itself present only by making itself pressing to the point of carrying man away—or, what amounts to the same thing, to the point of plunging him into darkness. The Nietzschean ambivalence harbors no incoherence but reveals an otherwise menacing aporia. Does the one who renounces the divine, by critiquing it, and therefore by constituting it as an idol, not expose himself, precisely in that he mediates, and then destroys the mediations of the (false) divinity, to its immediate—faceless and nameless—return? This barbarization of the divine could constitute the supreme danger both for man and for the divine. The metaphysical idol ensures, in its way, a named and imaginable mediation of the divine. The destruction of the idol delivers, more than a desert, the anonymous space of an anarchic invasion of the divine. That to which Nietzsche succumbs is perhaps such an invasion. But precisely, his proper task—to announce the death of the idols of the divine—did not require him to dominate such an advancing tide. To say it better, poets transgress the history that philosophers, in advance, scan historially; one poet knew, before Nietzsche, if in a profound familiarity with him, a similar alternative, in order there to apprehend its overcoming—Hölderlin. Indeed, the absence of the divine, in the form of a "nostalgia for Greece," occupies and commands "Hyperion, or, the Hermit in Greece" (1797–99). The immediate assumption by the divine leads to the "Death of Empedocles" (1798–1800), where death and communion coincide in a "Ganymedean" disposition of man in the divine, that is, in Etna. Hölderlin escapes this alternative only by risking to think an unthinkable paradox: the intimacy of man with the divine *grows* with the gap that distinguishes them, far from diminishing it. The withdrawal of the divine would perhaps constitute its ultimate form of revelation. This is what we attempt to delineate under the name of distance.[1] Two poems, chosen with neither measure nor decency, among the greatest, will, as privileged guides, be able to lead us to the evidence of this paradox: they are titled "In Lovely Blue" and "Patmos." Let us attempt to listen to them, and therefore, line by line, to read them.

---

[1] The same paradox, or at least a similar one, can be read in Rimbaud, at least if one understands his itinerary in the sense that Corinne Nicolas-Marion attempts to outline it; see "De la gourmandise à l'ardente patience: Rimbaud à la conquête du divin," *Résurrection* 42 (Paris, 1973), pp. 95–111.

The Withdrawal of the Divine and the Face of the Father: Hölderlin

> For without these distancings, souls would never learn to approach God.
>
> John of the Cross, *Dark Night*, I.14

> . . . his decline itself was for him a pretext to be: his final birth.
>
> R.-M. Rilke, *Elegies to Duino*, I

§ 8. The Measured Image

WITH AN ALMOST unbearable density, Hölderlin registers within a single poem the ultimate level at which his meditation was able to assume a position. And even more than that strategic position, the text "In Lovely Blue," marks forever, and hence enigmatically, the fundamental dimensions that outline the poetic figure of the whole oeuvre. That an editor should have counted it among the fragments of doubtful authenticity[1] does not impede an extraordinarily tight network of rapprochements, resonances, and references to other indisputably canonical texts from arising as the unfathomable center of the entire Hölderlinian word. Perhaps even this original and nodal situation—which saturates with meaning, irrigating the channels of the whole oeuvre—reinforces the amazement and the doubt: the poem becomes extraordinarily difficult and troubling because it concentrates *too* sovereignly the

---

[1] F. Beissner, in *Hölderlin, Sämtliche Werke*, Grosse Stuttgart Ausgabe, vol. 2, 1 (1051), p. 372 ff. I will cite according to this edition (hereafter GSA), indicating volume (except for vol. 2, 2, the most often used), page, and line or verse of the poem, and then referring to the corresponding place in *Hölderlin, Oeuvres*, published under the direction of P. Jacottet (Paris: Gallimard, "Pléiade," 1967). Because I sometimes dare to distance myself from them, I want to express my gratitude and admiration for the writers who attempted this transportation (J. Tardieu, M. Deguy, F. Fédier, R. Rovini, G. Roux, D. Naville, A. du Bouchet, and P. Jacottet).

particular character that authenticates the other writings as "Höld-erlinian." It is a rigorous and modest approach to such a center that we must, in the shadow of greater ones, attempt here.

"In Lovely Blue," lovely (*lieblich:* worthy of the love it in-spires)—lovely, as already, "lovely sounds the hammered scythe and the voice of the farmer / Who, going home with his bull, likes to command and curb" ("The Traveller," 82, 1–2 = 801; Hamburger, 139). Blue, in the sense that, for Empedocles, "The Ether bathed me in its breath like you / To heal my chest wounded by love / And ascended, like the smoke from a flame / To dissolve my cares in the supreme blue" ("The Death of Em-pedocles," 2nd version, 1, 3, GSA, 4, 1, 106, 427–30 = 553). Why does the Ether, which is adorned and approached in blue, merit the love to which it gives rise? The blued horizon condenses a space where adoration becomes possible, the adoration of the ether—of the "Father ether" ("To the Ether," GSA, 1, 1, 204, 2 = 107). In what way the mystery of the Father is put into play here is what remains to be thought. But the poet has no need of concepts or of substitutes for the concept (allegorical alterations of the conceptual discourse) since to him, as poet, the things themselves become explicit speech. What begins to speak, there-fore, would be, here, "the metal roof of the steeple," or rather the sun that makes it flower, as it colors the sheet metal. Sur-rounded by noises, the colors and the sounds mix in order to stand out all the better in a previously highlighted singularity: the cry does not contradict the silence of the weathercock any more than the cry of the swallow troubles the calm of the steeple. From these reciprocal constitutions there is born "a calm life, *ein stiller Leben*" (372, 5 = 939, 9): not a still life (*Stilleben* in German), but a calm of tensions counterbalanced by the whole that counterdis-tinguishes them and renders them visible—life. Life here issues from the calm from which it nevertheless, in a sense, results. From such a play arises the silhouette that is forever inscribed in the arched window, of a man who descends the stairs, returning from ringing the bell, shows through, then appears, and finally is out-lined—turned blue against the blue background—as a figure. Or rather, "with the figure thus distinguished, the imaging of man comes forth" (372, 6–7 = 939, 10–11; Sieburth, 249, mod.). When, instead of merging with others or vanishing in its apparition, the silhouette manages, in the "calm," to distinguish itself (*abgesondert*, 372, 6), it becomes visible in the blue that receives it. It stands out therein, like a blue collage by Matisse stands out: with an unforeseeable and irremediable rigor. And yet Hölderlin does not simply express the distinction of the figure. He does not see the figure alone, but what in lovely blue the figure itself opens up, for another vision. He indicates, starting with the figure, that an image (*Bild*) of man becomes possible. This is not to say that man admits only an image, one figure among others, but that he has the property, or the possibility, of letting himself be given an image within a figure (*Bildsamkeit*). To be sure, within the opening of the window of the tower, there appears the figure of the silhouette that is delimited and set off by "calm life." But through that apparition there appears above all the fact that man *can* appear in and as an image.[2] Within the sensible appearance of a silhouette the poet sees appear the mystery of the apparition of man: that man should be able to assume figure in an image, as one takes root (or not) in a soil.

Where then would this apparition be where man finds himself imaged? In the frame of a window—that of the tower—of a window inasmuch, however, as "The windows / The bells ring through / Are as gates to beauty (*an Schönheit*)" (line 8 = lines 12–13; Sieburth, 249). Beauty, here, is discovered in the opening of the windows, but above all the gates become gates to Beauty: beauty qualifies the rib (or the arch?) as window, in harboring the lovely blue that delimits, with its discretely haunting trait, the apparition as an image. But what are we to understand here by Beauty? "A flower itself is beautiful, because it flowers under the sun" (372, 24–25 = 940, 40–41; Sieburth, 251, mod.). Would the sun, which in its decline the poem names "beautiful sun" (373, 32 = 941, 94), free up Beauty? Perhaps, unless it refers itself, as to that from which it issues, to "powerful, divinely beautiful, Na-

---

[2] Even though *Bildsamkeit* was not employed by Kant, one cannot help thinking here of the doctrine of the schema in the *Critique of Pure Reason*, which is defined less as a *Bild* than as "the representation of a universal process of the force of imagination (*Einbildunskraft*) to create its image in a concept" (*KrV*, A 140–B 179). The *imagination* here indicates the power of imaging, through a staging that is without effect or deception but that gives form to the very essence of the thing, which it allows to take form itself. See, obviously, M. Heidegger, *Kant und das Problem der Metaphysik* (Tübingen: Niemeyer, 1929), §§ 19–23.

ture" ("As on a Holiday," 118, 12 = 833, 12). Nature where, as one of the poems of the *Umnachtung* says, "The deity kindly escorts us / At first with unblemished blue" ("The Walk," 276, 17–18 = 1026, 12–13; Hamburger, 333). But how can Nature divinely invest more than "the windows of heaven" ("The Nearest the Best," III, 237, 1 = 904, 1; Sieburth, 175), to bring about the image in human-made windows—the arch of the tower? Because, the poem enigmatically continues, "gates / also take after nature, / They resemble the forest trees" (372, 8–9 = 939, 14–15; Sieburth, 249, mod.). To the "also/*auch*" that introduces this resemblance answers in the following line "But purity is also beauty." What does this "also" link? To be sure, it links the beauty that defines and issues from Nature to the purity that humanly imitates it—as art imitates Nature—("imitate, *nachahmen*, l. 14). How does art imitate Nature? Hölderlin here thinks in concert with Aristotle: "On the one hand, art brings to completion what Nature is incapable of working, while on the other hand art imitates Nature."[3] Art imitates Nature only in order to complete it, which means that it completes it only by playing its role, by fulfilling its duties: art proceeds naturally precisely there where nature can no longer advance, unless artistically:

> Each one accomplishes in his own way, one more beautifully, the other more brutally, his mission as man, namely, to increase the life of Nature, to accelerate it, particularize it, mix, separate, bind it. It is indeed necessary to recognize that this original instinct, that of idealizing, of demanding, of fashioning, of developing and of perfecting Nature hardly animates the activity of men any longer. . . . You see, my dear, I have just formulated a paradox: the artistic and educational need (*Kunst und Bildungstriebe*), with all of its modifications and varieties, is a true service that men render to Nature.[4]

---

[3] *Physics,* II, 8, 199 a 15–16. See the commentary by J. Beaufret, "Hölderlin et Sophocle," in *Hölderlin, remarques sur Oedipe, Remarques sur Antigone,* trans. and notes by F. Fédier (Paris: U.G.E., 1965), p. 8 ff. I am greatly indebted to this remarkable edition.

[4] Letter to his son, 4 June 1799, no. 179, GSA 6, 1, 328–29 - 711. See all of the "Foundation of Empedocles," from the same period (Hamburg), and especially the following: "Art is the flowering, the perfection of nature. Nature becomes divine only through its tie to art, which is of a different but harmonious kind. When each of the two is entirely that which it can be, and when the one unites

This "paradox" alone clarifies the resemblance that we located: to be sure, purity is not, any more than the arch, confused with beauty; but the divine springs properly from the fact that "also" they "imitate" that which nature failed to give them. Or rather: it is a question neither of lack nor of failure, since the lovely blue bathes and overwhelms the pure arch as much as the beautiful trees. At issue is the divine: that purity can achieve in its way what beauty in its way attains. Beauty achieves "naturally" what, "culturally," purity augments. More precisely, the "native return" delivers culturally to art the task of augmenting nature, by establishing it in its truth: art itself opens to us a path toward that which remains most native to us. If the flowers owe to the sun the beauty in which they are figured, "The eye often discovers beings (*Wesen*) in life that it would be yet more beautiful to name than flowers" (l. 25–26). More beautiful than the flowers that the sun adumbrates as much as every being is the act of language that would name it as such: the poetic art.

No splendor surpasses beauty other than the gesture that, otherwise, designates beauty: the gesture of art, more native, in its "native return," than the naturally born native. The assumption of figure that man provokes and in which he evokes himself adds nothing to nature—except the delay of the man who measures its beauty. Better: who is measured by it as beauty. The figure assumed does not redouble nature any more than nature is exceeded by the man who, nevertheless, completes it: "But Frankfurt, to speak of man, / According to the figure that is a reproduction (*Abdruck*) of Nature" ("We Set Out from the Abyss," 250, 13–15; Sieburth, 199, mod.). Man and reproduced figure here indicate nothing more than Nature, unless that they take it into view in its radical nativity: the village is found humanly figured according to Nature. Thus it is that Aristotle introduces the polis.[5] The reproduction avoids opaque duplication because Nature it-

---

with the other, fills the lacuna of the other, a lacuna that is necessary for it, in order to be exactly what it can be as particular, then we are in the presence of completion, and the divine is found midway between the two. The organic, artistic man is the flower of nature" (GSA, 4, 152 = 659). It is in this sense also that one must certainly understand the following: "Read in life art, in the work of art life, / If you see the one rightly, you will see the other as well" ("For Oneself," GSA, 1, 1, 305).

[5] Aristotle, *Politics* I, II, 1252b27–1253a39.

self there imprints the incompletion that it gives to be filled. An impression (*Abdruck*) that becomes precise if the gaze, which receives it, discerns in Nature the figure that does *not* present itself there—the very one that remains to be (made) seen. Hölderlin names the sure precision that authorizes such a vision "purity":[6] "For where the eyes make their way, more perceptible / Is the spirit there, and openly and more serenely flower / the crepuscular figures of life / There where a more sure light appears" ("To a Dessau Princess," GSA 1, 1, 309, 17–20); in purity, like another optical milieu, the spirit becomes perceptible: the imperceptible there assumes figure; in the "serious spirit,"[7] the crepuscular weaknesses of Nature free up the opening where, as much "culturally" as all the more natively, the "sure" and "serious" light of the spirit makes them, like flowers, and better than flowers, flower. Such seriousness allows the light to endure wherein the spirit makes figures rise up in the crepuscular lack of figure: then, poetically, man can state its "seriousness and self-sufficient word."[8]

For the seriousness of spirit is necessary: the image, which arises from the gaze that images it (*Bildsamkeit*), is outlined against the lovely blue, an apparition of unbearable precision and of stupefying rigor. Not only does the image invest the entire essence (*Wesen*) of the thing in the silhouette where the figure is detached, but it is outlined at the same time as the figure that does *not* precede it naturally. This coincidence of the figure and the image is known by the painter, who sees the thing establish itself in the visible all of a sudden. This coincidence is designated and experienced by Hölderlin: "Yet so simple (*einfältig*) / These images, so very holy (intact, *heilig*), / One fears to describe them" (372, 11–12; Sieburth, 249). Sacred simplicity of the image that appears in a figure—man in the arched window: whoever has ever *seen* it has known the fear. Whoever reads the opening of the poem without experiencing it in his depths need not here con-

---

[6] "In Lovely Blue," 372, 9, 16, 20; 373, 2, 12.

[7] Ibid., 372, 10–11; 373, 13.

[8] *Remarques sur Antigone*, § 2, GSA, 5, 267. The question of seriousness does in fact qualify endurance (*dauern*, 372, 16; *bleiben*, 373, 2) before the purity of spirit. Most often man lacks that endurance ("Bread and Wine," § 6 and § 8, 93–94), with the result that the divine can no longer take shape in man's eyes.

tinue: what follows will escape him forever. The image does not need to be described, because the prodigious simplicity gives rise to the fear. That fear, calm and discreet, imperceptible and invisible for the most part, belongs to the imaging (*Bildsamkeit*), in its essence. To express the "emergence" of the invisible into visibility implies that fear halos the visible. Man, whose purity must endure the spirit, is offered as well to fear, because fear springs from the imaging. Man must endure that fear as long as he poetically receives the image. Pegged to *Bildsamkeit,* fear belongs to him. How to "remain pure," and to what point? To this question, the very question of imaging, Hölderlin offers no other response than a redoubling of the aporia: man must endure the trial of the image by "imitating" the Celestials, since he takes his image from them—the "image of divinity" (372, 22).[9] Image of the supreme native, the divine, how could man ever reassure himself before the fear of the images that provoke him round his purity?

The Celestials, to whom man must aspire, "ever kind in all things, / Are rich in virtue and joy" (372, 12–14; Sieburth, 249). Man, then, will without misfortune measure himself against—be the image of—divinity, "as long as kindness lasts, / Pure, within his heart" (372, 16–17; Sieburth, 249). Kindness, where purity is at work, aspires to the joy and the virtue (*Tugend*) of the Celestials. That no text—to our knowledge—comes here to clarify the obscurity, even with a low-angled light, perhaps indicates the obscure point of the poem that sustains it as a whole. The Celestials and, through them, the Divinity surprise the expected purity of man and provide for it by their virtue and their joy, where we recognize what is outlined by our kindness. Joy and virtue result—arise through an abrupt projection—from their wealth: wealth permits kindness, where joy and virtue are in accord. Kindness (*Freundlichkeit*) gives rise to "friendship," where the other remains at a distance that preserves its apparition. The Celestials remain at a distance, and thus can they *see* images. Their withdrawal alone receives the rise of the visible. Or rather, the visible

---

[9] An obvious allusion to Genesis 1:27, as is confirmed by "What then is the life of men?" (209, 1), "The Only One, I" (153, 25–26, etc.), but perhaps also to Colossians 1:15, where Paul defines the Christ as "icon of the invisible God": It is indeed sometimes to the Christ that the title "image of God" belongs ("To the Madonna," 216, 150).

receives the imprint and the homage of a rise (as one speaks of a rise of vigor) only through the reception saved by a withdrawal. The joy and virtue of the rich—this is well known—stem from saving, which allows one to "see come." But as opposed to our own, the celestial rich do not save in order to possess more, to solidify goods into capital; they save in order not to possess, to let "flower" the image where things take shape. What Hölderlin means, moreover, by "saving"[10] registers the step back that opens up perspective, as the altitude of an aerial view allows figures and contours to appear that are missed by the overly terrestrial gaze, in short, preserves the advent of the invisible image. The withdrawal of the gods would perhaps have to be understood first as follows: a discretion that allows to come, "expects to see," and gives distance to the thing. If the gaze of the Celestials properly saves a withdrawal for things in order there to receive their image, man will have to imitate that withdrawal: but doubly, because he receives the rise of images only by maintaining himself as an "image of divinity," which only a withdrawal can allow to appear. Before saving a withdrawal, man must benefit from a withdrawal that allows him to take figure in an image. This is indeed why the gods withdraw: they withdraw before the man who becomes for them an image, just as man must withdraw in order that the invisibility of the world should become an image for him. The evidence of the gods, or of God (the text here is in the singular), coincides strictly with his withdrawal: the sky withdraws in order to offer, "in lovely blue," the background and the basis for any taking the image (as one speaks of taking the veil) of things. Far from erasing it, this withdrawal ensures his prior and unavoidable attentiveness. "Is God unknown? Is he manifest as the sky? This I tend to believe" (372, 17–18; Sieburth, 249); to this sequence answers another: "What is God? Unknown, and yet / Full of qualities is the face / Of heaven, of him."[11] Evidence and ignorance are con-

---

[10] *Schonen;* see notes 13 and 51. Can one, not without forcing the letter a bit, here translate *Tugend* by *retenue* (and not the banal *vertu*), as is proposed, with some semantic but not philosophical justification, by A. du Bouchet (ed. Pléiade, 923, 22, and then 940, 65)? The other references of this term, which is rare in the Hölderlinian lexicon ("Dichterberuf," 477, 12, and "An die Madonna," 844, 30), do not seem to confirm this sense.

[11] "What Is God?" (210, 1–3 = 887, 1–3; Hamburger, 271, mod.). See "Menon's Lament for Diotima," § 7: "You, who teach me, inspiring (*begeisternd*), to

fused for the one who finally conceives withdrawal as the most radical mode of presence for God, and for him alone. Similarly, the withdrawal of the artisan finally models the *artefact* to the point of its irreducibility: thus, more than ever, the *artefact* constitutes, in itself and entirely, the mark of the one who withdraws therefrom. The one who would like an evidence of God other than this manifest withdrawal undoubtedly does not know what he asks for. Unless he asks that God himself be made *Bild*, εἴκων, and therefore that he there still remain in withdrawal so that his own image might be born. And withdrawal is established then at the very heart of God: kenosis. Elsewhere, Hölderlin thought this explicitly.[12] For no visibility gives itself to be seen in a figure without a withdrawal preceding it in order to receive it. This background, where the place of the Father is outlined, hence remains an abyss. Like a sky supports the images that are figured in it.

In aspiring to it, then, man could imitate nature: by withdrawing from the images that he receives. In this, he would imitate the one whose withdrawal he mimes—God, by all evidence unknown. This imitation of one withdrawal by another Hölderlin indicates as measure: "man does not measure himself unhappily against the divinity" (372, 12). Like a measure, where one simultaneously takes the measure of oneself and of the one against whom one is measured. But what measure does man thus find for himself? "Is God unknown? Is he openly manifest as the sky? This I tend to believe. Such is man's measure" (ibid.). Would the measure of man be to measure himself against God? Undoubtedly, provided that a triviality not mask the essential—that God himself, as welcoming withdrawal, establishes a measure, that of his very with-

---

see great things / And, like them calm to sing more gaily the gods" (2, 1, 77, 85). An earlier version gives for these lines "And like them silent to sing the silent gods" (2, 1, 73, 75). We might prefer the latter. See "The Vatican": "To keep pure and with discernment / God, This is what is entrusted to us" (252, 12–13), and the *Remarques sur Antigone*, § 3, GSA, 5, p. 78 ff.). Likewise J. Beaufret: "The most proper task of man, that which is entrusted to him *in service and in care* is henceforth to learn to endure *this lack of God*, which is the most essential figure of his presence. To know how to carry out such a task is to enter into the most proper dimension of the *tragic* and of tragedy (*Trauer-spiel*)" ("Hölderlin et Sophocle," in *Remarques*, p. 15).

[12] For this see H. Urs von Balthasar, *Herrlichkeit*, III, 2/1, *Theologie, Neuer Bund* (Einsiedeln: Johannes Verlag, 1969), pp. 196–211; and *Theologie der drei Tage* (Einsiedeln: Benzinger, 1969).

drawal: the blessed God "seems kindly, disposed to give life, / Generate joys, with us men, as often knowing the measure (*kundig des Masses*) / Knowing those who draw, the God who is patient and saves (*schonend*) / Sends well-allotted fortune to both the cities and houses."[13] That of which man takes the measure in order to establish his own measure is the measure established by the God through his withdrawal. But, just as the God gives his full measure only in his withdrawal, and only he who withdraws therein knows the number of steps, no one knows the measure of the divine withdrawal: "I never achieve the measure / I wish. But a God knows / When the best I wish comes true" ("The Only One," I, 155, 89–91 = 865). Imitating the divine requires not only that one share (and transpose into our own destiny) its withdrawal, but even that one not measure the measure of that withdrawal. The divine keeps a just measure, which man imitates (in achieving it) only by bearing the burden of having alone to determine his measure—that is, by doing it justice. To determine for oneself the measure in which one attains his most proper good is for man less an absurdly solitary destiny than a task where, by the grace of the divine withdrawal, he becomes an image thereof. The reserve offered by such a double withdrawal founds and convokes the development by man of the space that he has uncovered, like a tide uncovers a beach. The development that, with a rich and at times busy merit, man carries out toward a ceaselessly withdrawn end (the development of territory offers the technical face of this) should not mask the reserve that, attentive to the withdrawal, is measured by the measure. What purity[14] here maintains—that

---

[13] "Homecoming," 96, 24–27; Hamburger, 161, mod.. In this sense, see also "The Traveler": "Then, though, you said to me: here also gods are, and they govern, / Great is their measure, but men take as their measure the span" (80, 17–18; Hamburger, 137); "Bread and Wine": "whether it's early or late, always a measure exists, / Common to all, thought his own to each one is allotted" (91, 43, 45; Hamburger, 153); "Celebration of Peace": "For sparingly, at all times knowing the measure, / A God for a moment only will touch the dwellings / Of men, by none foreseen, and no one knows when" (this text, edited and published in 1954, is absent from the GSA; it is reprinted by F. Beissner in the *editio minor, Hölderlin, Sämtliche Werke* [Frankfurt: Insel, 1965], p. 344, which we cite; Hamburger, 211).

[14] Purity, moreover, is tied to measure: "For the brute also must be / Subjected to measure / In order that the pure might be known as such" ("The Titans," 219, 64–66 = 894).

man is the image of divinity—touches less on merit (*Verdienst*) than on the exclusive manner of traversing the distance that, in its withdrawal, man ensures for the image of the world—namely, "poetically": "It is to be presumed that poetry is above all a measure. Even more. In pronouncing the sentence, To be a poet is *to measure,* perhaps we have to accent it differently: *to be a poet* is to measure. In poetry is manifested what in the foundations of its Being all measure is. . . . Poetry is a taking measure understood in its rigorous sense, a taking by which alone man receives the measure suitable to the whole reach of his Being" (Heidegger).[15] The naming that respects withdrawal can alone inspect the image. Within poetic speech, language escapes the status of "language-object" as well as the servility of a means of communication. In a lordly manner, it keeps its distances, or rather preserves distance: not allowing man to take possession of the thing, it delivers the thing and man to an intimately and silently harmonized dialogue. This is what Hölderlin here means by "dwelling" [*habiter*]: this earth becomes, not "habitable" (as is said by worthy business), but a habitat in which to remain, if poetry there preserves distance. "But for that words must, like flowers, shoot up" ("Bread and Wine," § 5, 93, 90 = 811). That words here imitate, precisely, the native beauty of flowers, this is what closes the journey.

§ 9. The Weight of Happiness

"Is there a measure on earth? There is none" (372, 23 = 940, 37–38; Sieburth, 251). No measure: first and fundamentally because the withdrawal does not remain alone. What "endures" and "remains" (372, 16; 373, 2 = 939, 29; 940, 33) is only the purity whose endurance, like that of John, "remained pure" ("Patmos," III, 180; 73), a purity for which alone "a measure remains" ("Bread and Wine," § 3, 91, 44 = 809), since it reserves it, invests it poetically, in its withdrawal. "The enigma, that which is born of a pure springing forth" ("The Rhine," 143, 46 = 850) corre-

---

[15] "Poetically man dwells," in *Vorträge und Aufsätze* II, p. 70. It goes without saying that I will not ridicule myself by resaying badly what is thought thus. This text is presupposed by my reading, and renders it all the more exposed.

sponds strictly to the enigmatic destiny of man to dwell only as a poet. To remain a poet—to persist in the poetic posture in order to remain—constitutes man's task par excellence, but also the mystery for which "in this miserable time of darkness, [there are] poets" ("Bread and Wine," § 7, 94, 122 = 813). Without the poet there would disappear, along with measure, the figures of imaging. Can one remain poetically to establish the measure always to be preserved, without its ever being established itself? At the moment when the aorgic bursts forth in all its strength and attempts to swallow man up, the heroic thing is to remain in purity in order to maintain measure. "*To hold strong,* to resist being torn away, such is the heroic life of the man who, in a tragic time, precisely does not give tragedy any hold" (F. Fédier).[16] Poetic heroism removes itself from the tragic inasmuch as it remains pure enough to measure the withdrawal in measuring itself against the immediacy of the divine. In a second sense, measure can be lacking: not that it is not encountered as already established, but because its poetic establishment fails with man. Then tragedy arises: Oedipus's night hangs over the two last movements of the poem (373, 20 = 941, 2–3). The poem moves, then, up until its end, between the failure of measure and the poetic perdurance of man.

What is signified here by the gleaming of the flowers, of the birds of the brook; why is it brutally countered by "wisdom" and "virtue" (373, 4, 13 = 940, 51, 65)? The flowers are "beautiful" because the sun is charged naturally with imaging them. The brook, itself also "beautiful," owes that imaging only to the natural order that calms it. The "doves around the tombs" (373, 8–9 = 940, 58–60) proceed, Valérian, only to the bed of a creation in which, without their cooperation but for their benefit, a more light-hearted life "flowers." Their "figures" (373, 7 = 940, 56), calling up no measure, do not attain the properly poetic imaging. This is why, perhaps, the brook offers itself only "as the eye of the divinity" (373, 5 = 940, 54), but not at all, after the fashion of man, as its *image.* Man can therefore become ecstatic before the superabundant beauty that, naturally, obsesses him to the point

---

[16] F. Fédier, *Remarques,* p. 166, commenting on the beginning of § 2 of the *Remarques sur Antigone,* pp. 71–72.

of nostalgia. But he must understand that it is with measure, and not at all with superabundance, that it falls to him to be in agreement, "lest the eagle wing its way up to the Almighty" (373, 2–3 = 940, 48–49; Sieburth, 251) who, at that instant again, "seeks, as before, a ravished prey for the father" ("Germania," 150, 45–46 = 856). These songs remain those of birds, and man is not a bird catcher, nor a whistler of bird calls, he who "poetically" maintains measure. Suffering, envious of the painless figures given to things by Nature, can indeed make him "bleed both in figure and in heart" (372, 27 = 940, 45), can make "tears well up from his eye" (373, 6–7 = 940, 35–36)—that very suffering belongs to the essence of his insurpassable relation to Nature. For man suffers from not equaling the profusion of natural figures with his "cultural" imaging, only in that, more originally, it falls to him to preserve the measure in which his purity can manage to image that which the benevolent failure of Nature abandons. Man can hope for nothing greater than the "wisdom that is figure" (373, 3–4 = 940, 51). The same "virtue" that belongs to the Celestials (373, 13 = 939, 22 and 372, 13 = 940, 66), as a "restraint" that preserves, imparts to man his essential lot. Just as the profusion of spontaneous figures does not weaken the measure maintained therein, according to their measure, by God,[17] so the measure maintained by man loses nothing in being measured itself, with a modesty that never reaches the height of a "comet," and therefore never suffers any attack by it. "The nature of man cannot allow itself, without lack of measure (*sich vermessen*), to hope for greater" (373, 12–13 = 940, 64–65). *Vermessen:* to measure, as Heidegger notes, according to "a reciprocal delimitation of the domains within the Dimension";[18] *sich vermessen:* to be mistaken and to go astray in measuring with a lack of measure, hence in losing, strictly, all measure. In fact, man loses measure as soon as he wants to measure himself against the divinity and its standard. Not only through ὕβρις, but by forgetting that measure, which ensures his essence, imitates only a withdrawal of the divinity whose image that essence is. Precisely because the divinity gives itself in that withdrawal. That only a withdrawal imitates with-

---

[17] See "Greece," III, 257 = 917–18.
[18] Heidegger, "Poetically man dwells"; see note 15 above.

drawal indicates that lack of measure fails doubly: in failing to reproduce the divine measure, in losing especially the sense of measure—the essence of measure as withdrawal. Hence its erring as to the essence of man. Hence the insistent return of the poem to the "serious spirit," which maintains measure. For "life is made of acts, and audacious ones! / A high goal, a more sustained drive / The advance and the step, but also the happiness that virtue gives / Of a great seriousness still, and yet of limpid youth" (*Die Zufriedenheit,* 279, 29–32). Happiness is born from a restraint, which is kept only by the great seriousness that remains within the separation of a distance that imitates the distance of the divine. What merits praise is not, any more than the merit (*Verdienst*) of business, the lack of measure that dissolves measure, but indeed the "virtue" that, with the "elation" (373, 13 = 940, 66) of a "limpid youth," supplely, rhythmically, and modestly dwells in withdrawal.

Returning with a brilliant pertinence to the inaugural imaging, the poet nevertheless displaces it in a second one: the young girl in the garden—closed like the cemetery—receives from the grave spirit, through the columns, a breath (one can see in the passage the biblical ambivalence of the πνεῦμα, even that of John 3:8). The columns form windows again, as already the pointed arch of the steeple, so that the image of a human figure might there come through. Why does the figure here take on an image? Because to the seriousness of the spirit answers the measure that opens space for a visibility: the columns. However, Hölderlin modifies the vision: the young girl takes on an image because she *herself* (and no longer the space that receives her) "is simple according to her essence and feeling" (373, 16–17 = 940, 70–71). The "simple" of the "simple sky"[19] reaches simplicity without having to take any care of it. The young girl must, in order to arrive at "the simplicity / Of the disciple ("Patmos," I, 167, 78–79 = 869), place therein all of the care of her Being and of her heart. Indeed, such simplicity receives the praise of the serious spirit because it issues therefrom: it conquers, through the seriousness and patience, the suffering and the labor of withdrawal, the homage that renders it visible in an image. Does this with-

---

[19] See "What, Then, Is Life?" 209, 9 and 5 = 887.

drawal, which crosses the window of appearance, suffice to locate it within the columns? Not at all: echoing the hard test presaged by the second stanza of the poem (before, in the third, experiencing it), Hölderlin makes the conditions of the young girl's visible distinction point back as far as her essence and heart—in such a way that the face put in images kisses, as its frame, the crown in which the withdrawal is delimited that, ostensibly, presents it. What does the crown here indicate? It is woven with myrtles "which are found only in Greece." Without the Greek leaves, "No feast . . . and yet I would like to crown my head" ("Menon's Lament for Diotima," § 2, 75, 25 = 795); and yet Greece herself no longer weaves such crowns for her cities: "Where do they flower, the very-illustrious, the crowns / Of the feast? Athens has faded, and Thebes" ("Bread and Wine," § 6, 93, 99–100 = 812). Palmyra remains, among others, "forests of columns on the plains of the desert"; but "the spirits of the blessed" have nevertheless died, since "You were stripped of your crowns / Because you have transgressed the limits / Fixed for those who breath / By the smoking vapors and the fire / Of the gods" ("Ages of Life," 115, 5–9 = 832). Which indicates two pertinent things about the crown. First, if, in transgressing limits, mortals immediately strip their heads and their cities of any crown, the crown manifests, in the frame whose capital figure it highlights, specifies, and surrounds, measure. To lack measure is to lose, with one's head, the crown. They are both kept only by the one who endures poetically, with all of his essence and all of his heart, simplicity. The closure of the garden and the window of the columns do not replace the crown: one needs sober virtue and a serious spirit. Only man should be crowned, because he alone, in measure, triumphs. Only he triumphs because he must struggle. Only he struggles because he must take it upon himself to spare the sudden appearance of the world from its withdrawal. But then, what does it matter to mention the crown if, in attributing it to the myrtles "which are in Greece," one forbids weaving it, now that even Greece has lost her crowns? In what sense can one be "Greek" in order to be crowned with measure, without, however, such a coronation remaining possible in its Greek mode? It is necessary here to refer summarily to the reflection that Hölderlin conducts (or that conducts Hölderlin?) concerning the comparative situation of the Greeks and the Hesperians—we others, the latecomers, the Occidentals, that is, the descendants. What is naturally imparted to the Greeks as most proper to them is, within the Original One-All, the immediate relation to the fire of the Sky, by which they find themselves from the beginning and overabundantly overwhelmed. Thus do they undertake, culturally, to introduce there the differentiation and discretion that, alone, can maintain a Junonian sobriety.

With Homer, or more exactly with the "gift of exposition at which, since Homer, they excel,"[20] the Greeks distance themselves the most from the natural lot: immediate confusion with the fire of the sky. Gods and men, sky and earth, are distinguished from one another in the ring of their presentations. Aeschylus plays between these two poles. Hence Sophocles' *Antigone:* through a "native return" (*vaterländischer Umkehr*) the tragic, eliminating measure (Creon), breaks the Junonian sobriety in order to return to the most native = the One-All, the aorgic. What is proper to the Hesperians, on the contrary, is the original sobriety, the discrete distinction of the gods and of man, of the sky and of the earth; the very thing that the Greeks know only culturally we experience natively. Is it, then, that we maintain measure, and weave our crowns more easily than the Greeks? On the contrary. "This sounds like a paradox. But I affirm it once again, and I leave it to your examination so that you might make use of it: with the progress of culture (*Bildung*) what is properly national will ever more lose its primacy. This is why the Greeks are less masters of the *sacred pathos,* because for them it was inborn . . . With us, it is the reverse."[21] The native, precisely because original, loses its primacy, to the benefit of that which, culturally, in each epochal moment, occupies the foreground. Thus must the Greeks carry out, in *Antigone,* for example, a "natal return" that leads them back to their native *pathos:* the One-All, the aorgic. Conversely, but in parallel fashion, we must accomplish the "natal return" that leads us to reinvest *our* native lot: the "clarity" of representa-

---

[20] Letter to Böhlendorf, Stuttgart, 4 December 1804, no. 236, in *Remarques,* pp. 96–97, and GSA, 6, 1, 426. On the distinct exposition of characters in Homer, see "On Achilles," 4, 1, 224 = 597–98; see also "The Different Modes of Poetry," ibid., 338 ff. = 601 ff.

[21] Letter to Böhlendorf, Stuttgart, 4 December 1804.

tion (*Darstellung*), the clarity of imaging. *Darstellung* for a *Bild*, in a word, *Bildsamkeit*. What falls natively to the Hesperian, this latecomer, is hence indeed measure. If, then, it belongs to him alone to return here natively, as opposed to the "natal return" of the Greeks toward the aorgic, why demand of the Greek myrtle plaits for our crown? Because, if *Antigone* is perhaps the last word of the Greeks on their native destiny, *Oedipus* "is in the 'Greek' world the 'cultural' master-piece par excellence. . . . This is also why, for we who are the opposite of the Greeks, *Oedipus* constitutes an *indispensable* model if we want to cease shining in *excentric enthusiasm*, in order finally to write a true modern tragedy"[22] (J. Beaufret). The excentric and the cultural of the Greeks— *Oedipus*—mark out the path opposite the one that we have to follow in order to shoulder our native experience—measure. The "cultural" lot of the Greeks, precisely because it contradicts our own, favors us again, even in marking out our radically non-Greek "natal return." Measure, of which *Oedipus* would be for us the least Greek and the most cultural model, therefore comes to us, inasmuch as our own "natal return" does not yet provide for it, only from Greece—which nevertheless must turn away from it. In order to weave our crown, Greece, which undid it, alone still gives us myrtles.

The figure of Oedipus will henceforth dominate the poem up to the end. It is introduced, however, only after an imaging that, taking up those of man (first stanza) and then of the young girl (second stanza), offers in the third stanza its sensible support. Provided that he is a *man*, someone cannot look into a mirror without appearing to himself in that appearance to take on an image. Without any lovely blue, nor any window of columns or of an arch, without a crown, imaging is at work here. For every other being, these conditions must be fulfilled before any imaging takes: it is necessary that measure be kept, withdrawal preserved,

---

[22] J. Beaufret, "Hölderlin et Sophocle," in *Remarques*, 17. See F. Fédier: "It is here (*Remarques sur Antigone*, § 3, ibid., pp. 80–81) that we can see the way in which the destiny of Oedipus, even more profoundly than his character, is more Hesperian than Greek, seeing as he survives and finds death only at the end of a second tragedy, having lived here below an entire life, as it is necessary for us to do in order to answer to the lot of Hesperia" (ibid., p. 173). The preceding development refers, once and for all, to the understanding of the *Remarques* made possible by the approaches of J. Beaufret and F. Fédier.

and the serious spirit maintained. But if man wants the image of man, the false withdrawal and the fallacious depth of a mirror fill the role perfectly. For withdrawal reflection is substituted. No unbearable happiness has to uphold the appearance of the thing in its image: banally, brandishing the mirror suffices. The image thus mirrored demobilizes admiration. Paradox: in the imaging of the man "who" images, there lacks the distance in which he receives all other images, as man. Even more, the immediately mirrored image of man "is equal" to (*gleicht*, 373, 19 = 940, 74) the very man who images. His eyes no longer see a particular rising to visibility of a being, but more eyes—themselves. These mirrored eyes do not see without troubling the mirroring eyes: for if "the image of man has eyes," as opposed to the moon, whose borrowed light highlights all the more that it remains "the shadowy image of our earth,"[23] those eyes themselves still look at man. To infinity, the mirrored eyes, in their turn, mirror. The image without distance is multiplied and endlessly reproduces (*abgemahlt*, 373, 20 = 940, 74) man to the point of madness. Distance, which the mirror only mimed, disappears from the phantasm of images. This "imaginary," by imaging too easily, abandons both distance and the image. —"King Oedipus may have an eye too many" (373, 20–21 = 941, 76–77; Sieburth, 253): it is not specified whether Oedipus carries this eye in his body, cyclopsically, between the two other lost ones. The eye is indeed "too many" (*zuviel*), not just extra. It comes to him from the outside, which reflects his inward figure. Would not the eye "too many" be the one that, from the bottom of his image, looks at Oedipus? Does Oedipus not have this eye "too many" as one has the "evil eye"? The eye, through which the mirrored image mirrors Oedipus in return, throws the imaging into turmoil and sweeps over all measure. Now precisely, the turmoil of the measure that one must rediscover and maintain constitutes the very business of Greek tragedy and, in another sense, of the least "Greek" of tragedies, *Oedipus*. The eye too many that he has—to see measure thrown into turmoil—does not balance the two others that he lost, since this eye is not his, but the one that looks at him. Oedipus does not see, with an interior eye, what his lost

---

[23] "Bread and Wine," § 1, 90, 14 = 808.

fleshly eyes would not see in any case (as in "The Blind Singer" and "Chiron"). The eye that, in looking at him, annihilates distance for him, darkens him spiritually infinitely more than his lost eyes blind him physically. He confronts, through that blindness, the immediate concept of the One-All, of the aorgic, of the divine—a blindness in which he rediscovers himself as a son of fire, with neither withdrawal nor measure. "The sons of gods, though, are blindest of all."[24] The eye that disqualifies distance for Oedipus projects him, with neither retreat nor withdrawal, into the debate of a relation with the divine, in which all imaging (*Bildsamkeit*) fails and all sober distinction. In this, Hesperian, Oedipus strives nevertheless at the very heart of the blindness that makes him, thanks to his suffering, an immediate son of the gods.

The term of suffering now ceaselessly punctuates the text. Why? The suffering of Oedipus does not at all reside in the physical and moral blindness of his self-condemnation, but first, as for Hercules and the Dioscuri, in the abolition of measure, "namely . . . to battle God" (373, 28 = 941, 88; Sieburth, 253). In what way does this biblical episode—Jacob's battle with an angel (Genesis 33:23–37)—find its place here? Because "the presentation of the tragic rests principally on the fact that the unbearable, [namely] how God—and—man couple, and how, every limit abolished, the [panic] power of Nature and the inmost depths of man become One in fury, is conceived in the fact that becoming—an unlimited one, is purified by an unlimited separation." The tragic unfolds when "the faithful and sure spirit suffers in furious excess."[25] Oedipus seeks measure and misses it, experiencing in its place only the lack of measure in which the god appears in an immediate and abstract confusion. This is indeed why "at the extreme limit of pain, there remains nothing but the conditions of time and space"; the divine presence invests man so violently that at the limit every image, *including his own,* disappears, since all distance has disappeared that could have welcomed it. The divine presence is abstracted in a minimal image: the Kantian forms of sensibility as the simple conditions of possible experience.[26] In such an

---

[24] "The Rhine," 143, 40–41 = 850; Hamburger, 199.

[25] In order, *Remarques sur Oedipe,* pp. 62–63 and pp. 54–55; see the *Remarques sur Antigone,* pp. 62–63, 68–69, and 78–79.

[26] *Remarques sur Oedipe,* § 3, pp. 64–65, and the commentary of J. Beaufret, p. 21, as well as the note of F. Fédier, p. 164.

explosion, can one still speak of suffering, since the unbearable (*Ungeheuer*) destroys those whom it overwhelms? It is here that the suffering of Oedipus finds its singularity: not only does he suffer from the divine unmeasure, like Hercules; he suffers "also" (*auch,* and *doch;* 373, 30 = 941, 90 and 91), for and from not dying of that excess. Oedipus survives the transgression of measure and the immediate irruption of the divine: "To be of that which does not die, when precisely jealous life is also a suffering" (373, 29–30 = 941, 89–90). The jealous and indiscrete care of a life passing beyond all measure is not enough to kill Oedipus. His suffering makes him endure the immediate assault of the divine as if there were withdrawal. In the absence of measure, he does not renounce measure, but, blind, mad, and patient, tirelessly awaits it. Instead of succumbing to the fire of the sky (like Prometheus, or Antigone), he endures, in a withdrawal not established in measure, but maintained by force, "the beautiful sun" (373, 32 = 941, 95). A sun that here no longer decorates the image of things with natural beauty (stanzas 1 and 2) but burns immediately that very thing which would like to remain in withdrawal: during the summer, man endures the burning, without abandoning himself to the *jouissance* of being consumed in the solar fire, like Empedocles in Etna. The suffering of Oedipus becomes that of Hölderlin, and hence ours, we the Hesperians: if "I can indeed say that Apollo has struck me," it is necessary to learn to bear, in a withdrawal to be conquered, the presence of the divine, painfully, in being burned by it from afar, without being confused with it. "Previously I was able to exult in discovering a new truth, a better view of that which is above us and around us"—this was the "Greek" moment, that of *Antigone,* the regression of the Junonian sobriety to the aorgic of the sons of fire; "now I frightfully doubt that it should go to the end with me, as with the ancient Tantalus, who received from the gods more than he could digest"[27]—the "occidental" moment, already that of *Oedipus:* return from confusion to measure, in maintaining withdrawal even in the aggression of the divine. The overabundance

---

[27] Letters to Böhlendorf, respectively, from 2 December 1802, no. 240 (GSA, 6, 1, 432 = 1009 = *Remarques,* pp. 104–5), and 4 December 1802, no. 236 (ibid., 427 = 1005 = *Remarques,* pp. 96–97). The parallel between *Oedipus* and the destiny of Hölderlin is indicated explicitly by these two letters.

of the divine that Oedipus experiences, like a sickness with which
the gods crush him, must not mask how much more essential to
the divine gift than pain remains the gift itself. The most painful
is not the pain that the gods give but the divine gift itself. The
very overabundance becomes painful to bear. If Oedipus col-
lapsed under the happiness of a bacchic delirium, his pain would
be as heavy, or perhaps heavier, to bear. "But to each his
measure. / For it is a painful load to bear, / Sickness, / But that
of happiness is even heavier."[28] The proper task of Oedipus, and
his suffering, reside in precisely this: to bear the absence of measure, to survive its transgression, to work for its reestablishment.
All the complaints of Oedipus indicate in the end what superabundance—as well as he himself—"lacks" (374, 3 = 941, 98),
measure.

"Life is death, and death a life" (374, 1 = 941, 100; Sieburth,
253). The poem closes with the elliptical and rigorous pronouncement of its stakes. One can understand the idea that life
is a death according, again, to the *Remarks on Antigone:* "The presence of the tragic rests on the fact that the immediate God, wholly
one with man . . . , that *infinite* possession by the spirit, in being
separated salutarily, is of itself seized *infinitely,* that is in opposi-
tions, in the consciousness that sublates (*aufhebt*) [*relève*] consciousness, and that the God is present in the figure of death."[29]
The undifferentiated union of the divine and the human within
the tragic unmeasure demands that consciousness suppress its
limits, in order, at the extreme, to be itself suppressed and raised
again, in order absolutely to let itself be penetrated by the God.
God then takes on the figure, for consciousness, of death, since
death, as a condition, renders the union possible. When "life"
triumphs, not only as "still life" (372, 5 = 939, 9), but as a "life
that is jealous" (373, 29 = 941, 89) whose overabundance haunts

---

[28] "The Rhine," 148, 2-3-205 = 854-55. See also: "you have acquired the
strength / To bear a heavy happiness" ("Germania," 151, 63–64 = 857) and
"To carry all with him the burden that gives happiness" ("Stuttgart," § 6, 89, 94
= 807).

[29] *Remarques sur Antigone,* § 3, pp. 78–79. See also, perhaps, the letter to S.
Gontard, no. 182, GSA, 6, 1, 337 = 719: "I say to myself in hushed voice this
formidable word: living death!"

measure, far from its tension reconciling the human and the divine, its excess inverts it in death. When the "life that is jealous" annihilates the measure in which figure takes on an image, it allows to subsist, for itself, but one figure, a figure of the nonfigure—death. One can understand that death might "also" be life only by meditating on the new name that just previously comes to be attributed to Oedipus, "poor stranger in Greece" (374, 4 = 940, 99). Greece natively issues from, and through *Antigone* returns to, the original upsurge of the sons of fire. The divine is there aorgically overabundant. In Greece Oedipus remains poor and a stranger. He remains nostalgic for measure, in the extreme of the jealous solicitude of the divine with regard to him. How, in preserving withdrawal, would he be the depositary of a life, when his accumulated unhappiness has, and this is his most authentic trial, long ago put him to death, even before his physical death. Unless this long trial of an endless death does not constitute, precisely, the new face of life with the divine: "the unlimited becoming-one is purified by an unlimited separation," "the *infinite* possession of spirit . . . in being separated in a holy way (*heilig*), is seized *infinitely*." Purification and holy caesura perhaps indicate that only on condition of admitting withdrawal and its modesty, the "life that is jealous" disappearing in the figure of death, will solitude open the space of a presence of the divine. Here, Hölderlin adds, in a decisive aside: "The immediate God, wholly-one with man (for the God of an apostle is more mediate, is the highest conception in the highest mind)."[30] The God of the apostle is opposed to the immediate God of tragedy, because he is "more mediate." In a sense, in fact, the immediate God already admitted a mediation: in order to disappear, measure had to precede him. The apostolic God would therefore never make measure disappear, because his appearance would remain in distance, and therefore would remain, simply, an *appearance* visible in an image. Apostolicity indicates, theologically, that God never arrives more intimately than through the mediation of an envoy, to the point that, in the Christ, the misery of the envoy and the splendor of

---

[30] *Remarques sur Oedipe*, § 3 (ibid., pp. 62–63), and *Remarques sur Antigone*, § 3, pp. 78–79.

the one who sends him are embodied in the same figure.[31] To maintain withdrawal, as a definitive and no longer provisional distance, is the "more mediate" role of the apostle, who introduces a discrete God. But then, once again, what is indicated by the so hardly "Greek" solitary poverty of Oedipus? The fact that the apostolic discretion and mediation here join up with endurance and measure, over against Greek tragedy and "natal return," itself gives much to be thought. Is it not "one of the strangers"[32] who approaches at Patmos, after having left the natal dwelling? The solitude of the access is suitable to the discretion of that toward which one accedes: the permanence of measure. It remains, then, to be thought that measure, or more radically distance, renders possible the imaging of the world and of that which works man, only in that, more essentially, it arranges the presence, by all evidence unknown, of God. For God gives himself only within the distance that he keeps, and where he keeps us.

§ 10. FILIAL DISTANCE

It is necessary to learn from Greece how to leave Greece—which is the only way of remaining at its height. "I know now that outside of that which, for the Greeks, as for us, must be the highest, that is, the living relation, the living destiny (*Geschick*), we are not at all allowed to have anything *identical* with them."[33] We must leave Greece, which is led by its "natal reversal" ever further toward the One-All, toward the aorgic. Inasmuch as after the profusion of divine fusions, Greece, now, has been emptied of the gods: "Why then does a god not sign, as before, the face of man / Sealing with his seal, as before, the one whom he has seized?"[34] The migration that leads the poem from the Alps to Patmos can

---

[31] See R. Brague, "L'Apostolicité de l'Eglise," "Pour une exégèse apostolique," and "L'Esprit-Saint, témoin du Fils," in *Résurrection*, nos. 45, 46, 47 (Paris, 1974, 1975).

[32] "Patmos," I, 167, 67–68 = 869.

[33] To Böhlendorf, 4 December 1801, no. 236, GSA, 6, 1, 426 = 1003, and *Remarques*, pp. 98–99. See also the letter to Schiller from 2 June 1801, no. 232, ibid., 422 = 999–1000.

[34] "Bread and Wine," § 6, 93, 105–6 = 812.

be understood only in such a reversal: straightaway the hoped
for departure (to fly over the peaks) is inscribed in a "return"
(*wiederkehren*) of the "faithful hearts" that never go away except
in order to visit those who "dwell near" ("Patmos," I, § 1, 169,
9–15 = 867). The moving away and the proximity, the departure
and the return, seem to be confused within the same faithfulness.
When the god becomes too close, then we want to seize him, and
the danger, even more than the difficulty, floors us. That which
saves us grows with the danger itself: the most touching proximity
of the God teaches us that to move away from him—to take one's
distances—is what can be done by the highest faithfulness. The
proximity of God weighs on us (*schwer*) only inasmuch as we find
therein the occasion of a seizure (*fassen*), which, precisely, cannot
let us but seize and relinquish [*dessaisir*]. At the heart of proximity, would not the salvific be, precisely, to see distance deployed,
and all promiscuity vanish, hence to experience distance? That
which saves does not, here, spare us the trial, but prepares us to
endure it: the more proximity becomes pressing, to the point of
the promiscuity of the divine, the more the danger grows, and
the more also the salvific appears. Proximity perhaps is not to be
seized like a good to be stored away, but to be received, like a gift
in which distance remains irreducible just as much as presence
there delivers itself without return. The flight that a "genius" renders possible must also surpass Greece, reascend as far as Asia. Or
rather turn away therefrom: Asia, where the aorgic shines with its
most sumptuous glory, offers for any dwelling "palaces / Which
the gods themselves built" (166, 45 = 868)—where precisely "to
dwell poetically" becomes impossible: with the result that between Greece and Asia, worlds of the aorgic, it remains only to
"turn oneself toward" the obscure grotto, toward the isle that
dwells "without glory" on the ocean (166, 55 and 60 = 868 and
869) in order that, toward this discretion, an "approach" becomes possible (*nahen*, 166, 56 and 167, 67 = 868 and 869). Why
does Patmos allow the approach? It does not allow it so much as
it gives rise to it: "poor," it can let itself be approached by "the
stranger" without disfiguring him with a stateless munificence;
its silence "loving echoes / the complaints of men" (167, 72–73
= 869). Why so "full of welcome" in its poverty? Precisely because
poor: Patmos prepares the space in which the god neither obfus-

cates man with its presence nor, as in the henceforth "atheistic" Greece, saddens man with its absence. Apostolic island: the divine does not present itself there but is represented there; thus can the "disciple whom Jesus loved," because he is himself an apostle, dwell there. The sun that aorgically glorifies or burns, here uncovers only poverty: "But these three / Are this, that under the sun / They are like hunters of the hunt or else / Like a laborer who, catching his breath from work / Covers his head like a beggar" ("The Only One," III, 164, 92–96 = 866–67)—after Bacchus, after the work that Hercules experiences under the sun, the Christ. Under the sun, the Christ neither triumphs nor labors: with more difficulty, he begs. He refutes the aggressive plenitude of the sun with a poverty that takes its distance. Poverty indicates that the highest presence of God to man does not obfuscate the figure of man with light but, by means of distance, assures him of assuming an image.

Despite its numerous versions, "Patmos" never mentions measure among its themes. Nevertheless, nothing governs it more than measure. One can verify this by reintroducing, in the measure of its advance, each of the moments that are, in parallel, developed by contemporaneous poems that themselves attempt also to meditate on the figure of the Christ, namely, "Conciliator . . .," "Celebration of Peace," "The Only One," and "Bread and Wine." A synoptic reading of these poems seems, indeed, possible and correct.[35] What is lacking, then, for an experience of the divine? Above all not, at first, the divine itself: "too bright, dazzling, this joy enters in," and man fears it, like an overabundance that crushes him. If the gifts befall him from the gods, without consuming him immediately, like a barbarian, he cannot but wallow in them: "And he hardly knows what's to be done with such wealth, / Busily runs and wastes it, almost regarding as sacred / Trash which

[35] I am happy to acknowledge my debt here to J.-M. Garrigues, o. p., whose spiritual meditation on Hölderlin ("Hölderlin: De l'impatience de parousie à la passion d'apocalypse," unpublished) guided me from one end to the other of this work. It is from him that I learned about *Hölderlin: Eine Studie* (Nuremberg, 1949), one of the last achievements of E. Przywara, whose brilliant and painful destiny was so close to that of Hölderlin. See also B. Alleman, "Sein Ort war aber / Die Wüste," in *Martin Heidegger, Zum siebigsten Geburtstag* (Pfullingen: G. Neske, 1959), pp. 204–16.

his blessing hand foolishly, kindly has touched."[36] There is the same blindness in famine as in harvest: man always wants to possess the divine. The gods know this well, but bring it on themselves: "It is something the gods endure in the extreme," because they want to lead man to accustom himself to the gift of a presence, as much as to the presence of the gift. Hence the play between famine and overabundance, to the point that man might "see openly the Revealed ones." For the recognition of all these gifts man is missing the very god who prepares them: "Let him first bear it." What does "to bear" indicate here? No doubt, echoing "The Evangel," that "I have yet many things to say to you, but you cannot bear them now" (John 16:12). Man misses the divine because he does not know how to bear, and founders in indifference or possession. He lacks the knowledge of how "a measure always remains." If the God "sparingly, at all times knowing the measure," touches only with moderation the dwellings in which men find a place to live, that is because "were not the giver sparing / The blessing of our hearth long ago would / Have fired both the root and the floor"[37] ("Celebration of Peace"). The measure kept by the divine preserves us from succumbing to an immediate blessing. But, in fact, we must be able to welcome the divine even in its gifts, since "much that's divine nonetheless we / Received . . . / Much more than humanly only / Are these, the alien powers, familiar with us."[38] The scope of our reception will depend solely on our strength to "bear" that which confides itself to us: the powerful strangeness of the divine. To what point can we receive? To what point can the liberality of the divine abandon itself without reserving or preserving? "Knowing the measure," He who gives cannot give within the measure that we alone fix, that of our strengths, since it, precisely, does not suffice: "I never achieve the measure / I wish. But a God knows / When the best I wish comes true" ("The Only One," I, 155, 89–91 = 865). Only a god knows what measure is suitable to my desire and my song—man himself does not fix the measure within which his relation to the divine becomes an

---

[36] "Bread and Wine," 92, 74 and 92, 79–80 = 811, then 92, 81, 92, 83, and 93, 1 = 811; finally, 91, 44 = 809; Hamburger, 155.

[37] "Celebration of Peace," minor ed., 345, 52 and 345, 61–63 = 860; Hamburger, 213.

[38] Ibid., 345, 64–65 and 67–68 = 860–61; Hamburger, 213.

image. Would it be necessary that the measure that he maintains in order to image everything else escape him for his own imaging? The poem specifies nevertheless who must fix and maintain the measure in which the divine and man mutually image one another:

> For as the Master
> Once moved on earth,
> A captive eagle, . . .
> So too, the souls of the heroes are captive.
> The poets, and those no less who
> Are spiritual, must be worldly.
> (ibid., 156, 92–94, 103–5 = 865; Hamburger, 223)

It is the God "who knows" the amplitude of measure, only on the condition that, as Master, he know no less carcerally the earth and its limits. This double belonging is imitated by the poet who, for his part, must maintain a "worldly" (*weltlich*) spirit: a bipolarity in which the poet undergoes the trial of his measure, a bipolarity that allows man to dwell only "poetically," a bipolarity, finally, that the Incarnation of God, who manifests himself within human measure, radically founds. If the Son and the poet are superimposed here without being confused, that is perhaps because "all religion, in its essence, would be poetic."[39] Perhaps also, what Hölderlin means by "poetry," far from accounting for the Incarnation as one illustration of the divine among others (in the well-intentioned view of some critics, all of whom devote their energies to reading the most obvious texts as if it were never a question of the Christ), finds its properly poetic depth only within a christological debate. The measure of the sky and the earth, of man and the gods, is taken care of only by the man who, poetically, dwells—that is, the one who receives in his humanity the divine overabundance and who, so to speak, absorbs its shock in his flesh, to the point that the human and the divine are translated one into the other with neither confusion nor separation. The poem directly expresses this institution of the two extremes of measure:

---

[39] "On Religion," 4, 1, 281 = 650.

> And many who
> Looked on him were afraid,
> While the Father did
> His utmost, effectively bringing
> The best to bear upon men,
> And sorely troubled in mind
> The Son was also.

("The Only One, I, 156, 95–101 = 865; Hamburger, 223)

Why the fear? Because leaving aside all reserve, the Father alienates his divinity in actualizing it, with the ultimate actuality, among men: the overflowing of measure would have here to enflame the beneficiary with its blessing. But this beneficiary, the Christ, although "troubled," received the blow of God without succumbing to it. In this, precisely, he established *in Him* the insurpassable measure of what humanity can know of God. His body thus became the actuality of measure, and hence the poetic center of the world. The question imposes itself all the more of knowing why the most foreign thing (*das Ausserstes*) can remain the best (*sein Bestes*)—as much for humanity as for the divine—without the one and the other foundering in the aorgic. Why does the Christ come to maintain measure with neither confusion nor separation?

The divinity that invests the humanity of the Christ nevertheless does not confuse it in the monstrous, because it itself admits, in itself, distinction, "For never he reigns alone" ("The Only One," I, 155, 71 = 865; Hamburger, 223). Who? "And indeed I know / That he who begot you, your Father, / The same who . . ." (155, 61–63 = 865; Hamburger, 223). The divine that invests the Christ admits measure, because God is Father. Let us note that such a declaration immediately follows the very enigmatic word that registers Christ, in face of his "brothers" Bacchus and Hercules, as "the Only One": "And yet a shame forbids me / to associate with you / The worldly (*weltlichen*) men" (155, 59–61 = 865; Hamburger, 221). It is undoubtedly not because they are "men of this world" that the other gods fail before the Christ, since the end of the poem qualifies him also as "worldly," *weltlich* (156, 105 = 865). Why, then? Because the Christ alone comes from a Father: and he issues from a Father only inasmuch as he alone comes therefrom as his "only begotten, μονογενές" (John 1:14). He attests the paternity of God in manifesting himself, par excellence, in a filial manner. In the Christ, divinity becomes filial. Alone among the gods, the Christ experiences his divinity less as an investment or a dispossession than as the freedom of a gift received from the Father and returned. His qualification as "the Only One" does not reject the other gods, in disqualifying them as mediocre and poor appearances of the divine, so much as it grants him the distinction, separation, and, so to speak, the individuality of a person at the very heart of the divinity. The Christ does not merit the title of "the Only One" because in Him alone the divine becomes person. He is "the Only One" in himself, as Son of a Father—without any polemical reference to the other gods. Hence the profound inanity of those trivial debates that seek to decide whether Hölderlin leans toward the "pagan" side or toward the Christian side. "The Only One" first as Son, the Christ then transcends the other figures of the divine—not the reverse. This is indeed why the distinction of the Son is developed as explicitly as possible, for Hölderlin, in the "trinitarian" fullness:

> Yet to the All-Living from whom
> Many joys and songs have sprung
> There's one who is a Son, and quietly powerful is He
> and now we recognize Him,
> Now that we know the Father
> And to keep holidays
> The exalted, the Spirit of
> the World has inclined towards men.[40]

---

[40] "Celebration of Peace," 345, 71–78 = 861; Hamburger, 213. The editor, in the notes of the French translation (Pléiade) very judiciously relates lines 74–75 to John 14:7 ("If you know me, you also know my Father"), in order, less judiciously, to discern its inversion by Hölderlin (1216). The reality here, less contorted, is more revealing of the theological rigor of the poet. In John, the disciples' failure to recognize the visibility of the Father in the Son (14:5–15, the questions of Thomas and Philippe, the answers of Christ) issues from a radical impossibility: So long as the Spirit is not sent, man cannot see the Father in the Son. The reproaches of Christ to the disciples therefore culminate in the promise that the Spirit will be sent to them by the Son, returned to the Father (John 14:16 ff.). Immediately mentioning the gift of the spirit (lines 77–78) therefore fairly directly puts in place the trinitarian relation of the Father to the Son. Thus there is no reversal but a concentration of the discourse of John 14. As to the remark that "it is no less tendentious to want to confuse the religious thought

Such a trinitarian disposition allows one to confirm the unicity of the Christ. The unicity of "the Only One" refracts in the actual field of the human the filiation that constitutively affects the divine. The Christ is "the Only One" who finds his distinction precisely when the divine invests him, because God admits a Son in him, or rather welcomes in his essence the multivalent distance that polarizes him as Father, as Son, as Spirit—or rather, again, welcomes as his essence the field polarized by the triple play of the relation. We experience the distance that is properly constitutive of God only in the unicity of the Christ, who refers in filial manner to the Father. But this reference itself of the one to the other presupposes the distance that it traverses, and that the traverse consolidates, without ever reducing or destroying it. The Son appears in the splendor of his irreducible unicity, the "Only

of the poet with orthodox Christianity than to conjure away the presence in the text of the [biblical] references" (1212), we subscribe to it for the references that are too numerous and too explicit for it to be seriously possible to pass over them in silence. As to maintaining a narrow relation between Hölderlin and "orthodox Christianity," that becomes "tendentious" only if the question of the Greek divinity and the Christian divinity is maintained on a polemical terrain. In reestablishing a fraternity among Baccus, Hercules, and Christ, Hölderlin perhaps does not reduce the latter to an unprivileged figure of the polytheism in which the others bathe so much as he seriously considers the Greek gods as the figure, as much bygone as decisive, of a certain age of the divine. That the Christ should obtain a privilege over the Greek gods presupposes, precisely, his "fraternity" with them. Their recapitulation (in the sense, to be sure, of Saint Paul's Ephesians 1:10, of Saint Irenaeus, and of a few others) does not signify a polemical disqualification but a foundation of the Greek figure of the divine in another—that of the Father—which preserves it. Obviously, this way of seeing has become foreign to us, and we believe that we have to choose between vague, flat, and critical syncretism, and expeditious, sufficient, and Chateaubrianesque disdain. The first Fathers of the Church proceeded differently. Hölderlin invites us, here also, to meditate on the union of what our vain alternatives dissociate. Finally a last remark: To distinguish between Hölderlin and "orthodox Christianity," it is necessary to know both in their foundations. Other than that this double claim would quickly become untenable, why not admit that perhaps Hölderlin will teach us more about Christianity than the idea that we have of it—and reciprocally, that the Christian mystery will teach us more about Hölderlin than our polemical convictions ever will? One should not forget certain apparently explicit confessions of Christian faith: "To His Mother," no. 41, GSA 6, 1, 63–64 = 69–70; "To Breunlin," 10 January 1798, no. 151, 260–61 = 433; "To His Mother," January 1799, no. 173, 308–14 = 693 ff. There remains finally the strange declaration related by W. Waiblinger: "I am on precisely this point to make myself Catholic" (in P. J. Jouve, *Poèmes de la Folie de Hölderlin* [Paris: Gallimard, 1963], p. 130).

One" in the glory of his filiation, thanks to the gesture in which, in abandoning themselves to the Father, their insufficiency is underlined and rejected. This reference, which makes him "Under the sun . . . a beggar," attests that he who refers himself thus, because he refers *himself*, is the "Only" Son, and because He *refers* himself, is the "Only" Son of the Father. Poverty coincides with overabundance in the divine because God admits— what is shown by the Spirit—the distance of a Son.

The Son manifests the overabundance of the divine in stripping himself of it, through a stripping that testifies to the unique manner in which the divine dwells in him: through the filiation that carries one into the Father. There is no need, to reach this point, to force the Hölderlinian text; it is sufficient to read it in admitting both it and its resonances. Thus, the second stanza of "Celebration of Peace," which repeats almost word for word the christological hymn of the Epistle to the Philippians, superimposes the entire filial reference on the theological figure of kenosis (Incarnation and, indissolubly, Passion); who is the one of whom the poet says "you like to disavow (renounce, *verleugnest*) the distant country from which you come (*dein Ausland*)" (344, 16; Hamburger, 209, mod.), or, as "Patmos" will repeat, with regard to Holy Friday, "to contemplate, nevertheless bent over, before God the figure / Of the one who renounced" (182, 176–77 = 874), who is this if not the one who, being "in the condition of the divine," in the very figure (μορφή = *Gestalt*) of the Father, renounced "seeking equality with God as a possession to be defended," and who "on the contrary" (ἀλλά, 2, 7 = *doch*, 344, 16) emptied himself (ἐκένωσεν, Philippians 2:6–7)? What the poem means by "renounce" corresponds to what the christological hymn attempts to approach by "empty oneself." More, the "Prince of Peace" "renounced" only in order to "take upon himself the figure of the friend," to don the very figure of those who become his neighbors in the kenosis—men. The hymn declares, in parallel, that the Christ, having kenotically "taken on the figure, μορφή, of a slave, was born in the likeness of man, and was, as to his bearing, taken for a man" (Philippians 2:7–8). The exile from his divine figure does not lead the Christ to annihilation—no more for Hölderlin than for the hymn that cites Saint Paul. Or more exactly, the annihilation that goes to the point of death on a cross reveals, by its very radicality, the reference to the Father, who, in return, graces the annihilated one as All-powerful Son. The dispossession here is voluntary (*gern,* Hölderlin says, echoing the verbs of annihilation that, in the hymn, all have Christ as subject); it therefore marks the profound reference of the Son to the Father, as the source from which all his plenitude comes. The reference begins by annihilation, to the point of death. But, since death definitively manifests this reference, it also definitively opens the horizon onto the Father: the Son immediately shines there because annihilated, as He who receives from the Father that which he sends back to him in annihilation. Hence the evidence of his divinity at the very moment and by the very fact of his "renunciation": "In / Your presence I know; but one thing: mortal you are not. / A wise man could elucidate much for me; but where / A God as well appears, / A different clarity shines" (344, 21–24; Hamburger, 209–211). The appearance of a God no longer follows after annihilation: it coincides with it, or rather the annihilation finally shines with its true light, where it appears as filial reference to the depth of the Father who, by that very fact, invests the Son—triumphant—with his power. To which the hymn answers in a prior echo: "He humbled himself, making himself obedient even unto death, and the death of the cross; thus God exalted Him and graced Him with the Name that is above every name, so that at the name of Jesus, every knee should bend, in heaven, on earth, and in hell, and so that every tongue should proclaim of Jesus, the Christ, that he is Lord to the glory of the Father" (Philippians, 2:8–11). That this parallel should be pursued all the way to the end is confirmed by a final point: the very verse that most explicitly registers the abandonment by the "Prince of Peace" of his figure for the "figure of the friend" is completed by the paternal exaltation of the Father, following the very formula of the hymn: "Assuming the figure of a friend, you known to all men, yet / Almost it bends our knees, such loftiness."[41] The Hölderlinian meditation here fixes, then, on one of

---

[41] "Celebration of Peace," 344, 19–20 = 859; Hamburger, 209, mod., to which one should compare the first stanza of the different versions of "Conciliator . . .," GSA, 2, 1, 130, 1–4; 133, 1–13; and finally 136, 1–13 = 844: "Conciliator in whom none ever believed, / Who in this day is here, it is the figure of friend that for me / You took on yourself, immortal, but fully / I

the most decisive christological texts of the Christian tradition. There is nothing accidental about this, nor, to be sure, any arbitrariness to the reading, but the inescapable necessity of a convergence, in considering the same paradox. Or if one wants, on condition of understanding the paradox as a certain vision of glory and its oblique arrival (παράδοξος). The glory of the divine befalls us only obliquely, in the naked form of the Son. There is nothing more properly divine than masked glory and the absence of immediate appearance: because the question of the divine for man is expressed according to measure, because measure itself constitutes, through restraint, the most divine character of a God who "saves," instead of invading and investing, because, finally, the withdrawal of God in its very essence coincides with the humanly bearable measure of the divine in the form of the Son. The Son manifests his own glory of God in the very reference that attributes it fundamentally to the Father, but that attests it simultaneously as Son. Without the least contradiction, this reference puts into play both abandon and gift, as the two movements of one distance. To abandon oneself to the Father is, by designating Him in the distance, to receive, in the very gesture of the reference, an irreducible alterity: to remain, inasmuch as poor, the one who, only then, becomes the valid interlocutor for all overabundance. Only the Son is poor enough to be the other of the Father. Hence only the Son can, in the alterity that distance ensures him, receive everything from God.

Only in the "figure of the friend" does the Christ manifests his height—as Son. And hence the veil over his turn of glory constitutes the highest figure of God—not only the highest that we can bear without dying—but the highest that God himself gives of Himself; on his face as Christ, the Son does not always reveal the Father so much as God Himself is always received as Son, in the distance of the Father, which is traversed and brought about by the Spirit. That the reference of the Son to the Father traces the highest and most humble form of revelation—measure; that that presence in withdrawal does not mark any deficiency but testifies to a reference in which the distance of the Father is uncovered;

---

grant (you?) the height / That makes my knees bend." The end of the stanza corresponds to "Celebration of Peace," 344, v. 20–24 = 859, cited above.

that the distance of God as Father alone ensures the Son and, reciprocally, is ensured only by Him, is what the face of the "Only One," of the "Prince of Peace" conceals and reveals. His face opens onto the abyssal depth of the Father—whose distance he manifests in filial manner. Measure, which the divine establishes for man, is here deciphered, and here alone; the measure through which the human and the divine can encounter one another without dissolution, but without absence, is indeed founded on the internal distance of the divine—in the Christ, the divine distance also plays humanly. Distance becomes the distance from man to God, on the basis of its play as distance from the Son to the Father. When the Son takes on the face of man, the distance from the Son to the Father becomes the measure of the human and of the divine. Thus Hölderlin joins to the christological title this last name, "Conciliator," repeating very closely the qualifier that Saint Paul gives: "he reconciled with his peace (εἰρηνοποιήσας), through the blood of his cross, through Him, the things of the earth and the things of heaven" (Colossians 1:20). But, if such a celebration of peace can indeed be carried out forever, the Conciliator can, and even in a sense *must*, remain the one "in whom none believed." For we do not accept the measure whose salvific withdrawal tests us as a danger: that of "discovering the true Christian feeling that we are but one with the Father"[42] only at the price of the solitary gap that separates us from him as sons.

§ 11. THE ONLY ONE AND HIS DISAPPROPRIATION

For man, there is one way to accept the Christ that censures all the more his uncontrollable and definitive innovation: namely, to claim to maintain with Him a relation whose immediacy contradicts—at the very moment when it claims to state and announce it—the withdrawal where the Son appears in distance to the Father. The disciple whose "attentive eyes . . . / contemplate the face of the god most closely" ("Patmos," I, 167, 79–80 = 869)

---

[42] To His Brother-in-Law Breunlin, 10 January 1798, no. 151, GSA, 6, 1, 260–61 = 433.

indeed intends to approach "most closely," to the point of risking confusion with Him, the very One whose presence expresses the distance that unites him to, in distinguishing him from, the Father, as a Son. The Christ incarnates distance, not only for us, to whom He presents himself "mediately in the Holy Scriptures" ("The Only One," III, 163, 83–84), but already with his Palestinian incursion into the history of men. Such a god distinguishes himself massively and mysteriously from the others—without, however, giving up all fraternity with them—in that, far from obfuscating our horizon of presence with his splendor, he enters into corporal presence only better to conceal himself there:

> My Master and Lord!
> O you, my teacher!
> Why did you keep
> Away? And when
> I asked among the ancients,
> The heroes and
> The gods, then why were you
> Not there?
>
> ("The Only One," I, 154, 36–43 = 864; Hamburger, 221)

Withdrawal governs his relation with the invading and ravished disciples, because withdrawal governs the relation to the Father who, at every instant, for eternity, maintains him as Son. The withdrawal in the approach therefore has nothing to do, for example, with the dissimulation of the leader in relation to the troops or the governed, nor with a humility "buried in the human stuff" as is trivially repeated: the withdrawal of the approach refracts, with a paradoxical and maximal evidence, the withdrawal of the relation to the Father. In giving himself to be desired in the withdrawal, the Christ conceals neither himself nor the Father: on the contrary, he makes their most radically unthinkable secret burst out—that withdrawal, as distance, constitutes the sole place and mode in which the Son is united with the Father all the more insofar as he receives definitively from the Father the ability to distinguish himself forever from Him. If, then, the disciple, ignoring that the withdrawal of the relation is manifested in the withdrawal of the approach, attempts obstinately to know the Christ "most closely," he immediately misunderstands the only divinity in Him—that of the Son in distance from a Father. He seeks, then, to reproduce with the man of the divine withdrawal, who assumes under the sun the form of the beggar, the immediate and excessive relation that he maintained, perilously, with Hercules and Bacchus. A regression that goes, by the way, less from the Christ to the Greek gods (which remain forms of the divine, authentically) than from a relation measured by the standard of the divine withdrawal, to an unmeasured relation to the immediately present or absent divinity. To recognize Christ, then, presupposes that one admit the withdrawal that, between him and us, reveals that other and same withdrawal, in which the Father and Son recognize one another and are united. The withdrawal in which the Son appears slips away as soon as the spectator wants to put his hand on the body—lovingly or hatefully, for an embrace or for murder, it matters little: "And yet I know, it is my / Own fault! For too fervently, / O Christ, I'm attached to you" ("The Only One," I, 154, 48–50 = 864; Hamburger, 221). Such a fervor is faulty only in that its love does not reach the height of what it is necessary to love: the distance itself in which the withdrawal of the Father frees up the Son. The impatience of the excess marks, in fact, the insufficiency of the love; it does not reveal, on the contrary, a demand too strong for the divine to satisfy it.[43] Hölderlin is thus inscribed in a tradition whose theological scope he radicalizes and reactualizes, that which, for example, Saint Bernard had clearly formulated: the attachment of the disciples to the immediately corporal presence of the Christ remains a "carnal love" that attempts to take possession of it, with the infantile frenzy of a strained, distracted, and impotent desire. In approaching the Christ thus, "carnal love" effaces the withdrawal and

---

[43] Hölderlin here sets himself up in opposition to authors who, before him, fade. Vigny, Jean Paul, even Nerval and Hegel conceive the withdrawal of the divine only as an excess of human love over the guilty failure of "God," whose claims collapse in liberating the fantasmatic self-sufficiency of a human Eros that passes into hyperbole. That this hyperbole indicates the weakness of man, that on the contrary the silence of the Father reveals him with an unbearable evidence as Father, this is what Hölderlin alone gives to be thought, because he alone lent himself to the withdrawal sufficiently to encounter the Father in it. That this simultaneously arrogant and naïve attitude remains the most common in the piety-steeped atheism that holds sway in clerical milieux is what Father Louis Boyer well marks with the acerbic vigor of the converted and the righteous indignation of the believer in *Religieux et clercs contre dieux* (Paris: Aubier, 1975).

misses the testimony of the filial withdrawal: "Even though this attachment to the body of Christ is a great gift of the Holy Spirit, I still call it carnal, in comparison with that other love that has for object not only the Word made flesh but the Word as Wisdom, justice, truth, holiness, piety, virtue, and many other designations of this order."[44] The attachment to the body of Christ is "carnal" here not because a mark of infamy would taint corporeal reality—Christ sanctified it in assuming it—but because, in the proximity of a close familiarity, the body is banalized, with the result that one misses the divinity that delivers itself therein. The divinity, that is, the withdrawal in which the Son lets himself be named Such by the Father, even unto the Cross. The "carnal" love of the Christ does not see his relation and reference to the Father, and in fact rejects that by which the Christ is God. Since "under the sun they loved / This life and were loath to part from / The visible face of the Lord / And their habitual habitat (*Heimat*)," they cannot welcome as an enduring joy "the great decisive caesura (*Grossentschiedenes*)" ("Patmos," I, 168, 93 = 870; Hamburger, 235, mod.). The nostalgia of a life under the immediate sun of the divine ties them to what they hold as their habitat (*Heimat*); the corporeal face of Christ here, when men venerate it with puerile covetousness, masks, in the Christ himself, the revealed face of the divine—the icon, under a solar gaze, again becomes an idol.[45] In the end, the face of Christ, for "carnal" love, is identified with our habitual habitat, and there makes us assume or keep our usual habits. Thus ignoring the mediate approach to the Christ ("spiritual" and filial love), the disciples miss the mediate relation of the Christ to the Father, and hence steal away from

---

[44] *On the "Song of Songs,"* XX, 8.

[45] It is known that, during the iconoclastic controversy, in seventh-century Byzantium, the icon had been contested as an idol. The formula retained by orthodoxy avoids both privileging the icon (which would amount to monophysitism) and disqualifying it (to exclude Nestorianism); it concludes that "then honor rendered to the icon passes to its prototype, and he who adores the icon adores in it the person of the one who is depicted there" (Council of Nicaea, II, 787, *Dz.* 302). The reference of human nature to the divine nature expresses, in the very person of Christ, the reference of the Son to the Father. Without this reference, the Son, denying himself as Son, masks the Father, and collapses as God. See C. von Schönborn, *L'Icône du Christ: Fondements théologiques élaborés entre le 1er et le 2e concile de Nicée* (Fribourg, Switzerland: Editions Universitaires, 1976), pp. 217–27.

their fatherland (*Vaterland*, 176, 120), to be imprisoned in a desert-like and cellular no-exit where, anachronistically, they desert their destiny in awaiting a return of the flame of the immediate divinity. Whereby is effaced the decided and decisive event, the caesura that Christ in himself provokes: that the withdrawal that distinguishes him from the Father manifests as well on the face of Christ the highest form of all possible relation to the divine—the Son.

What the disciples miss, what provokes their sadness and withdrawal [*repli*], coincides exactly with what permits the Christ, "victorious, from the peaks of joy, to cast upon them" as upon friends "the supreme gaze of a conqueror" ("Patmos," I, 167, 89–90 = 869)—the filial abandon in the withdrawal of the Father. If Hölderlin passes quickly over the Cross and Resurrection (167, 89–90, and 168, 106–7 = 869 and 870), that is undoubtedly because, repeating Saint John, he honors with his silence the unspeakably superabundant—"Much could be said of it" (ibid., 167, 87–88 = 869; Hamburger, 235; see John, 20:30 and 21:25). It is also because the paschal mystery in itself is neither the question nor the object of a discourse: the Christ manifests his divinity all the more perfectly insofar as, in the unreserved abandon of his being placed on the cross, put to death and in the tomb, he plays absolutely the play of the withdrawal that unites him to and distinguishes him from the Father. The cross manifests the withdrawal as distinction, and the Resurrection, the same withdrawal as union. The distance of the withdrawal shows its two faces in these two events, whose chronological succession should not hide the theological and conceptual inherence. The question that here awakens the poet does not consist, trivially, in demonstrating (or dismantling), critically or apologetically, the paschal *tridum*. The believer in him avoids this ridicule. What gives rise to the question is something else: can the disciples, who misunderstand the withdrawal in the approach of Christ—that is, we, Hesperians, who ignore the mediating measure of our relation to the divine where, nevertheless, our most native destiny summons us—can they conceive that the divine manifests its highest glory precisely in the paradoxical withdrawal of the Cross/Resurrection? Obviously not: the profound sadness of the disciples does not even suspect the triumph of the paschal joy of Christ. The hermeneutic of the

decisive and decided event would demand, so that occidental
man locate it, that he penetrate the double withdrawal of the approach and the reference; he misses it, moreover, only because
he wears its mask, destinally. Hölderlin here mobilizes, to ensure
the transport of Hesperia into the hermeneutic place of its modernity (the paschal paradox of the withdrawal), the gift of the
Holy Spirit: "Therefore he sent them / The spirit, and mightily
trembled the house."[46] But as the second sequence indicates, the
Spirit, even in the episode evoked here of the pilgrims of Em-
maus, is still perceived by the disciples only as a dilatory remission
before the definitively catastrophic separation. The eucharistic
exegesis lesson given by the Christ (Luke 24:27, 30) intends precisely that his fleshly body be effaced, for the disciples, in the
corporally consecrated bread exposed by the delivered Word—
with the result that in "disappearing to their eyes" (Luke 24:31),
"suddenly . . . withdrawing hastily" (168, 130–31 = 870), the
Christ abandoned to men a more corporal and intimate presence
that the body (mis)understood by "carnal love." Now, precisely,
"carnal love" still tries to retain the one who remains only by "Far
off in haste [looking] back" (169, 131 = 870; Hamburger, 237,
mod.), by an awkward and inchoate mime of charity: "vowing, /
So that he would stay, from now on goldenly / Bound fast as to
ropes, / Calling the evil by name, they held out their hands"[47]
The disciples do not reach an understanding of the withdrawal,
and they do not glimpse that it is precisely in separation, which
they experience as a departure, that the advent of the divine becomes more intimate than ever: "departing / Once more he appeared to them" (168, 106–7 = 870; Hamburger, 235). Not that
the Christ disappears *after* having appeared a last time, nor that,
on the point of disappearing, he keeps himself an instant *more* in
his appearing: the appearance *coincides* exactly with the apparent
disappearance. God's present is not inscribed in a presence that

---

[46] "Patmos," I, 168, 100–102; Hamburger, 235, and 169, 125–27 = 870. These
two sequences allude respectively to Pentecost (Acts 2:1 ff.) and to the double
appearance to the disciples in Luke 24:36 ff., John 20:19–23, and John 10:26.
One should remember another text on the Spirit, in its trinitarian acceptation,
"Celebration of Peace" (345 = 861).

[47] Ibid., 169, 132–35; Hamburger, 237, mod., French trans. according to G. G.
Bianquis, *Hölderlin, Poèmes—Gedichte* (Paris: Aubier, 1943), p. 415.

a possessive gaze could bind. The present reveals itself in the withdrawal of presence, because that withdrawal harbors in itself, and delivers by a gift, the only presence of the present, and the sole present of a presence. It is only in such a withdrawal that presence and the present can be conjoined. This is what is rendered thinkable by the recourse to the Spirit, this is what the disciples miss. The latter do not reach, even after the gift of the Spirit (according to the "chronology" of the poem, in 168, 100 ff. = 870, not that of Luke), the hermeneutic place of their faith: the immediate relation—which binds man and where the divine does not cease to "seize him by the hair, present face to face (*gegenwärtig*)" (169, 129 = 870)—still remains dominant. Or rather, and here Hölderlin's theological exactness is amazing, the gift of the spirit, if it is full and definitive, is received only eschatologically. And only the withdrawal of the approach reveals the withdrawal of the relation to the Father in the Son's reference to him; the disciples—once again, we, the Hesperians—must also enter into the withdrawal of the approach (to the Christ) so that in their turn they experience the withdrawal of the relation and the reference to the Father. Which means: the insistent and poorly received gift of the Spirit becomes familiar only if the withdrawal, at first, that of Christ, is opened to us, as a danger and as a salvation. Thus, between the two mentions of the Spirit, there intervenes the death of the sun:

> For now the kingly one extinguished
> The day of the sun and broke
> The straightly beaming, the scepter,
> Divinely suffering, yet of his own free will,
> For it was to come back when
> The time was due.
>
> (168, 108–13 = 870; Hamburger, 235–37)

The sun is extinguished where the divine affects man immediately. Intentionally, the poet evokes together the falling of the sun, the darkness that comes upon the death of Jesus (Matthew 27:45), and the consent to break the scepter of the death willed by Jesus (John 10:17–18); but the episode is found as if carried over *after* the resurrection, mentioned above (167, 89–90 = 869). One must no doubt not overemphasize here the chronological rigor of the poem. One can nevertheless remark that it is as after the passion and the resurrection that men enter into the withdrawal of the sun. Or rather, as soon as the Christ has sublated the other forms of the divine, the immediacy of the divine sun must, itself also, enter into withdrawal, pull itself back into the darkness that leaves the space of a withdrawal of affiliation. The Holy Spirit thus finds its most effective name, "Serious spirit," which allows one to endure the measure of the withdrawal. Remarkably, the sole verses of "Patmos" (168, 115–21 = 870) that resonate, in a positive and calm serenity, with the first stanza of "In Lovely Blue" are inserted here: "Dwelling" became possible because solar immediacy yielded to the "loving night"; "joy" (168, 115) belongs to men, as much as to the gods, such that the night loves man even before he has to love the "lovely (*lieblicher*) blue." The same "joy" ensured by the withdrawal "preserves" the "simplicity" of the eyes; that is, it allows them to take into view, with neither drunkenness nor fear, the "abysses of wisdom." Hence, also, some "images" become visible, since they are ensured by simplicity, measure, and joy. The "abysses of richness and wisdom," taken up from Saint Paul (Romans, 11:33), connote a capital nuance: that the "mystery of the benevolence of God" moves in paradoxical ways. And this particularly: it is in entering into withdrawal, of which they for their part represent the crucial kenosis and where the double withdrawal of the Christ stands out, that men can enter into the right measure of their relation to God. Or rather, to God as Father: for the "dwelling" mentioned here is named by a later version of the poem "Vaterland" ("Patmos," II, 176, 120). This serene path appears, however, only between two sorrows, which are imposed by the repeated departure of the Only One. It immediately implies, in fact, the recognition that "it is a terrible thing to fall into the hands of the living God" (Hebrews, 10:31), or more exactly: "Yet dreadful it is how here and there / Unendingly, God disperses whatever lives" (168, 121–22 = 870; Hamburger, 237).

The greatest sorrow, however, remains to be endured. For the disappearing appearance of the Christ is engulfed in that of the Father. Or rather, because they experienced the withdrawal of the approach in death (169, 136 = 871), or again, because they experienced the withdrawal of the approach in death (169, 136 = 871), or more, in the departure of the risen Christ, the disciples suspect the filial withdrawal of the relation to the Father. When he "To whom beauty most adhered, so that / A miracle was wrought in his person and / The Celestials had pointed at him" (169, 137–40; Hamburger, 237, mod.) is obscured, then beauty is darkened (above Hölderlin also said "the day of the Sun, the Royal"), or more exactly the opening of beauty onto the divine. Here as in "In Lovely Blue," the Celestials are announced by the solar beauty that they consign in a figure of Beauty where their "brother" shines forth with the "glory" of a "demi-god" (169, 144–45 = 871). What "dies" here are not only, with the sand, willows, and temples, but with the temples, the suitability of the immediate Beauty, even contained in the form of the last "demi-god."[48] For when the immediate approach to Christ is closed (ascension of the Resurrected), it becomes manifest that, in the Christ himself, the Father remained in withdrawal: for us the two withdrawals, because we misunderstand them equally in the terrestrially given Christ, shine forth all of a sudden, for a double desertion. Trial imposed by the Father, of a withdrawal in the approach of the Christ. "Yet dreadful it is how here and there / Unendingly, God disperses whatever lives"; trial opposed to the Christ, of a withdrawal into the relation to the Father:

> When even the demi-god's glory and that of his friends
> Is blown away by the wind and the Most-High
> Himself averts his face
> Because nowhere now
> An immortal is to be seen in the skies or
> On our green earth, what is this?
>
> (169, 145–51 = 871; Hamburger, 239, mod.)

The Christ and the Most-High are effaced simultaneously, for us, in the inexorable evidence of a double withdrawal. Who thus turns his face away? The Most-High, or more precisely, the Father: "For when some time ago now—to us it seems ages— / Up rose all those by whom life had been brightened, made glad / When

---

[48] "Demi-god" undoubtedly indicates less a restriction of the divinity (Bacchus, like the Christ, sometimes receives this qualifier and sometimes receives that of "god") than a mode of the divinity: he who reveals himself in Beauty and immediately and provisionally takes shape in it, without man in any way being able to reach it, except in losing himself in it.

the Father had turned his face from the sight of us mortals." Why the Father? No doubt because the gods, in turning away, do not die, but remain in another guise: "But my friend, we have come too late. Though the gods are living / Over our head they live, up in a different world. / Endlessly there they act."[49] The gods, in turning away, do not disappear, but recover their proper good: the unfathomable and unquestionable anteriority that, in this very withdrawal [*repli*], makes them become paternal; or, more radically, because the anteriority is rooted in it alone, an abandon unthinkable to itself, *the* Father. Above all, because in the withdrawal, where the gods plunge into the invisible face of a Father, never, in a sense, yet crypted, the divine was never more actually at work: "Endlessly there they act . . ." "But where the Spirit actually works, we are also."[50] The withdrawal, here, reinforces the attraction of the Father who, obscurely, works most closely to men. Why can he, in his absence, reinforce the infinitely reserved intimacy that he imparts to men? "Endlessly there [the gods] act and, such is their kind wish to spare us, / Little they seem to care whether we live or die."[51] The appearance of withdrawal announces the indifference of the gods with regard to men. This appearance, although less trivial than the "death of the gods" in an empty sky (which Nietzsche, we saw, precisely does *not* say), lacks the paradoxical foundation—the withdrawal of the foundation as the only founding. The appearance of an absence (God would have "some absences") masks that of which it is the result: in the withdrawal culminates the affectivity of the gods, since they "spare" men. Fools see in such a sparing a failure, even though their foolishness remains possible only as protected by that which it ignores. The withdrawal of the divine overabundantly manifests the ultimate figure of God—as Father. For only he becomes paternal who survives the withdrawal. Of God, the "hand that spares" touches man only in respecting his nature,[52] that is, in pulling

---

[49] "Bread and Wine," § 8, 94, 125–27 = 813; Hamburger, 157; then § 7, 93, 109–111 = 812; Hamburger, 157.

[50] "Celebration of Peace," 346, 80 = 861.

[51] "Bread and Wine," § 7, 93, 110–12 = 812; Hamburger, 157.

[52] "Conciliator," 1, 131, 44 = 845. See "Conciliator," II, 134, 51, and "Celebration of Peace," 345, 52 = 860. *Schonen* in this sense can be located also in "To the Earth Mother," "Spare nevertheless, O Powerful one, he / Who sings alone" (124, 31–32 = 840); "Mnemosyne," I and II, "Without benevolence

back in the very gesture of the gift, in order that measure should thus be established. The withdrawal [*repli*], or what seems to us "in appearance" a withdrawal, deploys the gift in its singularity to the point of giving to the beneficiary the gift of appropriating it to himself. The obvious absence of the giver is not an obstacle to the gift, but a path between the gift, the giver, and the recipient:

> Even higher beyond the light, does the pure, neverclouded
> God have his dwelling, whom beams, holy, make glad with their
>   play.
> Silent, alone he dwells, and bright his countenance shines now,
> He, the aethereal one, seems kindly, disposed to give life,
> Generate joys, with us men, as often when, knowing the measure,
> Knowing those who draw breath, hesitant, sparing the God
> Sends well-allotted fortune to both the cities and houses.

("Homecoming," § 2, 96, 21–97, 1 = 815–16; Hamburger, 161, mod.)

Such sparing echoes the "measure" the concern for which occupied "In Lovely Blue" from one end to the other. Nevertheless, something decisive has been established since then: the sparing of the Father saves *sons*—"A God, however, wishes to spare his sons / A life so fleeting" ("The Rhine," 144, 76–77 = 851; Hamburger, 201). What qualifies men as the sons of gods is, precisely, the withdrawal in whose reserve the gods achieve the figure of the Father. The withdrawal of the approach reflected, in the Christ, his divinity, since, filial, that divinity wells up in him from the withdrawal of the relation to the Father. Men, in their turn, become sons of God only if, as the Rhine accepts banks that hem in the growth of its continuous power, they learn how to "bear the divine plenitude" in the "holy night," which "strengthens" because it mediates the divine, transforms the aorgic irruption into filial donation ("Bread and Wine," 93, 114, 116 and 94, 124 = 812 and 813). Would not what we, ignorant, call the flight of the gods, or the "death of God," be the precise and precious occasion to experience the filiation in us, and hence the double withdrawal presented by the Christ? Would this not be, precisely, the desert in which every idolatrous form disappears, and hence where there shows through the nothing that makes everything,

---

indeed / Are the gods, when someone, sparing his soul, has not contained himself," 194, 49–51, and 196, 48–50 = 880; *Remarques sur Antigone*, § 2, pp. 70–71.

our confrontation with the withdrawal of the Father? Would not the empty desert of the divine where we err offer the place of the divine, since of the Christ "the place was nevertheless / The desert" ("The Only One," III, 163, 74–75 = 866)? Would not that confrontation demand only to be recognized as such, so that the knowledge qualify us paternally as sons, in the manner of the Son, "first born among a multitude of sons" (Romans 8:29)? In a word, "erring helps" ("Bread and Wine, § 7, 93, 115–16 = 812), just as "there where the danger is grows / also that which saves" ("Patmos," I, 165, 3–4 = 867), because above all "the lack of God helps" ("Vocation of the Poet," 48, 64 = 780). It is the testing of this word, or rather the testing of oneself in its approach, that the whole end of "Patmos" risks. Thus Hölderlin attempts to follow its rigor to the very deepest mystery of the Christ.

For the poem, in prolonging its meditation on the man who can be affiliated with the paternal withdrawal, encounters as its summit the ultimate and unique privilege of the Son. From here on it is necessary to approach him, since he inspires the stanzas dedicated to the situation of man. How can the Christ "dwell" in a withdrawal where, humanly, one experiences less paternal affectivity than the flight of the gods? If they love me, why do the gods love him first, and much more? "For one thing I know: / The eternal Father's will / Means much to you" (171, 200–203 = 872; Hamburger, 241). The Celestials paternally love the Christ, who values in the highest degree the will of the Father. Why the will of the Father? Because the sole thing that remains, even in the withdrawal from all representation (whether a conceptual idol or not), is the naked will. This is less the injunction that persists in imposing itself in the collapse of its origin, than the most subtle and sustained intimacy which no absence can undo, since it alone ensures, in the distance, the place of an absence. Will of the Father: in a sense, this is a pleonasm, since only the will is poor enough to agree with and to grant the discretion of the Father. It is to that poverty that the will owes its ability to subsist even during the collapse of representations. Poor and pure, the will has nothing to lose in the withdrawal where the Father manifests himself. And it offers as well the primordial splendor thereof. Nothing else would bear the withdrawal, since all other riches (idol, name, attribute) would be dismissed in the withdrawal itself. The will persists only at the price of radical poverty, which harmonizes it with the restrained discretion of the Father. To the will of the Father, the Christ gives his highest regard. In what way? A later version of "The Only One" perhaps indicates it: "But the Christ imparts to himself his part. / Like a prince is Hercules. Spirit of community, Bacchus. The Christ, however, is / The completion. No doubt he is of one nature; but he accomplishes / What still for the presence / Of the Celestials lacked in the others."[53] In the other gods, what was lacking for the completion of the presence of the divine was precisely this: that the figure of the divine, also human like Hercules, be experienced as divine in a voluntary limitation. Giving himself his part in lordly manner, the Christ also limits in lordly manner its department. The fact that the limit that guards measure is voluntary is itself divine. For the divine does not signal itself by overabundance but by withdrawal: only the will is suitable to discretion. Hence the Father remains intimate to all through the will. Through the will, then, that, lordly, imparts to itself a limited department, man ratifies the divine. The "presence of the Celestials" therefore does not at all find the completion of its failure in an overflowing that would surpass what Hercules and Bacchus already accomplish. It is accomplished in the paternal withdrawal, where a will is sufficient to give rise to the measured will of a son, who "dwells in" distance. Only these two wills can subsist in the distance that they measure, endure, and consume. Hölderlin here speaks in symphony with Maximus the Confessor, according to an encounter that chance, no more than an improbable "influence," does not suffice to refute or to found.[54] Only wills can

---

[53] "The Only One," III, ed. Hellingrath, *Hölderlin, Sämtliche Werke* (Berlin, 1923), vol. 4, p. 234 = 867. *Bescheiden* refers to "Bread and Wine": "at noon or just before midnight, / Whether it is early or late, always a measure exists, / Common to all, though each his own is allotted" (91, 43–45 = 809; Hamburger, 153). This partition effected by the Christ, with the reserve of a sovereign, for himself and for others, refers to that of the Father in relation to him: "And me, I have at my disposal and allot to you, as the Father has at his disposal and allots to me, a kingdom" (Luke 22:29). Luther, by the way, translates διατίθεσθαι by *(sich) bescheiden.*

[54] The an-historic, but perhaps all the more striking, relation that unites Maximus the Confessor and Hölderlin will have to be taken up for itself. On the eminent role of the will in the relation to the charity of God, see H. Urs von Balthasar, *Kosmische Liturgie, Maximus der Bekenner: Höhe und Krisis des griechischen*

traverse distance. And their measured accord delivers the perfection of the divine. By Christ "the works of the Father / All known forever" ("Patmos," I, 171, 210–11 = 873): the works of the Father are laid out in the distance that only the will traverses. He whose will traverses distance knows the terrain and the ground of the works. In filial manner, he considers their heritage. Henceforth, the withdrawal of the divine qualifies it as Father, and qualifies as son he who, willingly, endures this withdrawal.

"What is this?" the poem asked about the withdrawal. The answer becomes audible: "It is the cast of the sower" (169, 153 = 871; Hamburger, 239, mod.), who throws the wheat over the threshing floor, with losses and gains, until there remains the grain. The withdrawal judges men according to whether they are driven to distraction as before an absence or whether they endure it as an affiliation. The trial must with patience endure, for "Not all things at once does the Most-High will" (170, 161 = 871; Hamburger, 239, mod.). To claim exception to this, by producing in and by oneself an immediately completed relation with the divine, is again to miss the paradoxical affiliation of distance: "And so I should have wealth / With which to form an image and see / The Christ as he truly was" (170, 164–66 = 871; Hamburger, 239). But in this way I would still proceed according to the Empedoclean overabundance of an Etna whose aorgic figure, here mentioned, contradicts absolutely the withdrawal of the divine, who does not want all at once. The image of the divine, here, is doubly disqualified. First, because it ignores the withdrawal of the approach of the Christ, and hence it produces an idol; the qualifier "similar" (*ähnlich*) undoubtedly bears as much on the Christ as on the imagining subject. The image gives to be seen the one who imagines as much as the imagined. Above all, besides the fact that it claims to reach the Christ all at once, in being mistaken about the withdrawal of the approach, the image unconsciously neglects the withdrawal of its relation to the Father: "I tried / To copy the God's own image, I as a valet" (170, 169–70 = 872; Hamburger, 239, mod.). The "valet" claims to imagine the Father

Weltbildes (Fribourg-in-Breisgau, 1941), of which the second edition, *Kosmische Liturgie: Das Weltbild Maximus des Bekenners* (Einsieddeln, 1961), modifies and largely completes the first version; and J.-M. Garrigues, *Maxime le Confesseur: La charité, avenir divin de l'homme* (Paris: Beauchesne, 1976).

with an ignorance that is as miserable as is dangerous the Empedoclean overabundance that threatens to idolize the Christ. A double, inverse, neglect of a double, unified, withdrawal. The destiny
proper to man, on the contrary, between the valet and Etna,
comes back to remaining, enduring, in the withdrawal. Thus it is
desired by the "Lords of heaven": "Benign they are, but what
they most abhor, / While their reign lasts, is falsehood, and then /
What is most properly human no longer counts among human-
kind" (170, 173–75 = 872; Hamburger, 239, mod.). Nothing
threatens man so much as not seeing in what withdrawal it falls
to him to remain. The withdrawal does not distress as much as
ignorance of it threatens. For man then forgets what remains
most proper to him, in withdrawal, namely, "poetically to dwell"
in it; he disfigures himself in figuring for himself, outside of all
measure, a double idol of the divine; with the divine he loses,
in the sole distance, his filial status. That—a lack of concern for
measure—the "Lords of heaven" abhor. In their way the Greek
gods preserve measure among the men they inspire. This is why
they can, as his "brothers," efface themselves before "the jubilant
son of the Most-High" (170, 181 = 872; Hamburger, 239, mod.).
Remarkably, indeed, the triumphal advent of the Christ repeats
the concern of previous gods, in order to impose on men the
same endurance: "the wand / Of song, signaling downward, /
For nothing is common" (170, 182–84 = 872; Hamburger, 241).
The wand extinguishes the song. Why? The answer follows. The
poem announces a first resurrection, in which the Christ awakens
those who have not yet rotted away. But in addition "many timid
eyes / Are awaiting to see the light" (170, 186–88 = 872)? Resurrection in two moments, which alludes, obviously, to Saint Paul
(1 Thessalonians 4:13–18), which is also rendered noticeable by a
bridle: "They are reluctant to flower / Beneath the searing beam,
though it is / The golden bridle that curbs their courage" (170,
183–71, 180 = 872; Hamburger, 241). Resurrection therefore
does not become the object of a desire, nor of a nostalgia, but
only of an enduring wait, where the tension already mimics completion, without claiming to anticipate it. If the wand suspends
the song, and falls with it, that is because no one knows the day
or hour of the final resurrection, neither the angels of heaven,
nor the Son, but only the Father (Matthew 24:36). The Son sus-

pends the triumphant desire of a resurrection; he therefore manifests the irreducible anteriority of the Father, in his withdrawal. He likewise initiates men into remaining in the withdrawal, that is, "Rejoicing in grace, they / May practice upon the quiet gaze" (171, 195–96 = 872); Hamburger, 241). During the same time that the Son, suspending the song, brings back to obedient waiting, hence to the will, everything that unites him to the withdrawal of the Father, men, in waiting serenely for a resurrection, enter into the withdrawal of relation to the Father—and by that alone, the salvific recovers them. Affiliation joins them together in the trial; in the waiting prepared by the Son—the withdrawal of the Father, they discover themselves as sons.

§ 12. To Dwell in Distance

To discover oneself as a son, through the withdrawal of the Father—the poem would be finished here if the ultimate stanza did not specify that the endurance receives, as an aid as much as an injunction, a will of the Father:

> But what the Father
> Who reigns over all loves most
> Is that the solid letter
> Be given scrupulous care and that what stands
> Be well interpreted.
>
> (172, 222–26 = 873; Hamburger, 243, mod.)

The letter must remain, as in the trial of the withdrawal "that stands (*bestehendes*)." This is because Scripture, in the imperious insufficiency of a closed text, must not be read as the fossil of a discourse that the Father would revive, or would have revived, if he had wanted to, by his authority. On the contrary nothing indicates better the paternal provenance of Scripture than the withdrawal of its speaker, who disengages himself from it in order to leave it, hard and naked, amidst the words of men, as a silent, frightening, and derisory injunction. Paternal, because in it withdraws the immediate presence of the Father, which it comes, among other authorities, to mediate, such that the paternal obsession is veiled. Paternal discourse because the author detaches himself from it, and retires, in order to disappear—or rather to appear—in the figure of the Father. The letter keeps from the discourse what the will keeps of presence: the possible communion, in distinction, with distance. Because the Father retires from it, Scripture becomes paternal for us, that is, a place in which to dwell "patriotically." Paternal through withdrawal, it becomes holy for us. "A quietly shining strength falls from holy scripture" (171, 194 = 873; Hamburger, 241), which thus exerts its strength through the permanent poverty of its injunction, without ever imposing, with the jealousy of the other gods, any other offering than that of a pure heart. The eschatological expectation punctuated by the exasperated exclamation of impatient nostalgia—"Too long, too long now / The honor of the Celestials has been invisible"[55]—is doubtful in that it risks forgetting that with the letter is revealed the withdrawal, and the withdrawal in which the restrained brilliance of the Father is adorned. "But the Father loves / Who reigns over all" (172, 223–24 = 873; Hamburger, 243, mod.). To be sure, He loves, the poet continues, that we respect the letter. But one must understand: the Father loves that we respect the letter only as a consequence of what the letter reveals—that the Father loves in and through his withdrawal. Because the Father loves, he entrusts to us the letter, in which he abandons himself. "The German song" (172, 226 =873) must "follow" the letter, in the sense that the voice must follow a melody, even more than an injunction. To follow: to remain in harmony, with neither fault nor false note, with "what remains," so that such a counterpoint render explicit what remains and "interpret" it. To interpret: to make oneself, through the song, "poetically" the interpreter of that alone which remains—the indication of the paternal withdrawal. He who thus sings respects and marks measure, the measure in which man dances with the divine—at a good distance and in the right rhythm. The eschatological cry mars, then, the final neglect, in not seeing that the highest presence already and definitively, because obscurely, fills the man who "follows the letter." The silences and withdrawals

---

[55] "Patmos," I, 171, 212–13 = 873 (Hamburger, 241, mod.). One cannot help but find an echo here of the biblical formulas concerning the interruption of prophecy and the silence of God (1 Samuel 3:1; Micah 3:5–9; Maccabees 4:46; 9:27; 14:41, etc.).

place—or allow one to place—his song in symphony with the music of the sole star, for "heavenly talk is now his" ("Ganymede," 68, 24 = 791; Hamburger, 107).

The permanence of distance as the highest revelation and manifestation of the divine in the form of the Father—such, perhaps, is the unthought legacy that Hölderlin was preciously though carelessly building, and that our time will indeed have to attempt to possess if it does not want to miss the ultimate significance of its trial. It remains to "dwell" in that permanence with measure. Hölderlin does not spare us from seeking how to manage it—alone. Of his own unrepeatable attempt, "there would be many things to say." Let us outline three. "A sign we are, without interpretation (*deutungslos*) / Without pain we are and have nearly / Lost our language in foreign lands" ("Mnemosyne," II, 195, 1–3 = 879; Sieburth, 117, mod.) How could we "interpret" well that which remains if no sign gives us our signification? But a "sign" is nevertheless given to us, a memory of the presence of the Only One, a guarantee of his return—a second presence ("Bread and Wine," § 8, 94, 131–32 = 813). Since a more open presence would be unbearable to us, since indeed "there is still a lack of hearts strong enough for the highest / Joys" (95, 135–36; Hamburger, 159, mod.), the presence remains humbly given, in the bread and wine. "Bread is a fruit of the earth, yet touched by the blessing of sunlight, / From the thundering god issues the gladness of wine" (95, 137–38; Hamburger, 159). This double blessing of the terrestrial by the divine gives us the presence of the divine, like a guarantee that the gods will return. Based on this guarantee, our patient endurance of the divine can produce a "praise" (94, 142), for and by which "silent some thanks do live on" (94, 136; Hamburger, 159). The reprise of the Christian Eucharist, which seems to me obviously identifiable,[56] here indicates

---

[56] That God himself blesses the gifts that are given to him, that the eucharistic sacrifice is a memorial of previous manifestations of God as a token of their future completion by the coming of the Messiah, that the Eucharist conveys to us a presence otherwise unbearable for our weakness—these are all, precisely, Christian themes. See J. Jeremias, *Die Abendmahlsworte Jesu* (Göttingen: Vandenhöck und Ruprecht, 1967); L. Bouyer, *L'Eucharistie* (Paris: Desclée, 1966), and *Le Fils éternel* (Paris: Cerf, 1973), pp. 140–52, 217–37, etc.; and finally G. Martelet, *Résurrection, Eucharistie et Genèse de l'homme* (Paris: Desclée, 1972), despite a few disputable points.

that, with the remaining of the Scripture that accompanies us, another viatica is given to us. Or rather, in the bread and wine, the Eucharist delivers to us a sacramental and therefore absolutely real presence only with the goal of a path and a journey. Bread and wine are blessed for us, because we endure the withdrawal of the Father, a withdrawal that puts us on the path of awaiting the return of the Son, in us. On this path, they become viatic for us: food for those who remain, and hence attempt to "dwell" in withdrawal, respectfully—what we will henceforth call traversing distance. Because it gives to us the sign of the present divinity, the Eucharist of the bread and wine brings us to our senses, by interpreting us. In the pain thus conquered, we remain awakened to what remains, in order to render it the praise of a correct interpretation. In this way we hasten the advent of the Son to us, and of us to his figure. Praise, for no other speech respects, rhetorically, the divine: "When we bless the meal, whose name may I speak and when late we / Rest from the life of each day, tell me, to whom give my thanks? / Will I name him the Most-High?" ("Homecoming," § 6, 99, 96–99 = 818; Hamburger, 165, mod.). Is any naming suitable to the divine? To name, we might also say to predicate, or to formulate categorical statements, is to presuppose an object so that praise should state it correctly, that is, take its exhaustive measure within a formalized and axiomatized language. But can this God, whose withdrawal manifests his paternal figure, offer himself within an immediacy, whether trivial or aorgic matters little, through which he would become the object of a discourse, without being dissolved as the God of withdrawal? And moreover, could we bear such an immediacy with the gods, their virtue and their "joy"? "A God does not love what's unsuitable, / Him to embrace and to hold our joy is too small" (99, 99–100 = 818; Hamburger, 165, mod.). The unsuitable (*Unschickliches*), that is, what is not suitable to our destiny, would be precisely to claim to include the God verbally in an immediate relation with the human. The first suitability requires admitting the withdrawal of the divine as its paternal figure; similarly, it is necessary, linguistically, to let the withdrawal distend the discourse: "To silence ourselves, such is often our duty; for the divine names are lacking" (99, 101 = 818; see Hamburger, 165). But silence here must not seem to give up on "blessing," even if it must no longer attempt to "name": the recognition of distance within discourse, even if it must keep silent before its evidence, must speak it in some way. To honor him with our silence, we must keep silent before God but not silence him: it is necessary that the discourse still speak, without making claims to naming, because the divine never struck those who discover themselves at a distance from it as much as in that silence: "the hearts beat, and yet the discourse stays back?" (99, 102 = 818; see Hamburger, 165). The discourse should speak, without unsuitable predication, in order to express only the recognition of distance. Only the poet manages this, or rather the man who "poetically dwells" in distance. For "a lyre to each hour lends the tones / And perhaps delights the Celestials, who draw near" (99, 103–4 = 819; Hamburger, 167, mod.). The symphonic accord of a song with a time would constitute our only language with respect to the gods: respecting distance, it could save the space of an approach. Thus, Danaeus, according to Hölderlin's translation, for lack of the Sophoclean text, "counted to the father of time / the strokes of the hour in gold timbre."[57] Thus above all, the speech rendered to God sings, that is, it *praises*. The divine names, which are lacking for any categorical statement, are valid only when taken up within a discourse of praise. Hölderlin inscribes himself here at the properly theological center of what at its best gives rise to what is habitually (and wrongly, we will see) called "negative theology."

A final point, in passing, should be raised. In what, mixing up and masking everything, one sometimes crudely calls his "madness," and what with modesty and respect it would be necessary to approach as his exemplary serenity, Hölderlin still wrote; but little has reached us from his intense production. In a few dozen amazing poems, however, the formal intangibility of the terms and themes raises our washed-out language up to a quasi-sacred discourse, with a power whose unheard of density reaches a level perhaps ignored by the greatest of the moderns: let us dare not to say anything about these. We can, nevertheless, sense something of them, through the equally formal character of the letters from the same period. What to say in considering each of them? All of them, or almost, can be reduced to the prodigious schema that, for example, Letter no. 287 (= 1055) clearly shows:

---

[57] See *Remarques*, p. 91, and J. Beaufret's commmentary, pp. 34–36.

Venerable mother,

I have the honor of wanting to write you again. The letters that you have written me have always greatly delighted me. I thank you for the goodness that you have shown me. I must end again. I give you the assurance of my highest consideration, and am [literally: give myself as]

>Your
>[very] obedient son
>Hölderlin

What is prodigious here? This: that the letter does not transmit any information or any "idea." What does it signify? It describes the separation between the son and the mother: the mention of the mother opens the letter, as that of the son closes it, and two adjectives in it hyperbolically mark reserve ("Venerable . . . very obedient"). There follows the recognition of a relation, which appears all the more intense insofar as it remains abstract and strictly epistolary. The abstract relation becomes the very content of the relation: there is nothing more precise and precious than to recognize the "goodness" that is delivered here, a "goodness" that has no other substance than the epistolary relation, itself empty because it refers to other similar letters. The object of the letter coincides with the bare epistolary function: a sending to the other of a sign from me. Hence "letters" that are reduced to the absolute minimum: "I have equally the honor of offering you my best wishes" ("To His Mother," no. 306 = 1062).[58] The relation appears all the more precisely insofar as mediation purifies it. Hence the tendency to write to his mother only through the intermediary of Zimmer, who is taken for an indispensable relay and a precious aid, as if natural affiliation had lost all its own efficacy before the intermediary of an institution: "I seize the occasion that Mr. Zimmer had the goodness to offer me to address myself to you" ("To His Mother," no. 248 = 1039; see letters no. 268, 274, 305). If mediation commands the relation, that is because the face-to-face relation constitutes the harshest trial and task, even though the most urgent. It engulfs and exhausts one's strength: "My means of communicating are limited to the expression of my attachment to you, in anticipation that my soul should

[58] See Letters no. 261, 262, 271, 277, and 303, for the most significant.

gather the necessary conceptions to express myself in words and to be able to interest you" ("To His Mother," no. 250 = 1040–41). This is why each letter includes the moment where the relation, purely formal, mediated (recourse to extreme politeness, to Scripture, to Zimmer, etc.), must nevertheless be suspended, because it surpasses the strength of the spirit: "it is again necessary that I end."[59] The relation for itself is valid, through mediation, in the measure of our endurance, as a gift. And the gift, which the heart of the letter names "goodness," becomes all the more precious and sumptuous, insofar as the separation grows.

The distance that keeps a relation possible with his mother is sufficient, moreover, to establish Hölderlin's non-"madness," in the trivial sense of the term. The maintenance of numerous relations (letters to his mother, his sister, and his brothers; visits from friends and administrators) is doubled by an ostensible reserve and a hyperbolic humility (hence the signature of the poems with the formula "With humility, Scardanelli"). In fact, it is undoubtedly a question of the emergence, in his human relations, of the full reserve at which the poet arrived, in his relation with the divine. What is at play between Hölderlin and his mother reproduces the exercise of distance between the poet and the divine—mediation, measure, meditation on withdrawal, discourse of praise. The withdrawal in the relation to his mother holds off the blazing return of a poorly resolved Oedipus complex, because the withdrawal in distance ensures the divine the face of a Father. With the same eye too many that he has, Hölderlin measures himself against the divine paternity in distance and imposes on human maternity the withdrawal of an insistent politeness. Similarly for the other "social" relations. One could trace, in a whole other study, how it is sometimes the maternal restraint that introduces the divine distance (letters no. 250, 274,

---

[59] See Letters no. 253, 271, 274, 275, 277, 280, 283, 284, 286, 287, 290, 297, and 298 ("for what I say I must say in as few words as possible, and I have now no other way of speaking"), 300, 303, 310, and 312. It is not a question of brachylogy, nor, to be sure, of disrespect, and even less of polite mockery. It is a question of the impossibility of maintaining the measure that ensures a face to face the serenity of a conversation. It is necessary to keep for a time, and then to renounce the relation, until another time that dispenses anew the grace of encounter; for "time is of a literal precision and wholly merciful" ("To His Mother," no. 307, GSA, 6, 1, 467 = 1062; see also Letters no. 250, 251, 257).

284, etc.), and sometimes the distance of the divine that mediates the relation to the mother (letters no. 307, 251, etc.).[60] This double play avoids at one and the same time the alienation of the other to the self, and the alienation of the self to itself, within the right distance, which ensures his "most intimate thoughts" in "recognition, religion, and the feeling of relations of obligation" (letter no. 259 = 1045). Distance remains most profound, without its exercise between humans devouring or masking the properly divine measure. Humble, serene, and full, the *Umnachtung* in which Hölderlin experiences the "loving night" manifests, with the highest brilliance, that "To keep God pure and maintain distinctions / Is entrusted us" ("The Vatican," 252, 12–13 = 915; Sieburth, 203). Thus is our purity, in distance, suitable to the God whose purity preserves and safeguards.

---

[60] This would have to be taken up following what is already indicated in the remarkable article by A. Besançon, "Du modèle chrétien de résolution du complexe d'Oedipe," in *Contrepoint* 6 (Paris, 1972), pp. 79–94.

Interlude 2

The withdrawal that preserves us simultaneously conceals its safe-guard. For the one not educated by the round-trip between exile and the crater, nothing distinguishes the withdrawal of the Father from the retreat of the gods. One must therefore undertake *to say*. To say in order to identify the silence. One might object: does not Hölderlin, precisely, come to speak and, poetically, to discover the retreat of the gods as a withdrawal of the Father? Does not Hölderlin come to say what is to be said, and definitively, since poetic speech, once again, has preceded and surpassed conceptual discourse? Absolutely. But, strangely, the question can be reversed: the poet has said everything, but what status are we to grant that speech? I am not asking, strategically and trivially, "From where does Hölderlin speak?" To this the poems respond sufficiently. I am questioning concerning the mode of discourse that Hölderlin utilizes, or rather that he allows to speak in him. Two points highlight the pertinence of the question.

My reading has perhaps seemed at times "to force the text." And the text has, to be sure, been forced, not as one violates, but as one forces a door. For the very frequent ambivalence of certain decisive terms gives rise to ambiguity and invites one to read a bit too much (or too little). Thus "*Vater*" can be understood of the father, of Zeus, of the Ether, or of the Father of Jesus the Christ. Thus the fraternity of the Christ and the gods oscillates between the assumption of the latter in the former, and the half-divinity of Jesus. One must therefore choose. And the polemic of the commentators finds, at bottom, the means to feed its vigor, even if it does not find any justification for its partiality. Here, as elsewhere (one can always think of Rimbaud), the poetic text gives room to a multiplicity of readings, among which also the theological reading. But whence this multiple play of meanings? To invoke poetic looseness here would be foolish—and above all because rigor culminates in poetry. It remains, then, to recognize that theological indecision is not of a piece with poetic rigor.

Indecision, here, does not belong to some supposed looseness, nor to the connected blur of the worst syncretism. It reflects a difficulty that poetic saying can bypass but that it cannot abolish, nor even *state* for itself. If the poem remains theologically ambivalent, the insufficiency does not arise from the poetry—which goes as far as ever—but from the divine. Even and especially when poetry assigns them to their highest reach, the unsuitability of words becomes blatant when the unsayable enters into play. The text that says betrays this entrance into play of the unsayable through its permanent polysemy, as also its celebration through its verbal alchemy. It remains to the concept to specify how the poet can speak ambiguously but nevertheless rigorously. Of this, the poet says nothing, since it is in this way that he can say everything.

Another question: how can the unsayable enter into play in the Hölderlinian discourse? Not the unsayable in the form, which is still wholly sayable, of the supreme being, but the unsayable of distance. It is no longer a question of speaking an object, even a transcendent one, even one that is supremely "personal." It is a question of signifying the distance in which withdrawal becomes the supreme insistence. The divine exerts itself paternally when advent coincides with recession. It is a question, then, of saying, more than a being, a separation (God makes a separation), a nothingness, then, the very nothingness of the distance in which the Son spreads out under the paternal withdrawal. The unsayable is to be said, doubly: as a supreme nonbeing, a hyperbolic separation. What mode of discourse is suitable to these two requirements? Or better: what mode of discourse works already in the Hölderlinian text and ensures its pertinence? In question, Hölderlin says, are "the holy names" whose failure gives rise to the song of praise: "the lyre to each hour lends the right tones." By virtue of the same contemporaneity that puts him in accord with Nietzsche, Hölderlin refers expressly to Denys. He whom one rightly calls the Areopagite, in memory of the Athenian converted by Paul, and whom one treats improperly with the *pseudo-*, elaborated, decisively for the tradition, a nonpredicative theory of discourse. What one here a bit lightly calls "negative theology" has nothing negative about it, but ensures a discourse in the modality of praise. There is nothing more suitable, then, to honor Hölderlin and that god of whom Nietzsche suggests that he wants to be praised, than to meditate on the *Divine Names* and *Mystical Theology.*

The Distance of the Requisite and the Discourse of Praise: Denys

When we bless the meal, whose name may I speak, and when late we
   Rest from the life of each day, tell me, to whom give my thanks?
Him, the most High, should I name then? A god does not love what's
   unseemly,
   Him to embrace and to hold our joy is too small.
Silence often behoves us: for the divine names are lacking,
   Hearts may beat high, while the lips hesitate, wary of speech?
Yet a lyre to each hour lends the right tones, the right music,
   And, it may be, delights heavenly ones who draw near.

Hölderlin, "Homecoming"

. . . what is the spirit worthy of question and this god, who wishes likewise to be praised?

Nietzsche, Beyond Good and Evil, § 295

Segnen sinnt.

Heidegger, Aus Erfahrung des Denkens

§ 13. UNTHINKABLE EMINENCE

PATERNAL DISTANCE OFFERS the sole place for a filiation. Since in it the intimacy of the divine strictly coincides with withdrawal, the paradox can lead to confusion: distance must, in order that we might inhabit it, be identified. It will be identifiable only if we can say it and speak of it. We will be able to speak of it only if we come from it and remain in it. To speak of distance: concerning it, and also starting from it. But what language can be suitable to distance?

It is not a question of speaking the supreme Being within a predication of which it would be the object. Nor is it a question of letting the supreme Being, as absolute subject, state a predication about itself and by itself. It is a question of designating the advent of a withdrawal to us. No being, even supreme, gives itself to be grasped, since the gift surpasses what any being could here give. Doubly unspeakable, this stake is characterized no less by the very conditions of its ineffability. For if, as Denys posits in principle, "it is necessary to understand the divine things divinely,"[1] the impossibilities of thinking coincide with the authenticating conditions of that which gives itself to be thought. As a censure and as a condition, distance requires one to think the doubly unthinkable according to excess (supremacy over beings in general) and according to lack (withdrawal as insistence, without being). Thus one cannot dismiss the duty to (attempt to) think distance by invoking theoretical impossibilities. One cannot, in order to disqualify the discourse of distance, invoke the impossibility in which an entire side of linguistic science finds itself of maintaining a relation to the referent: for distance bears upon a nonreferent whose indubitable resistance presupposes a withdrawal, that is, in common terms, an absence. In other words, radically prohibiting that one hold God as an object, or as a supreme being, distance escapes the ultimate avatar of a language of the object—the closure of discourse, and the disappearance of the referent. Or, if one wants to maintain that God pertains to the play of reference, one must understand the latter with so many corrections (referent without the status of object, etc.) that the referent admits in itself the separation of distance. The closure of discourse and the reference to a supreme being come together on this point, which distance rejects: to treat God as an object (attainable or not). The stakes of distance have to do first with the fact that it prohibits one from claiming any ontic treatment concerning God. On this condition alone could the divine things be understood divinely.

The idolatrous objection could take another turn and say: since we cannot think distance, nor speak of it, since it offers "nothing" to be stated, must one maintain its legitimacy, even problematic?

---

[1] *The Divine Names,* VII, 2, in *Patrologia Graeca,* vol. 3, column 869a. All references refer to this edition, cited PG 3, 868a, etc. The works of Dionysius will be abbreviated as follows: *The Divine Names,* DN; *The Mystical Theology,* MT; *The Celestial Hierarchy,* CH; *The Ecclesiastical Hierarchy,* EH; Letters, L.

This useless concern could disappear without any harm—unless, precisely, the unthinkable is not that through which one thinks the unthinkable. If "incomprehensibility is the formal reason of the infinite"[2] (Descartes), the unthinkable can be aimed at as such only in remaining unthinkable. In that way we approach the point of view of the absolute. Not by finally lending it the status of subject, borrowed from our *ego* and univocally metaphorized, but in admitting it as ab-solute: undone from any relation, and therefore also from any thinkable relation, that would tie it to an absurd "other than it." The ab-solute dissolves the tie that ties it to our thought. It undoes itself, whence our undoing, which, rigorously, is attuned to the ab-solute as such and, in its undoing, honors the ab-solute. Far from it being the case that the factually and theoretically unavoidable impossibility of thinking the ab-solutely unthinkable should end the enterprise of thinking it, that impossibility authenticates and, in a sense, inaugurates the enterprise. The experiential verification that the unthinkable is not illusory consists precisely in the fact that thought does not manage to think it. Thought is intensified by failing before the unthinkable. That failure becomes its first recourse and a new incitation. —I would therefore say: not only is it necessary to speak distance, but the impossibility of speaking it in the mode of other statements guarantees it as such, and even accomplishes it. What we a little too quickly call an aporia harbors, in fact, the sole suitability of the discourse to that which it concerns: "divinely of divine things."

The rigorous coincidence of accomplishment and impossibility makes itself clear in an example that is both remarkable and, through the immemorial tradition to which it gave rise, memorable. It adds above all a third characteristic of the discourse of distance, namely, that it is up to distance itself to speak that discourse. When Moses hears God reveal God's name to him, he hears אהיה אשר אהיה (Exodus 3:14), which has always been under-

---

[2] Descartes, *Cinquièmes Réponses: Oeuvres* (Paris: Vrin, 1964), vol. VII, p. 308, 2–4. See L. Wittgenstein, " 'the finite cannot comprehend the infinite,' which must certainly be a war cry of the theologians, but not of the mathematicians" (*Zettel*, § 273; French trans., *Fiches* [Paris: Gallimard, 1970], p. 77).

stood in two opposed ways. Either: "I am the one who is (par excellence)," to the point of recognizing the affirmation of a Being, even of a supreme existence (Saint Thomas, according to what E. Gilson names the "metaphysics of Exodus"), or, on the contrary: "I am what I am," without my presence receiving the explication or commentary of any name other than that, silent, of my acting presence. There is nothing more false than to oppose the two translations and traditions. Their contradiction appears only to the one who dissociates them outside of all distance. For the fact "that God should express himself is what allows one to name and approach him—and it is what reveals at the same time his incomparable and inaccessible character" (Hans Urs von Balthasar).[3] The two sides of the same pronouncement find their clear status only once they are related to the unique one who gives his Name. The Name has no name in any language. No language says it or understands it. This is why the Jew never pronounces the tetragrammaton, which he nevertheless reads. By orally substituting other titles for it, one indicates that the Name does not belong to our language but comes to it from elsewhere. The Name appears as a gift, where, in the same gesture, the unthinkable gives us a name as that in which it gives itself, but also as a gift that gives the unthinkable, which only withdraws in the distance of the gift. The name therefore delivers the unthinkable, as the unthinkable that *gives* itself; this same unthinkable also gives *itself*, and hence withdraws within the anterior distance that governs the gift of the Name. The Name delivers and steals away in one and the same movement. Of course, this convergence, which rediscovers in the biblical word the two fundamental characteristics of distance, is rooted in another characteristic: the Name that distances does not issue from a predication that a human speaker—whether gifted or lucky—would have finally performed successfully. No one gives God his Name, but rather it is God who delivers it. That deliverance of the Name by the unthinkable, which reveals itself therein as unthinkable, gives to the re-

---

[3] H. Urs von Balthasar, *La Gloire et la croix*, III, *Théologie, Ancienne Alliance* (Paris: Aubier, 1974), p. 58, French trans. of *Herrlichkeit*, III, 2/1, *Theologie, Alter Bund* (Einsiedeln: Johannes Verlag, 1967).

quirement of thinking the divine things divinely its ultimate exigency. One must think them according to God. This means leaving to God, the unthinkable, the care of delivering them. The unthinkable gives itself to be thought as unthinkable. The name does not result from a predication that, in transit over the border of the unthinkable, we would effect from the thinkable to the unthinkable, like an arrow that, hurled against the sun, manages miraculously and stupidly to arrive there. The Name comes to us as unthinkable within the thinkable, because the unthinkable in person delivers it to us, just as a perfect, unknown, and anonymous poem reveals all of the poet and conceals him infinitely. It is up to distance to use the language that identifies it. The unthinkable speaks even before we think we hear it, anterior distance holds out to us a language that precedes and inverts our predication. More essential than the predication that we can (not) exercise concerning the unthinkable, there appears the donation of the Name, whose unthinkability silently and overabundantly graces us, at a complete distance.

Supposing that one accepts this reversal, which is dangerous at the least, how is one to conceive precisely the language that would be suitable to the donation of the anterior and silent Name? What status can our discourse henceforth assume? Denys speaks of "honoring the unspeakable things with a sober silence."[4] But this silence still speaks, or rather completes a discourse that is sublimated into silence. What are we to say, then, of the Name that gives itself and thus makes itself in saying itself? The divine Word remains "beyond any name that one names, not only in this world but in the world to come" (Ephesians 1:21). But if the Word, humanized through incarnation and glorified through resurrection, receives from the Father "the Name that is beyond every name," it is in the manner of a grace that he receives it (ἐχαρί-σατο; Philippians 2:9). It is at the very moment that he escapes any human naming that the Son receives, at a full distance and as a grace, the Name, of/from the Father. But how do things stand with men and their discourse, which is thus subverted and contorted by the divine conversation? "At this Name which is now

---

[4] DN I, 3, 589b.

that of Jesus / at the name of Jesus, every knee should bow in heaven, on earth, and in hell, and every language should confess in homology (ἐξομολογήσηται) that Jesus Christ is Lord, to the glory of God the Father" (Philippians 2:10). What the given Name names as to the *Logos* is on the part of men a homology, or, if one prefers, a communion of word and thought. One would weaken the homology, however, if one did not understand it starting from humanity as lived in a Christic mode. For the operative model of homology issues from the Christ; concentrating in his person the status of the human, the Christ receives a homology from men only after having rendered homology to the Father: "I confess you (ἐξομολογοῦμαί) in all homology, Father, Lord of heaven and of earth" (Matthew 11:25, and Luke 10:21). The Word receives the Name, as his, from the Father. For that, he remains in a confessing homology with the Father. Man, likewise, receives the Name that precedes him in distance only in order to inherit it by a homology—such that "each on his own account shall give his *logos* to God" (Romans 14:12). The homology of the Son with the Father measures that of our discourse with the Name, which is received for predication. To put it clearly: human language must receive the Name, as the Christ received the Name from the Father. Reception imposes dispossession and abandon to the point of death. Likewise language carries out its discourse to the point of negation and silence. But just as the death that is refused according to the justice of love matures into Resurrection, so silence nourishes infinite proclamation. Language indeed dies from renouncing a predication of the unthinkable, but that aporia violently ordains it to another reception: to speak in homology with the Name. To move from a model of language in which the speaker makes an effort to take possession of meaning to a model in which the speaker receives meaning, with the Name, through homology: "to say divinely."[5] Nothing less would be necessary than a linguistic model of the dispossession of meaning in order to begin approaching what is at stake here. In his

---

[5] Michel Costantini, "Du modèle sémiotique au modèle chrétien du langage," in *Résurrection* 46 (Paris, 1975), and "La Bible n'est pas un texte," in *Revue Catholique Internationale, Communio,* I/7 (Paris, 1976).

way, Denys attempted nothing other, in what is conventionally called "negative theology."[6] We are perhaps now in a position to follow an elaboration of this as the conceptual response that, in a sense, Denys gives to the injunction of Saint Paul: "Knowledge puffs up, but love builds up. If someone thinks he knows something, he does not yet know in what way it is suitable to know: but if someone loves God, he is known by God" (1 Corinthians 8:1–3). Only love can claim to know Love. But knowledge presupposes conceptual and, minimally, linguistic mediation. Can language, including conceptual language, become homogenous with Love?

In naming God, thought, in a sense, encounters no difficulty. It is indeed self-evident that He whom one must think as "the cause remaining beyond every thing" must legitimately receive, starting from all things, all the qualifications that are outlined in those things: "Every thesis regarding beings must be established and affirmed for him." It is the least of matters to acknowledge that God is as much as any other being, that he lives as much as any other living thing, that he thinks as much as any other thinking thought, etc. The infinity of perfections presupposed by a nominal definition of the absolute demands, obviously, the infinity of its names. Affirmation will therefore indicate without rest or difficulty the "perfections" of "God." Without rest, without difficulty, but not without danger. First, because in relying on all beings, one risks "characterizing the cause that remains beyond all things on the basis of the least of things, and saying that it does not transcend any of the multiform and empty images of God that one has idolatrously formed."[7] If everything must be affirmed of God, will one say that even the most trivial things belong to him (hair and dust, as Plato asked)? To avoid this "impure" and unworthy idolatry, one corrective would be self-evident: one must select the attributes that offer the most suitable support for a predication concerning the Absolute and proceed "starting from what is most related to it."[8] But how can one determine that

---

[6] To my knowledge, Dionysius uses nothing that might be translated as "negative theology." If he speaks of "negative theologies," in the plural, he does not separate them from the "affirmative theologies" with which they maintain the relation described here (see MT, III, 1032 ff.).

[7] MT, I, 2, 1000b.

[8] MT, III, 1033c.

which is more or less related to the Absolute, without applying to it our own valuation? The refutation of naive idolatry leads, here again, to a second-level idolatry: an anthropomorphist critique. Naively idolatrous is that critique which decides between the divine and the nondivine, as if we could on our own ensure the suitability of any particular attribution with regard to unthinkable transcendence. To avoid such an idolatry, one must no longer "start from the primordial terms, in order to descend, through the intermediaries, to the last ones"—which presupposes, idolatrously, that we *affirm* perfections, and that we attribute them as *perfections*—but rather *deny* attributions as imperfections: "Starting from the lowest, ascend the ranks up to the principal terms";[9] or again, "starting below ascending toward the sublime," the spirit attempts to suppress (ἀφαιρεῖν) all attributes, even the most elevated, and even the most "divine" (or supposedly such): "freeing up by suppression the one who is beyond all suppression." Ascent coincides with the negation of attributes.[10] It is necessary to note that the denials bear, as much as on the names taken from the sensible (corporeal, figurable, measurable, variable, etc.), on the intelligible names themselves, including the most conventional within Neoplatonism: "nor One, nor Unity, nor Divinity, nor Goodness."[11] The most appropriate name is found, therefore, no more in the Plotinian One than in the grossest sensible idol. Thus the negative way plays a double role: first, in denying of God that which obviously cannot be affirmed of him (the names drawn from the sensible, which are infinitely removed and unsuitable), it eliminates the first idolatry. Next, and above all, it denies of God that which it seems one might legitimately affirm of him (the names drawn from the intelligible). At a certain point within the negative ascent, apophasis rediscovers the intelligible names that kataphasis affirmed. From then on, apophasis no longer only frees discourse from the obvious improprieties; it also eliminates the highest conceptions as impertinent. Struck in their assurance, they are inverted and abolish their illusory primacy: "The most divine and sublime of the visible and intelligible terms

---

[9] MT, II, 1025c.
[10] MT, III, 1033c.
[11] MT, V, 1048a.

are types of hypothetical statement (ὑποθετικόυς τινας λόγους) for suggesting that which remains subjected to Him who transcends all things, and through which is shown his presence which surpasses all knowledge,"[12] because "it knows more divinely the divine things"[13] by freeing them from every idolatrous substitute. Negation maintains, to be sure, a relation between God and our language, but by employing it only as an inversion and for inversion, it avoids at least the obvious idolatry. In this sense, "with regard to the divine, negations are true, whereas affirmations are deformed."[14] But it is necessary to understand the meaning here correctly. It especially does not mean that negation constitutes the last word of the discourse on God. For in being taken only as an inverted affirmation, negation would persist in its categorical pretension. In place of saying what God is, it would say what God is not. Who does not see that the same intention is at work, which, in both cases, means to reach the essence of God, as if he were organized around any essence whatsoever? Negation, if it remains categorical, remains idolatrous. When, therefore, by force of negations, it literally dissolves what those negations supposedly aim at, and eliminates the Absolute, this is only at the price of an idolatry—that of "negative theology." In this sense, there is no doubt: "Negative theology is the negation of all theology. Its truth is atheism" (C. Bruaire).[15] Negation becomes ignorance, because in it the mind experiences only an inversion of the category, on the basis of an idolatrous naïveté. Negation imagines itself only to invert the predication concerning a given object. In this case, the object is emptied little by little. But negativity remains as vain as

---

[12] MT, I, 3, 1000d; see also MT, III, 1033c: "Since one establishes a thesis concerning that which is beyond any thesis starting from that which is most appropriate to it, it was necessary to establish an affirmation that is supposed—or in order—to suggest (ὑποθετικὴν κατάφασιν)." Affirmation is valid only as a base for negation. These two occurrences of ὑποθετικος are the only ones in the Dionysian corpus, according to Van den Daele, *Indices Pseudo-Dionysii* (Louvain, 1941).

[13] DN, VII, 3, 872a. Likewise, "It is stronger to deny," MT, I, 2, 1000b; "The theologians have preferred ascent through negation," DN, XIII, 3, 981b.

[14] CH, II, 3, 141a.

[15] C. Bruaire, *Le Droit de Dieu* (Paris: Aubier-Montaigne, 1974), p. 21 and ch. 2. See *L'Affirmation de Dieu* (Paris: Seuil, 1968), p. 184 ff. On the diverse meanings of the phrase "negative theology," see M. Sales, "la Théologie négative," in *Axes* III/a (Paris, 1970).

positivity. For it does not reach that which it alone might have allowed one to glimpse: a beyond of the two truth values of categorical predication.

It is necessary to meditate more exactly on the status and the scope of negation. It does not deny that of which it is a question, by successively tearing away from it all of its attributes, but rather it frees it all the more insofar as certain nominations seemed to be more essentially suitable to it. Negation clears away and highlights a silhouette, far from opening onto a void. As sculpture frees from the brute and visible material that which renders invisible the invisible thing to be seen—the form itself—such that the stone no longer masks what it contains, "we deny and remove every thing in order to know without concealment that unknowing, which is concealed by all the knowledge that knows beings."[16] To know the unknowing that our knowledges conceal does not amount to ignoring or to foundering in the emptiness of the thing as some kind of knowing. It is much rather a matter of using denegation in order all the better to know—without any idea. This (un-)knowing is opposed to the idolatry of categorical predication, because in it the negative way encounters, in "ascending," the names that, precisely, the affirmative way, in "descending," managed to pronounce. Negation and affirmation bear upon the same attributes, only envisaged from two points of view. Instead of neutralizing one another, they reinforce one another with a properly unthinkable tension. No statue would ever appear if the stone only masked, and if, in another sense, its visibility remained the sole possible face of what in it remains all the more invisible— the statue itself. Even more: once the statue is brought out, the brute visibility of the remaining material must again become, so to speak, invisible, so that the face of the form might appear; the invisible, the form as that which does not belong to any particular material, remains invisible, all the more that the material offers it the concealing visibility of a mass; the play of the visible with the invisible, in their indefinitely reversible tension, produces and results from the statue as a figure of art. Is this play not a kind of beauty? When, therefore, negation plays with affirmation, its superiority comes from the fact that it does not destroy it but, in

---

[16] MT, II, 1025b.

a sense, restores it. It restores it by establishing it within a nondia-
lectical but quasi-aesthetic relation with itself. In fact, aesthetics
itself perhaps offers no model to the appearance of the theological figure; negation, which, exactly, mobilizes the aesthetic
model, opens indeed onto a different depth. Denys underlines
that it negates "according to transcendence and not at all according to insufficiency,"[17] which is to say that it does not register the
insufficiency of that of which it is a question, but indexes the
failure of our linguistic approach. Instead of being fixed in denegation, or of entering into the aesthetic game, negation pours
itself out into the transcendence of the thing itself, to the point
of becoming equivalent to it—"in the negation and transcendence of all things."[18] But what transcendence enters thus into
play? How could it avoid falling back into affirmation, safely baptized the "way of eminence," or marking a radical ignorance,
modestly baptized the "night of the understanding"? Negation
cannot affirm, at a second level, since it has just rejected affirmations (which precisely come from above). Nor can it deny, since
it admits to containing in itself the motives and impetus of its own
sublation [relève]. As for sublation (Aufhebung), it could not offer
the least help in thinking a transcendence whose strangeness refers, precisely, to an inexhaustible elsewhere. In order that sublation might operate here, it would be necessary that it display the
titles that justify its pretension to account not only for the play
between affirmation and negation but especially for its overcoming. It would be necessary therefore to attest that the Absolute is
at play in it, instead of postulating it; that is, to establish that the
negative concerns the Absolute, as it is experienced in consciousness. Supposing that this pretension might be justified, which remains doubtful, it would be necessary to do the work. For now,
sublation does not serve us in any way. We have to disqualify the
question that one cannot satisfy, in asking whether transcendence

---

[17] DN, VII, 2, 869a; "through transcendence and not through privation," see
L. I, 1066a and L. V, 1073a.

[18] DN, VII, 3, 872a. The "and also, τε καὶ" found elsewhere (as in "beyond all
negation and affirmation," MT, I, 2, 1000b; DN, II, 4, 641a, etc.) marks the
moment that attempts to contradict the categoric antinomy of the true and the
false in order to reach, without saying it or being able to say it, the (un)speak-
able that exceeds the very opposition between speakable and unspeakable.

does not intervene as a "bad infinite." For what is it to decide between the "bad" and "good" infinite if not, precisely, to decide on the undecidable? To decide on infinity does not allow one to reject it but only to miss it. Does the infinity that I define still remain infinity, or does it vanish all the more that I grasp it? The illusory definition of infinity leads one back to receiving it as a "natural and inevitable" horizon, which no thought can objectify, unless (as with mathematical infinity or infinities) by substituting *another object* for it. One can treat infinity "only in order to submit to it, and not at all to determine what it is or what it is not" (Descartes).[19] We do not comprehend infinity because it is infinity that comprehends us. Liberated from any human decision, from any categorical predication and from any reduction, there is then the Ab-solute, absolved through our defeats from any dissolution. What to say of it? Nothing is suitable. But silence would lie again, since only transcendence would have, through overabundance, to mobilize it; in keeping silent, it is of insufficiency that we make ourselves the false witnesses. What is signified by this impossible eminence, neither silenced nor said? The passage to eminence does not open to any third way, as has often been said; it registers the aporia of a predication that can only affirm and deny, there where neither one nor the other is suitable. To this aporia, which one must first of all not conceal, one must not respond too quickly either, in underlining, for example, that "the most divine knowledge of God is that which knows through unknowing."[20] As for spiritual experience, which this paradox announces, *here* at least it has no decisive value, since it does not pertain to the question of predication. Spiritual life can well find a plenitude in knowledge through unknowing, but the theoretical question of divine language would not be changed. The spiritual life here remains an oddity, which abolishes naming as inessential much more than it carries out such naming. For theoretical research, the spiritual life remains, *here* at least, a view of the spirit—that is, the inverse of a vision by the spirit. Nothing guarantees that the spirit is the place of naming. For the aporia of the spirit of man

---

[19] Descartes, Letter to Mersenne, 28 January 1641, ed. Adam and Tannery (Paris, 1971), vol. III, p. 293.

[20] DN, 3, 872a. See MT, II, 1025a; DN, I, 1, 588a; I, 6, 596a; L. I, 1065a; L. V, 1073a, etc.

covers perfectly that of naming, where nothing is tenable, neither affirming nor denying, nor above all passing to eminence.

§ 14. THE REQUEST OF THE REQUISITE[21]

Now, it happens that at the very moment when nothing is any longer tenable, there insistently repeats itself something like a naming, which nevertheless emphasizes, and perhaps provokes, the abolition of all naming: "and we pass toward what is beyond all things . . . in negation, transcendence, and the Αἰτία, cause of all things."[22] By "cause," one must here understand αἰτία. To be sure, the "cause" sometimes intervenes to justify affirmations: "Since it is the cause of all beings, we should posit and ascribe to it all the affirmations we make in regard to beings."[23] Most often, however, it renders possible, like an inward point of support, the negation that provokes the Ab-solute because it comes from it: "Αἰτία/cause of Being for all things, itself non-being inasmuch as beyond essence [*estance*] (οὐσία)"; "we say, therefore, as Αἰτία/cause of all things, beyond all things, it is without-essence (ἀνουσίος)," "beyond all things, as their cause/Αἴτος"[24] How to understand the intervention of the αἰτία/cause here? To interpret it as a privileged denomination that would escape the conceptual asceticism that it renders possible would imply a crude paralogism. In the same sequence, Denys would contradict himself quite impudently in order to cobble together a solution to the aporia of predication. Can we give him credit for a greater speculative rigor? Before responding, let us remark a patent lexical fact. The cause/Αἰτία maintains a privileged relation with a

---

[21] I translate Marion's *Requisit*, with which he renders the Greek term αἰτία, as "Requisite," and I will translate Marion's *requérant*, with which he signals the Greek αἴτιατα, as "requestant." Marion is appealing here to the senses in which the "cause" or "Requisite" (αἰτία) of all things caused (αἴτιατα) is that which all things require, and hence that which all things petition, that to which all things make request (αἰτέω, *requérir*) in prayer. [Trans.]

[22] DN, VII, 3, 869d–872a.

[23] MT, I, 2, 1000b.

[24] Respectively, DN, I, 1, 588b; MT, IV, 1040d; L. V, 1076a. See also MT, V, 1048b and DN, I, 5, 593c: "Because it (the Trinity) is the cause/αἰτία of all beings, it itself is nothing (οὐδέν), inasmuch as superessentially transcendent to all."

precise co-occurrence, *to praise:* "The theologians praise the cause/Αἰτία of all things with multiple names starting from all things caused/τῶν αἰτιατων"; "the cause/Αἰτία of all beings must be praised starting from all things caused." Maximus the Confessor had already made this remark with his prodigious theological exactness, in his *Scholia on the Divine Names* of Denys: "It is as cause/Αἰτία of all things that God is praised; for Denys does not say: these things are predicated (κατηγορεῖται) of God, but properly that he is praised for them (ὑμνεῖται)."[25] What is indicated here by the substitution of praise for predication, and by its relation with the irruption of the cause/Αἰτία? The concept of Αἰτία which we have just translated, following the usage imposed by the history of metaphysics, as *cause,* does not offer a new naming that the previous operations (affirmation, negation, eminence) would have omitted through simple carelessness or crude ruses. If one means by Αἰτία, when applied to God, the modern "cause of self and of the world," then one most certainly falls back among the idols of the divine (§ 2). But the cause intervenes here in order to mark precisely the reverse: namely, that we have no naming suitable to God, not even in negation. The cause enters into play precisely inasmuch as it puts itself out of play. This enterprise of disqualifying the predicative game is marked by Denys through the transcendence of the cause: "The exceedingly transcendent cause/Αἰτία of all things," "supereminent cause."[26] The cause acts as that which excludes from predication that which claims to concern the Ab-solute. Clearly, the adjective *transcendent* only comments on it without in any way modifying it. Thus "between the creature and the creator can be seen no resemblance so great that there would not also have to be seen between them a greater difference."[27] It remains to meditate on what transcendence can mean. It reactivates the aporia of eminence: negation refers to our world as much as affirmation. Since it claims to pass beyond what we constitute in and as a world, transcendence becomes strictly unthinkable: neither passage to the limit, nor nega-

---

[25] DN, I, 6, 596a and I, 5, 593d. See other references below, notes 66 and 68. See also Maximus the Confessor, *Scholia on the Divine Names,* V, 8, PG, 4, 328a.

[26] DN, II, 7, 645b and MT, I, 2, 1000b. See also DN, I, 5, 593c; V, 8, 724b; XIII, 3, 980d–981a, etc.

[27] Fourth Lateran Council, in Mansi, *Collectio Concilium,* vol. XXIII, p. 986.

tion of the negation, nor infinity completed in itself, etc., but the beyond of the limit that revokes both *limit* and *beyond* while saying them. It is unthinkable, which every expression, even simply mental, misses: the word that is written here and the thought that thinks in this instant can neither be silenced nor continue. Defective silence lies as much as the word reeled off, the white left in the text obfuscates as much as the text, and the full text remains as empty as the emptiness of a blank. Whoever does not experience and test himself in this oscillation has no business here. If the cause/Αἰτία remains unthinkable, if it disqualifies every naming of God and if transcendence slips away from the speaking grasp, perhaps one can agree that the cause does not have to be thought but indeed received. Or even: the inconceivable remains irreducible, and surpasses every conception. The distance of the Ab-solute precedes every utterance and every statement by an anteriority that nothing will be able to abolish. Anterior distance escapes every conception. But precisely, must distance be conceived? Anterior distance conceives us because it engenders us. Distance is given only in order to be received. Anterior distance demands to be received because it more fundamentally gives us [the chance] to receive ourselves in it. Distance, precisely because it remains the Ab-solute, delivers the space where it becomes possible for us to receive ourselves—to receive ourselves in the sense that the athlete, having cleared the bar, completes the jump by landing [literally, in receiving himself, *en se recevant*] on the ground, prepared for this purpose, of the landing pit [*fosse de réception*]—a pit that is not at all an excavation, since it is elevated above the ground (as know those who haunt stadiums). We discover ourselves, in distance, delivered to ourselves, or rather delivered for ourselves, given, not abandoned, to ourselves. This means that distance does not separate us from the Ab-solute so much as it prepares for us, with all its anteriority, our identity. It denotes, therefore, the positive movement of the Ab-solute, which, through its being set in distance, is ecstatically disappropriated from Itself in order than man might receive himself ecstatically in difference. In receiving himself from distance, man comprehends not only that distance comprehends him, but that it renders him possible. Distance appears, then, as the very disappropriation through which God creates—not the break of alienation, but the ecstatic place that saves irreducible alterity. The incomprehensibility of the unthinkable seems then to be the mark of anteriority; the seriousness of anterior distance is attested by the unthinkable. To admit that the incomprehensible cannot, must not, and does not have to be comprehended amounts to recognizing, receiving, and revering distance as distance. To claim to comprehend distance or to lament that it remains incomprehensible betrays a double inconsistency: not only does distance reject absolute knowledge by definition, but it symptomatically reveals the disappropriation of the Ab-solute by itself; to appropriate distance to oneself would mean appropriating to oneself through (human) knowledge (divine) disappropriation. The renunciation of any knowledge of distance is founded not only on a factual impossibility but also on a deep suitability to that which is in question with distance.[28] What the Christian tradition names sin is perhaps first this error of taste—the appropriation to oneself of the divine disappropriation. Anterior distance therefore governs positively that which it allows to be received in it. We have not thus distanced ourselves from Denys's position, but we have slowly approached what he indicates under the name of Goodness, when he assigns it to the cause/Αἰτία. Indeed, the cause/Αἰτία is thought in close relation with Goodness. This name, "the most venerable of names,"[29] would have to undergo the test of negation, if it were meant alone; here it is taken up by the transcendence that introduces it into the unthinkable: "all the gifts from the cause/Αἰτία as Goodness"; "the universal cause/Αἰτία loves all things through the hyperbole of its Goodness"; "cause/Αἰτία of beings, since all things were led to be by its Goodness, which was their essence."[30] The fact that Goodness

---

[28] See our outline, "Intimität durch Abstand," in *Inernationale Katholische Zeitschrift* (Frankfurt: Communio-Verlag, 1975), pp. 218–27.

[29] DN, XIII, 3, 981a.

[30] DN, II, 5, 644a; then IV, 10, 708a, and DN, I, 4, 592a. See also DN, I, 5, 593d: "inasmuch as subsistence of the Good, through its very Being, it (the Trinity) is the cause/αἰτία of all beings," etc. In DN, III, 3, 640b–c, the expression "all the terms-of-the-cause, the good, the beautiful, Being, the fertile, the wise, and all that which comes from the gifts of goodness suitable to the divinity" indicates well that the good—taken in the sense of one perfection among others—does not number with the Good intrinsic to the divinity, and hence to distance, but flows therefrom like the other names and goods. Hence the capital.

and Αἰτία are two sides of the same thing does not signify first that God has no other motive to create—to bring about distance—than Goodness (the thesis of the *bonum diffusivum sui*); rather, it indicates that Goodness remains as unthinkable to us as distance itself. Goodness, which a hyperbole refers to the cause/Αἰτία, refers in distance, to the point of being conjoined with the unthinkable. It escapes our investigation since, thought as an acolyte of the cause/Αἰτία, it ends up being typified therein. The same unthinkability makes the same transcendence rise up equally from "the cause/Αἰτία of all things and from the Goodness that surpasses them all."[31] Hence, the hyperbole of Goodness, become synonymous with the transcendence of the cause, requires that one perceive that very transcendence as the face proper to Goodness. The unthinkable distance, as cause, manifests Goodness, or better manifests itself as Goodness. Goodness in itself manifests itself, and of itself manifests itself as ecstatic transcendence. Distance offers the sole, unique form of manifestation suitable to Goodness. Because Goodness deepens infinitely within a hyperbole that we will see later refer finally to the Trinity, it remains unthinkable to us. The unthinkability of distance within it constitutes the mark and the seal of love, which "came down [to us] from heaven" (John 6:50). The unthinkable, as the distance of Goodness, gives itself—not to be comprehended but to be received. It is therefore not a question of giving up on comprehending (as if it were a question of comprehending, and not of being comprehended). It is a question of managing to receive that which becomes thinkable, or rather acceptable, only for the one who knows how to receive it. It is not a question of admitting distance despite its unthinkability, but of preciously receiving the unthinkable, as the sign and the seal of the measureless origin of the distance that gives us our measure. If love reveals itself hermetically as distance (which is glossed by *cause* and *goodness*) in order to give itself, only love will be able to welcome it.[32] If

---

[31] CH, IV, 1, 177c.

[32] The Good is qualified by hyperbole in DN, IV, 10, 708b, which is to say that "the good is transcendence itself" (E. Levinas, *Totality and Infinity* [The Hague: M. Nijhoff, 1971], p. 282). I here use the concept of *distance*, which commands all of the present work, with reference to that which H. Urs von Balthasar named "the areopagitic feeling of distance," and which he comments on by seeing in it a "distance which preserves, *wahrende*" (*Kosmische Liturgie* [Fribourg, 1941],

distance manifests love itself as unthinkable, then distance will disappear no more than charity will pass. Distance refuses nothing, nor does it separate enviously, but it brings about the separation where we experience love. Love (like Goodness) requires distance (as unthinkable), in order that participation be fortified in, and reinforce, the mystery of alterity. Distance brings about separation in order that love should receive all the more intimately the mystery of love. Alterity grows as much as union— solely in distance, anterior and perennial, permanent and primordial. In other words, the participation of caused things (αἰτιατὰ) in the cause/Αἰτία prevents one from passing beyond distance. It is even "the proper trait of the cause/Αἰτία of all things, and of the Goodness that surpasses them all, to summon beings to participation in it."[33] An amazing text when you look at it closely: what is proper to the hyperbole of the Αἰτία that is, of the unthinkable, consists in the participation it offers to the very thing that it surpasses immeasurably. *Because* it forever "remains in an inaccessible light" (1 Timothy 6:16) the unthinkable calls to participation beings that have no common measure with it—no common measure other than a reciprocal disappropriation in distance. Participation therefore never jumps over distance in claiming to abolish it, but traverses it as the sole field for union. Participation grows by participating in the imparticipable as such, and it increases the imparticipability of the imparticipable all the more insofar as it more intimately participates therein. The fundamental paradox of participation issues here from distance: "It is a common, unified and single property of the entire divinity to be participated in fully and entirely by each of the participants, and by none only in part . . . ; nevertheless transcending any dwelling, the imparticipability of the universally causal divinity, in that there is no contact nor any kind of communion that mixes it with its participants." "As much as beings carry the day over non-beings, . . . and participated terms over the participants, so does that which surpasses all beings remain beyond all beings, and so does the imparticipable cause/Αἰτία remain above both the participat-

pp. 177 and 248 = French trans., *Liturgie cosmique, Maxime le Confesseur,* pp. 138 and 190, despite a mistake in the translation of this last citation).

[33] CH, IV, 1, 177c.

ing and the participated."[34] It is not that transcendence refuses (itself to) participation, since it convokes and gives rise to participation. It is participation itself that presupposes and reinforces transcendence. To participate in the unthinkable is to do so in order to know it, to acknowledge it as such—as unthinkable. That of God which gives itself to be received covers exactly the withdrawal of distance (Hölderlin). Revelation communicates the very intimacy of God—distance itself. Thus participation is achieved all the more insofar as it underlines the imparticipable from which it arises. This is why, in the prodigious and lapidary Letter 3, the Christ, mediator and thus distance made flesh, places obscurity at the center of revelation: "The darkness remains, even after the manifestation, or, to say the most divine thing, at the heart of the manifestation itself. For it is this, of the Christ, that remains cryptic, without any mind or any discourse being able to come to its end, so that, spoken, it remains unspeakable, and known, unknown."[35] To suppose that manifestation coincides with obscurity in Denys because, as is too often repeated, the Christ occupies only a secondary, superficial role, would here be a misinterpretation. For that which finds its "paradoxical face" (R. Char) on the face of Christ, in order there to dazzle with a blinding evidence, is nothing less than the distance of imparticipable participation. It is on the face of the Christ that, par excellence, vision is exhausted in sustaining with a blinking gaze the darkness that makes up bedazzlement. Advance coincides with withdrawal because it is withdrawal that advances therein. Far from remaining marginally less hidden (or manifested) than the trinitarian thearchy, the Christ paradigmatically receives the paradox of distance and renders it absolutely (in)visible. There, as often, Denys's christology, which one so often and so lightly claims to be abstracted from the Jesus of history or purely Gnostic, touches in one stroke upon the mystery of the figure of apparition.[36] The distance of God is experienced first in the figure of

---

[34] DN, II, 5, 644a–b; then DN, XII, 4, 972b.

[35] L. III, 1069a. Pascal will speak, in this sense, of the "presence of a God who hides" (*Pensées*, ed. Br., § 556).

[36] On the figure of apparition, see H. Urs von Balthasar, *Herrlichkeit*, I, *Schau der Gestalt* (Einsiedeln: Johannes Verlag, 1961 = French trans., *La Gloire et la Croix*, I [Paris: Aubier, 1965]). We barely comment here on two of Balthasar's opinions concerning Denys: "God himself is causally superior to all surpassing,

the Christ: there, it finds its insurpassable foundation and its definitive authority.

The distance of the unthinkable, which mobilizes the "cause of Goodness," therefore provokes to participation. But, since it revokes immediate assimilation, distance must remain. It offers itself to be traversed, not at all so that one might abolish it. The scope of participation therefore absolutely does not depend on the greater or lesser liberality of God, who, in distance, unreservedly gives himself imparticipably to participation. The traverse through distance is measured solely according to the measure of the welcome that each participant can or cannot offer. If distance delivers the unthinkable unreservedly, the measure of the imparticipable participation will be set by each participant. This, moreover, is what is indicated by the texts that announce the imparticipable participation: "it is proper to the cause/Αἰτία of all things and of the Goodness that surpasses them all, to convoke beings to participation in itself, in the measure that each of them is defined by the fact of its proper analogical measure";[37] the "analogical" openness of each thing to distance measures only the participation which that thing manages to reach: "According to the analogy of each mind, the divine things are unveiled," "the superessential ray manifests itself in illuminations that are analogical to each being in the full suitability of Goodness."[38] Only the openness of the participant limits and measures

---

and hence also to that of the knowing mind," and "the third step, often mentioned, which goes beyond affirmation and negation, the movement of passing beyond, is not a 'method' of knowledge but the demonstration that beyond all the positions and negations of which the creature is capable, there is nothing but the objective transcendence of God" (*La Gloire et la Croix,* II, 1 [Paris: Aubier, 1968], p. 188, and note 202 = *Herrlichkeit,* II, *Facher der Style* [Einsiedeln: Johannes Verlag, 1962], p. 209). Likewise, W. Völker understands the "cause" as a denomination of "the creative activity of God" (*Kontemplation und Ekstase bei Pseudo-Dionysius Areopagita* [Wiesbaden, 1958], p. 150, note 5).

[37] CH, IV, 1, 177c.

[38] Respectively, DN, I, 1, 588a; DN, I, 2, 588c. See, among others, DN, II, 4, 641c; DN, IV, 20, 720a, etc. Analogy/ἀναλογία here refers to Saint Paul speaking of an "analogy of faith" (Romans 12:6). The Dionysian ἀναλογία implies no activity of the participant, nor any power that man would have to exercise in order to reach a higher divinization: Distance is not, indeed, given to be conquered but to be received (despite W. Lossky, "La Notion des analogies chez le Pseudo-Denys," in *Archives d'histoire doctrinale et litteraire du Moyen Age,* 5 [Paris, 1930], pp. 279–309).

the scope of his participation in the distance of Goodness; he gives himself every excess simply in welcoming it; to give oneself— the two acceptations are rigorously merged: it is inasmuch as he gives himself (abandons himself and opens himself) to the distance of Goodness that the participant gives himself (acquires) the chance to participate therein more intimately. The Good "at first deals out the light in moderate amounts and then, as the wish and the longing for the light begin to grow, it gives more and more of itself, shining ever more abundantly on them because they loved much; and it keeps pushing them ever forward (ἀνατείνειν) according to their analogical capacities of advancement."[39] Citing, in relation to capacity and its amplitude, Luke 7:47, "she loved much," Denys underlines that love alone governs participation, and thus access to the distance of Goodness. Once again, love alone perceives love correctly: as to be received. Capacity alone limits the participation that could and can become infinite, because "God is not jealous." God is not jealous of his divinity—but man lacks ambition. He does not grasp that nothing less than the distance of Goodness offers itself to be traversed through an imparticipable participation. For the analogical capacity receives nothing less than to receive distance, and hence that which brings it about—the cause/Αἰτία: "It is necessary to recall what Scripture says, 'I did not reveal these things to you so that you might attach yourself to them,' but in order to ascend, as much as it is in us, through the analogical knowledge of them, toward the cause/Αἰτία of all things"; "starting from that order of all beings, to the degree that God establishes it, and that he offers certain icons and similitudes of his divine paradigms, we reascend in order and rank, according to the possible, toward He who is beyond all things, in their negation, their surpassing, and their cause/Αἰτία."[40] The imparticipable participation allows one

---

[39] DN, IV, 5, 700d–701a; see also DN, I, 4, 592c. The growth of participation through receptive ἀναλογία makes one think of the *participatio/capacitas* couple in St. Augustine and, parallel to this text, in his *Commentary on the First Epistle of John 4:6*. It seems to me henceforth legitimate to translate ἀναλογία as capacity, on condition that one strictly maintain the passive semantic that modernity has forgotten and rejected (see my study "De la participation à la domination: Etude sur la sémantique *capable/capax* chez Descartes," *Revue philosophique de Louvain* 73 [1975], pp. 264–95).

[40] DN, V, 9, 824d–825a, and DN, VII, 3, 869d–872a. See also CH, IV, 1, 177c, etc.

to traverse the definitive distance. The traverse maintains with distance the same relation as participation with that in which it participates—that of intimate respect. The traverse, and the anagogy that makes it, as also the acknowledgement of the distance of Goodness, depend on the analogical capacity. But this measured receptivity depends, in its turn, on another instance, which alone can hollow out the space where a capacity might contain a greater participation. That instance, in a sense ultimate, on which depend the analogy and therefore the distance that announces itself therein, Denys names prayer: "We must first reascend toward the Trinity as principal Goodness through prayers," "we force ourselves to lift ourselves through prayers to the sublimity of the divine rays of Goodness."[41] By prayer, one must not understand first or above all the subjective act of a sensitive heart, but the concrete and locatable figure that signals the traverse of distance. Praying, man acknowledges the unthinkable, which anteriorly exceeds the traverse where its perpetuity is attested. That distance cannot be comprehended but must be received implies that a global (psychological but above all intellectual and spiritual) comportment should welcome and pass through it. Now, prayer for Denys is defined by the cause/Αἰτία that it reveres and reveals. Even more: prayer (εὐχή), but also αἴτησις, demands (αἰτέω), in the sense that, for the Evangelists, demanding amounts, in its fullness, to praying. What does the praying demand? It "demands with regard to the Father" (John 15:16), and it "demands in my Name" (John 14:16) the sole possible term of an absolute request, the Αἰτία itself. Hence, what we have just translated here exactly, but all the less correctly, as "cause" must perhaps be understood as that which all those beings request (αἰτέω, αἰτιάομαι) who for their part fundamentally receive themselves therefrom as requestants (τὰ αἰτιατά). The Αἰτία that Denys mobilizes undoubtedly does not correspond to Greek thought as such; it certainly does

---

[41] DN, III, 680a and c. See also the prayer (αἴτησις) of the bishop who "demands (αἰτεῖ) that (the promises of the Scriptures) be realized, and that their holy rewards be given to those who have lived well; immediately he is fashioned in imitation of the divine, in the fashion of Goodness, and demands (ἐξαιτῶν), as if for himself, gifts for others," CH, VII, 7, 561d–564a. Prayer allows one to imitate the Good in that which is proper to it—namely, to diffuse itself in a distance, where it moves ecstatically in an inconceivable alterity. Prayer presupposes the mystery of the αἰτία since it traverses the distance of the Good.

not belong to the Aristotelian doctrine of the four "causes," where it is already a question less of "causes" in the modern sense than of what is required, by the thing, in order to let it appear as a being. But here the relation between the Αἰτία and the αἰτιατά, already quite rare in Greek thought,[42] is invested by a relation even more foreign to the Greek essence of metaphysics (including, perhaps contrary to appearances, Neoplatonism)—distance, and therefore analogy, prayer. It is necessary here to understand this relation, in all of its lively rigor and simplicity, as the praying request in which requestants appeal, by hurling accusations or by making an appeal, to a Requisite.[43] We understand better, perhaps, why the Αἰτία in no way constitutes a new, surreptitious, or terroristic naming that would side-step negation. It pronounces as Requisite the unthinkable that, without ignoring it or knowing it, without comprehending it but being comprehended in it, without abolishing in it the ever anterior distance but in receiving itself therein, the very prayer of requestants traverses. Only on condition of removing the Dionysian Αἰτία as much from the Aristotelian topic of a fourfold condition of beings as from its modern reduction to the "efficient cause" (Descartes, let us say) does it become possible not to treat it as a false name of the Ab-solute, and, a fortiori, not to locate in it a metaphysical Idol. On the contrary, taken up as the Requisite of a prayer wherein all requestants receive distance and acknowledge it as anterior, the Αἰτία,

---

[42] This relation hardly appears except in Aristotle, *Second Analytics* I, 9, 76a 20; II, 16, 98a 36, and in Diogenes Laërtius, *Vies des philosophes illustres* IX, 97.

[43] It is known that Αἰτία signifies the accusation, the grief, the charge brought against the one toward whom one makes request. It is a matter, then, of that which is aimed at by the action of *accusing on a point that concerns me*, αἰτιάομαι. Indeed, the Platonic relation between αἰτιάομαι and αἰτία/αἴτιον (*Philebus* 22d; *Phaedrus* 98d; *Republic* 329b), as between that which one demands and the request, reproduces the juridical relation of the terms: to accuse one presumed guilty (*Iliad* XI, 654; *Odyssey* I, 32: "O misfortune! as today men accuse the gods!" etc.). In this context, I would underline that αἰτιάτον depends on a middle, αἰτιάομαι, *to accuse in that which concerns me;* one therefore cannot translate it as "effect," but one must conserve the nuance of the middle: *that which the requestant requests/requires for itself.* On this conceptual constellation, see the *Commentary* of Pachymere on CH, III, 3, 2: "Called requestants, αἰτιατά, are the terms that, in order to be in whatever way one might want, need an exterior requisite (αἰτία). Requisites (αἰτίαι), the completed terms, in view of which, in tending toward them, we complete the requestants and those of which they are the terms" (PG, 3, 456c).

when one reflects on it, consigns within itself two prodigious privileges. It announces itself as the operative concept within the critique of all idols of the divine, including the conceptual:
representing nothing, it signifies the very operation through
which the mind exposes itself to the unthinkable as unthinkable,
advancing without any mask toward the unthinkable that no
longer conceals its (in)visibility; not only does it not proceed idolatrously, but it proceeds to the disqualification of idols, in order
to find in that very disqualification the beyond of any disqualification. It passes beyond disqualification because it receives the
unthinkable as the Requisite of a Goodness that is itself hyber-
bolic and therefore unthinkable. The anterior and offered distance reveals itself, in the decency of its withdrawal, as love;
metaphysics, here, no longer pertains, and love, which gives itself
only in giving itself to be received, itself appeals to love. The communion of two loves becomes the ultimate traverse of distance,
which, far from abolishing it, properly speaking *consecrates* it. One
can thus understand why "before all things, and especially before
theology, it is necessary to begin with prayer":[44] Prayer performs
distance. The traverse of distance, or the praying request posed
to the Requisite by each requestant, covers the totality of that
which is a world for us; likewise, the question of the language
suitable to the Ab-solute is integrated within the task of traversing
distance, and constitutes only a particular case of that task. Thus
we cannot treat it profitably until after having specified what is
indicated by the traverse of distance.

§ 15. IMMEDIATE MEDIATION

To traverse distance does not imply that one abolish it but that in
traversing it one attest to its anterior incommensurability. How to
avoid having the traverse reduce distance to a space that is possessed because well known, and known because traveled at
length? But also, how to admit that distance offers to each being
the place of an effective (analogical) ascent, if on the other hand
that ascent remains forever caught in incommensurability? To re-

---

[44] DN, III, 1, 680d.

spond to this question, Denys mobilizes a term that our modernity forbids us straightaway from understanding correctly: hierarchy.

By hierarchy we spontaneously understand a nonreciprocal relation between two symmetrical terms, the superior and the inferior, the benefactor and the debtor, etc. In this sense, what one calls, ironically, the "hierarchical way" offers only little or no opening to ascend it, because it pours itself out unilaterally from above to below. In withdrawing and concealing itself in the measure that one attempts to take it from below to above, the "hierarchical way" is denounced as a power that one must renounce. Concealing its origin, it everywhere increases a power without identity. Unworkable, it becomes all the more so inasmuch as it remains hierarchy—a narrowly royal way that increases the effects of power ad infinitum in order to conceal all the better its unattainable cause. Hierarchy gives itself as a sacred power in that it refuses to give itself. The sacred supports and hides the origin of the asymmetrical relation—an origin that sacralizes itself by hiding itself, because its very absence fills it with fantasies of authority that the subordinates fabricate. The leader must conceal himself in order better to remain present to the mind of all. To reject this hierarchical structure, it would not suffice to revoke its beneficiary. It would be necessary to call into question the repetition of the asymmetrical relation at each link of the chain, even the most humble: the "petty tyrant" is more aware of the "hierarchical way" than is Orwell's Big Brother. For the "petty tyrant" puts the power game into play without really having any power: if power is not a hazing, hazing, in its very inanity, reveals all the more the machinery of the "proof of power" or of the "exercise of power"—the maintenance of the asymmetry. To maintain asymmetry is to retain power for oneself, to exercise power amounts to not giving it. The "hierarchical way" rests, as much as on its sacralized origin, on the captation of power at every level. Power is to be kept, not to be given; it safeguards itself only in keeping itself. This vulgar concept of hierarchy thus brings together two characteristics according to two possible points of view. From the point of view of the origin (the "master"?), it is defined as a power to be kept through a relentless appropriation. From the point of view of the inferior, it is experienced as an order that sacralizes concealment, unintelligibility, and anonymity. A sacred power that exerts itself by not giving itself—this would be the common concept of hierarchy. Of course, the political diatribes have an interest in not examining this concept's limits, attentive as they are to maintaining bad press for it. Of course, the petty marquis of theology, like the authentic despots of the para-episcopal apparatus, transpose this concept uncritically and without precaution to the ecclesiastic and therefore spiritual questions of divinization. But precisely, before speaking of the "Church hierarchy," would it not be necessary to attempt to understand what *hierarchy,* understood starting from the theandric mystery for which the Church offers us the sole place, can even mean and imply?

It is here that Denys appears as a decisive thinker, since he originally undertakes to understand hierarchy.[45] He defines it as "a sacred order," "a certain universal arrangement," an "arrangement of all sacred things."[46] In what way, however, does this definition modify the common concept? First in that the order under consideration does not give orders to be executed, but lays out "sacred things." The sacred intervenes not only to conceal an origin, but also to qualify that which gives order. Sacrality therefore plays on two fronts: at the origin and at the completion of the order. That the sacred qualifies the two extremes of the order equally is shown clearly by the goal of hierarchy. Indeed, "in my opinion a hierarchy is a sacred order, a state of understanding and an activity approximating as closely as possible to the divine"; "the goal of a hierarchy is a conforming and a union with God, as far as possible; . . . completion, for each being in the hierarchy, consists in ascending, according to their proper capacity, toward the semblance of God"; "the common end of every hierarchy is love for God and for divine things."[47] Hierarchy aims, therefore, to produce relation with God. The sacred, or rather holiness (ἱερός connotes both terms) does not dissimulate its origin so

---

[45] It is known that the very term hierarchy (ἱεραρχεία) is a neologism owing to Dionysius himself, and that it will barely appear afterwards except in Maximus the Confessor, and in his friend, Sophronius of Jerusalem. On immediate mediation as the foundation of Dionysian "hierarchy," see L. Bouyer, *L'Eglise de Dieu* (Paris: Cerf, 1970), p. 317 ff., and *Le Père invisible* (Paris: Cerf, 1976), pp. 325–26.

[46] Respectively, CH, III, 1, 164d; III, 2, 165b; EH, I, 3, 373c.

[47] Respectively, CH, III, 1, 164d; III, 2, 165a and b; EH, I, 3, 376a.

much as it manifests itself in and as its completion. Holiness issues
from the origin and leads back to it. The sacred order, far from
concealing the secret dignity of the origin, produces holiness—
places it forward—at the ultimate limits of the order. Hierarchy
must be understood, more than as a sacred principle, as *the origin
of holiness*. Origin of holiness: in order to understand this pleonasm correctly, it is necessary to conceive the fact that holiness
cannot—as anterior distance—but give itself. Hence that the gift
does not impose any exteriority on it. As ecstatic origin, charity
does not demean itself when it goes out of itself, since it is defined
precisely by that ecstasy. Or again, charity does not leave itself
when it goes out of itself, since it gives itself as that which gives
itself. Thus no misinterpretation would be more complete than
to reintroduce into the hierarchy/origin of holiness the Plotinian
model of an emanation in loss: in multiplying itself, the One undoubtedly loses and dissolves itself; but charity in giving itself
manifests itself all the more authentically. Each redundancy of
the gift, where it abandons itself without return, attests its unique
and permanent cohesion. Thus Denys can define hierarchy by
"ascent" as well as by "emanation." Not that the two movements
succeed one another or compensate for one another, but they
overlap one another, or even are identical to one another. The
gift that issues from the origin never attains the hierarchical terms
except in giving itself, but these do not welcome it except in giving themselves to that which they welcome thus. The essential
perhaps is this: each member receives the gift only in order to
give it, such that this gift, in the same gesture, regives the gift in
redundancy ("emanation") and, giving, sends the original gift
back to its foundation ("ascent"): "overwhelmed in a holy manner by the splendor that is given to them, they (i.e., the associates
of God) reflect it in their turn, without jealousy, to those who
follow"; "those who purify through the overabundance of their
purity must transmit (μεταδιδόναι) it to others. Those who give
illumination, since they possess a transparent mind, as much to
participate in the light as to transmit it (πρὸς μετάδοσιν), and are
happily overwhelmed by the radiance of the sacred, must transport the light, which everywhere inundates them, to those who
are worthy of that light. Those who lead toward perfection, since
they know the perfect tradition (μετάδοσις), must perfect the im-

perfect through a holy initiation into the silence of the holy things which they have contemplated"; "the bishop . . . allows himself to be lead to completion following the divine things, to be divinized and to transmit (μεταδοῦναι) to those subject to him, according to their dignity, something of the sacred divinization that comes to him from God."[48] The gift is received only in order to be given anew. The beneficiary, moreover, does not follow the circulation of the gift through simple altruism, as if it seemed to him decent and well intentioned, or even charitable, to share the gift with others. If the beneficiary must ensure what we call the redundancy of the gift, by putting it back into circulation as soon as it is received, this is for an otherwise radical reason: the gift cannot be received unless it is given, for otherwise it would cease to merit its name. The basin is not filled up by the cascade from above unless it ceaselessly empties itself into the basin below. Only the abandonment of that which fills it permits that the stream to come should fill it without cease. For that reason again, the gift can be received only if the recipient receives it as a gift, which means only if the "content" comes to him in an indissolubly giving act; the gift demands not only of the giver but of the recipient as well to be received by a gift. To receive the gift of God, as gift, requires of man that he himself immediately welcome the gift in its essence—as a giving act. In supposing that he wants to take possession of it (Philippians 2:7), he clutches onto a "content" that is in fact not at all valid if it is not carried by the giving act—unless it is valid as an idol. To receive the gift amounts to receiving the giving act, for God gives nothing except the movement of the infinite kenosis of charity, that is, everything. Man therefore does not receive the gift as such except in welcoming the act of giving, that is, through repetition by giving himself. Receiving the gift and giving it come together in one and the same operation, re- dundancy. Only the gift of the gift can receive the gift, without appropriating it to oneself and destroying it in a simple posses- sion. He who would not give would not receive anything that he does not immediately freeze in his possession. Receiving and giv- ing are therefore achieved in the same act. In this way hierarchy functions rigorously: the gift passes from one end to the other

---

[48] Respectively, CH, III, 2, 165a; III, 3, 168a; EH, I, 2, 372c.

without loss, and necessarily, since reception provokes propaga-
tion within an unfailing redundancy. And yet, does Denys not
indicate, through the expressions "inasmuch as it is possible,"
"according to their analogies," a diminishing transmission of the
gift, in the very measure that it propagates from the origin? To be
sure, but the limitation of the transmission does not issue from
divine jealousy, nor from the envious self-possession of the divine.
It results from the relative and variable impotence of each among
the givers/recipients to carry out the redundancy themselves also
"without envy." Let us consider the Dionysian but also Pauline[49]
term of tradition (παράδοσις, μετάδοσις). Tradition, or more habitually, transmission: of what "transmission" is it a question?
Within the transmissions practiced by men, through concern for
economy and rapidity, one is careful to transmit the most objects
possible with the most reduced means possible: transmitting an
electronic pulse is better than transporting a sheet of paper, but
transporting a letter is better than sending a courier. Is it the same
here? We have just said that the "content" of the gift constitutes
nothing in itself, separated from the act of giving and from the
recipient donor who ensures its redundancy. Here the means of
transmission (redundancy) win out infinitely over the object
transmitted ("content"). The transmission transmits no object,
although it transmits infinitely more. Infinitely more, since the
initial gift is transmitted only if the man presented with it receives
it, as one receives a blow. The gift is transmitted, or better propagates from one man to the other if one repeats the gift, reproduces it and sends it off again in order to receive it, such that, in
a sense, the other no longer welcomes the same gift as the first
but rather its redundancy. Each one becomes the interpreter
(and not the deliverer) of the gift, transmits it in the measure
than one welcomes it, and welcomes it in the measure that one
becomes oneself a gift. Interpreter and not the deliverer of the
gift, man can and must replay it and perform it anew, marking
with his character a gift that remains inalterable only inasmuch as

---

[49] In order to situate CH, III, 3, 168a, it is necessary to think of St. Paul, 1
Corinthians 11:23–25: "And that which I received by tradition (παρέλαβον)
from the Lord, I also gave to you by tradition (παρέδωκα), namely, that on the
night he was given over—by tradition (παρεδίδοτο), the Lord took some (given)
bread and, having given thanks, broke it, saying . . ."

each one reinterprets it faithfully. Even more than heredity, culture, or knowledge, charity must pass through our bodies—the mind and the soul—in order that we might be able to transmit it. Tradition: certainly not the transmission of an object, but the gift translated into another gift, there taking on a body. Tradition: that which can be transmitted only in identifying the transmitter with itself, such that the information is delivered only if the body where it is embodied delivers itself for that information. This is indeed why the same term that denotes the tradition of a Revelation describes the betrayal that delivers the body of Christ to death. The truth of the tradition culminates in the act where the Christ delivers himself to men, in order there to deliver the mystery hidden from all eternity. Denys notes in this way that those who purify must do so in taking "from their own purity" to justify the others: the tradition presupposes that one should pay with his person, the sole acceptable currency in matters of charity.[50] A gift is not repeated, nor is it received as a gift unless the recipient donor becomes integrally and in person—hypostatically—a gift. When, on the contrary, a limit affects the hierarchical tradition, the fault obviously is not due to the original gift, which, without envy, abandons itself kenotically therein, but to a defect of the redundancy. Its play is worth as much as the repetition of the original gift by each of the gifts that must liken themselves to that gift in order to transmit it. The seriousness of the hierarchical community appears here: that which a redundancy does not manage to translate of the original gift, when a man fails to have likened himself to the gift, will be missed by all the other redundancies. This means that a failure defeats not so much the one who commits it as the one near him, and so on. Hierarchy can transmit the failure of abandonments as much as redundancy delivers a gift. This is also called sin. Such a negative solidarity underscores perfectly that the Dionysian hierarchy, in its correct functioning, puts into play what would seem to distance itself the most therefrom—the concrete community of charity. The hierarchies (legal: Old Testament; ecclesiastical: Church of Christ;

---

[50] This is a commentary on John 16:14–15: "He [the Holy Spirit] will glorify me, because he is going to take from me and announce it to you. For all that the Father has is mine. This is why I said that he takes from me and announces it to you."

celestial: angelic world) constitute the models of spiritual intelligibility of the community of saints, that is, of the rigorous, absolute, and hidden interdependence of spirits in the transmission of charity. Far from passing into some kind of gnosis, Denys deploys in intelligibility the most concrete logic of a double solidarity, in charity as in its refusal. Here, each person relies rigorously on the other, since the gift of grace arrives only through redundancy. The other becomes my neighbor since grace comes to him only inasmuch as it can, through me and, so to speak, as me, reach him or miss him. Each man becomes, for the other, a sacrament of the Christ, or of his absence. Each person becomes ineluctably responsible for his neighbor and offers on his face the sole vision of God that the neighbor will perhaps ever see. "What have you done with your brother?" (Genesis 4:9)—such seems the question that hierarchy renders rigorously intelligible. There is nothing more concretely and profoundly inscribed in the Christian event.

Hierarchical mediation undertakes, then, the tradition of the original gift. But that tradition conjoins two apparently contradictory characteristics: first, the perfect transitivity of the gift that, through redundancy, passes without loss, safe and unchanged, from one term to the other; next, the ballast of a body that receives the gift only in delivering itself totally, in order, by making itself harmonious with that tone and that theme, to interpret it all the more scrupulously insofar as it totally "gives itself therein." Transitivity of the gift in a body that delivers itself: immediacy is conjoined with mediation. It remains to comprehend that here mediation neither troubles nor retards immediacy but rather completes it. One could simply think that mediation, attempting to repeat the gift, endeavors to reduce the part of imperfection and obscurity that it cannot not leave therein. It is precisely not in this asymptotic sense that mediation becomes immediate, as if mediation had, as such, to disappear so that then an immediate transparency might appear. Fundamentally to the contrary, mediation and immediacy grow together, far from making up for one another. The recipient mediatizes the gift in regiving it through redundancy: he does not receive only in order to give again, but he receives only in opening himself to the gift, that is, in giving (or being given) himself. The moment of mediation (the redundancy of the gift) does not mask immediacy but delivers the gift (which absorbs all "content") within an unadorned actuality. The gift itself consists uniquely in the act of receiving/giving, and in no other "content"; immediacy has nothing other to offer than this unique and infinitely repeated act. Even more, only mediation, in repeating the unique act (redundancy), delivers what is necessary to deliver within the greatest proximity possible—the gift received because given. In the end, what must arrive immediately at every point in the hierarchy is mediation itself. Mediation constitutes the sole given that merits immediacy, because it produces that immediacy. Only mediation produces immediacy; abolished, it would give way to barbarism. Mediation offers no "content" that might constitute an obstacle, or that might lack, but ensures an act that aims precisely to give in order to receive, to receive in order to give. Immediacy is not assured by the simple transmission of some labeled "gift," delivered directly to whoever would demand it, but by the always recommencing, memorially repeated mediation of the given and giving gift, which each person delivers to his neighbor only in delivering himself to it. The gaze always bathes in the same stream and cascade, but the basins ceaselessly cast out again their overflow. The same flame would not perpetuate itself from torch to torch if it did not transmit the flare-up that each time gives rise to a fire from out of nothing. Hierarchy allows an immediate mediation. To speak, in this case, of hierarchical conflicts between, for example, the priesthood of the baptised and the apostolic priesthood, or, even more vulgarly, between the "hierarchy" and the "people of God," indicates the application of the political model of hierarchy, there where it is a question of immediate mediation. Certain questions of ecclesiology deserve no response, because the terms within which one formulates them place them outside of any authentically theological situation. Powers are neither to share nor to balance nor to separate, but to reject, there where it is fundamentally a question of communion—of immediate mediation. The political model of hierarchy has nothing to do with the mystery of the hierarchy that opens to the communion of saints. Equivocation, kept or naive, betrays the perversion of the gaze and does not even merit refutation. It is a question only of seeing or of not seeing.

The mystery of hierarchy indicates therefore that mediation (separation) does not contradict but reinforces immediacy (unity): it testifies, then, to distance. From what does this mystery issue?

To respond, Denys indicates two theses. —First, hierarchy and its mediation find their principle in the Christ: "May Christ command my discourse, if I might say, He who inspires every hierarchical manifestation!"; "Jesus himself, the most thearchic and superessential spirit, Himself the principle and the essence of every hierarchy, sanctification, and theurgy, Himself the most thearchic power"; "We see every hierarchy culminate in Christ."[51] People are often surprised that the Christ seems almost absent from the Dionysian position, as if he were found in the margins of a scheme of autonomous mediations that would suffice, without him, for divinization. But it is necessary to ask oneself, on the contrary, whether the whole hierarchical scheme does not generalize the Christic operation; in other words, one must ask whether Christ alone does not render possible the hierarchical machine of immediate mediation, and whether, precisely because in a sense the Christ is found nowhere within the scheme of hierarchical mediations, the latter do not find their place in the Christ himself. What is proper to the Christ, indeed, as God incarnate, consists in the thearchic action that he deploys in the eyes of men. Within that action, and therefore within the hypostasis that it presupposes, are radically conjoined the Requisite and the requestant, immediacy and mediation: "Jesus himself, the superessential Requisite of the essences dominating the heavens, after having condescended to take on, without change, that which is ours, did not withdraw from the human disposition which he had chosen and established, but, obeying, he subjects himself to the orders which God the Father gives through the angels"; "How did Jesus, who is beyond all things, find himself placed, in his essence, among the ranks of men? To this question we respond that it is certainly not as the Requisite of men (requestants) that

---

[51] Respectively, CH, II, 5, 145b–c; EH, I, 1, 372a and V, 5, 505b. See EH, V, 7, 512c: "Our divine principle and the head of the hierarchy, Jesus, philanthropic . . ."

one declares him here, but inasmuch as he is man, in truth according to his essence.''[52] Christ, as Requisite, introduces himself, however, into the hierarchical play. There is no contradiction in this, since the double identity alone ensures the hierarchy's functioning as an immediate relation: in subjecting himself to the Angels, the Christ remains nonetheless the Requisite who, transcending the angelic mediation, consecrates and justifies it by ensuring its effective immediacy. It is even necessary to go further: precisely inasmuch as the Christ renounces—in human terms—presenting himself as the Requisite of every requestant, and inasmuch as he plays to perfection the role of requestant, he manifests all the *better* the perfection of the request. By coming in person to play the role of requestant with the means of the Requisite, he opens distance in all its fullness. Through his request, the requestant appears finally in his truth. The divinity of the Requisite never appears more obviously (to anyone who indeed wants to see) than in the practice, exercised divinely, of the human request by a divine and human requestant. What attests to us the divinity of the requestant Christ is the divine manner (absolute abandon) in which he exercises the human request. What attests the immediacy of the human request (and not its fall outside of its origin) is again the manner in which, without demeaning himself, the Requisite can exercise it in the capacity of a man. God plays the human role *divinely;* he appears as God, even while and all the more that the Request, as a whole, and as distance, has a divine status. That the mediation of the hierarchical request is immediate is attested by the divine Requisite in person.

The human role is played, like a second nature, by the divine person, because the exercise (the art and the manner) become adverbially the ultimate manifestation of a divinity that renounces the nominal possession of its glory. This transfer of divinity from the noun to the adverb becomes conceivable, however, only if its immediate mediation should offer adverbially an absolute place for the divinity. Or again: it is not sufficient that the hierarchical

---

[52] Respectively, CH, IV, 4, 181c; L. IV, 1072a. See also DN, II, 10, 648c: ''The Requisite of all things, which fulfills them all, is the divinity of the Christ, etc.'' On the role of Christ in the Dionysian corpus, a fair number of imprudent judgments find a first guardrail in the anthology of texts collected by Dom Philippe Chevalier, *Jésus Christ dans les oeuvres du Pseudo-Aéropagite* (Paris: Plon, 1951).

game be played by the Requisite himself in order to establish its divinity, it is still necessary to be assured that the immediate mediation concerns the divine as such, aside from "the expansion of infinite things" that announces it to us. The Requisite plays off of hierarchy, and divinely; but does immediate mediation belong for all that to the divine?

To this question Denys responds with a second thesis, where, perhaps more than anywhere else, he breaks, even to the point of the most decisive contradiction, with his Neoplatonic influences. Hierarchy and immediate mediation do not only govern the economic dispensation of the divine that reveals itself; or rather, it could do so only by keeping an intimate relation with the eternal intimacy of the divine, with the Trinity itself: "Whoever speaks of hierarchy indicates a certain sacred order of universal extension, which offers the icon of its thearchic [i.e., trinitarian] splendor within hierarchical dispositions and knowledge"; "the principle of this hierarchy is the source of life, the essence of goodness, the unique Requisite of beings—the [trinitarian] Triad—whence issues, through Goodness, the Being and well being of beings."[53] This means that between hierarchy and the trinitarian thearchy is reproduced the distance between the Requisite and the requestants. That distance, however, does not intervene accidentally, since it offers, in its hierarchical functioning, nothing less than an icon of the Trinity. Icon, not idol, such that distance also concerns the Trinity. Distance comes back from the Trinity because

---

[53] CH, III, 2, 165b; then EH, I, 3, 373c. See CH, III, 3, 168a: "Thus, each rank of the hierarchical order is led, in the measure of its own analogy, to cooperate with the divine activity, completing through the grace and power that God gives the things that are united naturally and supernaturally with the [trinitarian] Thearchy, those that are accomplished superessentially in order to advance toward the latter, and those that manifest themselves hierarchically in order to resemble as much as possible the spirits that love God"; CH, I, 3, 124a: "With the goal of our divinization (according to our capacities) the perfect [i.e., trinitarian] principle, which loves man, which shares liturgy, . . . leads us back . . . as far as the pure and simple summits of the celestial hierarchies"; EH, I, 4, 376b: "We say, then, that the thearchic [i.e., trinitarian] beatitude, divinity by nature, the principle of divinization, from whom their divinization issues to those who must be divinized, through a properly divine Goodness, granted the hierarchy in order to save and divinize all rational and intellectual essences." These three last texts announce that the hierarchy issues, as a gift, from the Trinity. They say less than the first two, which establish an "iconic" relation between the Trinity and the hierarchy. It is this relation that gives rigor to the gift of the hierarchy.

it dwells therein. Distance determines (and is determined by) the Trinity. Indeed, if in the withdrawal that it saves distance does not at all separate, if it betrays no fall outside the original, if mediation produces immediacy and conversely, perhaps the persons of the Trinity also play among themselves according to distance. Or rather, distance intervenes in the divinity only inasmuch as the divinity plays in three persons. The highest mystery here allows itself not to be spoken but to be sensed and—we repeat—to be praised. Each person, and primarily the Son, trinitarily admits receiving himself from a paternal gift that he did not order; the anterior distance that we located between the Requisite and created requestants plays *more* radically (and not less, as one often claims, with Hegel)[54] within the divinity itself. And this because the divinity, ordered essentially to the love with which it is identified, delivers itself without reserve or heaviness, without any concern for itself, to the rigor of distance. Thus the Son receives from the Father not only everything that it comes down to him to concentrate in himself—that is, everything—but especially the very impetus of the gift, through which the paternal gift gives with neither reserve nor return [*reprise*]. In his infinite and inconceivable dependence and poverty, the Son experiences the gift as gift, received in filial poverty and given from the overflowing anteriority of the Father. He in fact receives, in the dimensionless infinity that overwhelms him, only the givenness and the giveability of the gift. Inasmuch as he plunges into a desert-like poverty—that about which the Christ's kenosis and death on the cross give us a *small idea*—distanced through the irrecusable and watertight mediation of nothingness, the Son receives himself immediately as Son, by receiving, in that very condition, the givenness of the gift,

---

[54] The *Encyclopedia of the Philosophical Sciences* explicitly attempts (§§ 564–71) to substitute for the supposedly abstract relation of the Father to the Son the more radical seriousness of a separation operated by the negative: A new relation manifests the truth of the Son in the alterity of the world and, finally, because blasphemy always crowns Gnostic pretension, in evil. Since the preface to the system of science opened by *The Phenomenology of Spirit,* the question has remained hidden behind its peremptory dis-solution: Does the trinitarian love find more "seriousness" in the negative, or, on the contrary, would it not rather find therein an overly futile caricature? Distance disappears from the Hegelian meditation at the very moment when the analysis of difference and relation comes to its culmination.

given in full paternal anteriority, as such. Only a mediating poverty allows the Son to receive himself immediately as He whom the Father gives to himself. The Son receives himself and saves his life—as the life of a Son—only if he receives it all the way, and therefore only if he does not subsist outside of the anterior gift that constitutes him from all eternity as a Son. The Son receives himself integrally from the Father: nothing precedes the gift or escapes it, not even the filial pole of the Trinity. "Whoever wishes to save his soul will lose it, whoever will lose his soul for me will save it" (Matthew 16:25). This word addresses itself hierarchically to us only inasmuch as it rises trinitarily from the filial distance: the Son is He who ceaselessly and from all eternity loses his life for the Father, and who, by that very fact, ceaselessly and from all eternity saves it, in receiving himself from the Father as eldest Son, in whom the paternal kindness is found—that is, the anterior will of Love, the Father himself. If the "death of God" could assume a nonidolatrous meaning, that could only be the following: the distance from the Son to the Father, within the trinitarian play, surpasses in its seriousness, its patience, its labor, but not its suffering, all the separations, negations, exclusions, and debarments that we could ever imagine, precisely because we ignore distance in its fullness. The distance that unites and separates God and men (his "death") turns incommensurably short in face of the distance that *unites* the Father and the Son in the Spirit. Since what we understand by "death" represents almost nothing in relation to the trinitarian distance, that "death" disappears, as a trivially inadequate and therefore idolatrous concept, within the immensity of the trinitarian distance, where the gap remains too great, and too immediately tied to the union that produces and provokes it, for "death," even that of God, to suffice to glimpse it. Trinitarian love gives rise to a distance that, within the gap and the union that here cross in concert, is too powerful for the "death of God" to permit the least approach toward the eternal kenosis of the Son. Conversely, only our vacillating gaze could misunderstand that the final word of Christ on the cross, "It is finished" (John 19:30), expresses, within human suffering, but through it and its words, infinitely more than it, a cry of victory, a properly trinitarian jubilation, and, if one could say it without impropriety, a howl of filial *jouissance* unknown to us, with which the ecstatic joy of the Resurrection strictly coincides. The kenotic abandon of the Cross declines, in the mode of our finitude, the trinitarian play of distance. Thus the same distance plays within the Trinity and, iconically, in the hierarchy. Thus what we experience as "death" must be interpreted starting from the trinitarian truth of the distance that is at play, and that conceals itself, therein. The death of Christ on the cross, like ours also, offers only a particular—that is, irreducible—case of the finally trinitarian distance. Everything else oscillates between idolatrous pretension and existential insignificance.

Immediate mediation is founded in the trinitarian play (Thearchy). It renders the hierarchy possible and rigorous as icon of the hierarchy. How does one yet pass from one to the other, if not in the person of Christ, "icon of the invisible Father" (Colossians 1:15)? Can one say that the hierarchy is valid as icon of the Thearchy, in the same way and with the same rigor that the Christ presents the sole icon of the invisible? Perhaps, indeed, the hierarchy reproduces the immediate mediation only in a devalued and deceptive mode, since it offers us the sole possible exercise of that immediate mediation for requestants, just as it maintains the site therefore "in the Principle," within the Christ. The Son made man does not offer a reproduction of a god who is himself otherwise visible, according to a relation of resemblance or dissemblance measurable by some norm other than his face. He brings into visibility the definitive invisibility of the Father, who remains all the more invisible insofar as no face [*visage*] will ever be suitable to him other than the face [*face*] of his Christ. In this sense, the Christ indeed offers the icon, and not the reproduced image, the primordial visibility and the normative figure. For the invisible Father, the original, as to visibility, remains once and for all the figure of the Christ. Immediate mediation reaches us in this way only in the Christ who commands and completes every hierarchy. Hierarchy, grafted on the Christ and effected by him, becomes for us the sole possible icon of immediate mediation. More, in it alone the icon becomes thinkable as such. Hierarchy functions then as an icon of the Trinity, for immediate mediation makes it function as an icon, and then gives rise therein to an infinite play of icons. In a word, since hierarchy functions as an icon of the trinitarian Thearchy, it sets into operation the same immediate mediation between its terms and gives to them also the status of an icon. The double play of immediate mediation governs in its turn the icon, at once resembling and dissembling. "Between the requestants and the requisites, there is no precise relation, but the requestants comprise icons that retain their requisites, even though the requisites still transcend the requestants and remain beyond, in conformity with the definition of their principle."[55] What is remarkable here is the conjunction between the impossibility of resemblance, which a precise relation would come to ensure, on the one hand, and, on the other, the maintenance of icons that "retain the requisites." These two terms would appear contradictory, however, only if one failed to understand them within distance, where they nevertheless give one another their reciprocal reinforcement: "There is nothing utopic in ascending from obscure icons to the Requisite of all things, to contemplate them all with eyes that are from another world, held in their Requisite. . . . For he is the principle of beings, starting from which the character and very Being (αφ' ἧς καὶ αὐτὸ τὸ εἶναι) is received of all beings whatsoever, every principle, every limit, every life, every immortality, every wisdom . . . , every unity . . . and all the beings that are by Being."[56] The icons, however obscure and without measurable resemblance, allow an ascent because the latter reproduces, for knowledge, the praying ascent of the request, of the requestants to the Requisite. Every icon, however obscure it may be, in principle, remains previously in the Requisite, before freeing itself therefrom for itself. The icon allows one to reascend to that from which it issues—it is in fact a matter of a traverse through distance, where separation coincides with intimacy under the form of a resemblant dissemblance. The icon thus appears in its essence: the evident dissemblance of the icon requires its relation to the Requisite, far from prohibiting that relation. The dissemblance expresses in its way, in the visible, the invisible, by rendering inevitable the traverse of distance. That the icon owes its resemblant dissemblance solely to its relation to the origin is indicated clearly by an example. If one considers the image of the son as such, it offers, through hyperbolic use, but an icon

---

[55] DN, II, 8, 645c.
[56] DN, V, 7, 821b.

infinitely far from the Requisite: "Just as our sun illumines with-out reasoning or deliberation, but by its very Being . . . ; so the Good . . . distributes to all beings, according to the measure of their analogy, the rays of its full Goodness." As one here relies at first on the image of the sun, which is supposed to suffice to itself, the dissemblance follows inevitably; for the Good transcends "the sun, as the archetype transcends by nature an obscure icon."[57] But it is not the sun as such that here provokes the obscurity of the icon; the weakness belongs to the relation that does not suf-fice to qualify the icon as icon. It is not a question of understand-ing the Good on the basis of our sun, but of situating this impossible relation within the distance of Goodness, and there-fore of admitting that the light of the sun would have no right to the iconography of the Requisite, if it did not come to us from the Requisite as a gift; "for light comes from Goodness, and there-fore finds itself to be an icon of [the distance of] Goodness."[58] Not to name the unthinkable in the image of the world, but in-deed to receive the world as an icon of God—to relate the world back to him. The sun then becomes an icon of Goodness only inasmuch as, first, we admit that it issues from Goodness—whence, syntactically, the inversion of the comparison, whose term of reference (principal analogue) here becomes Goodness itself in its distance:

> Just as the divine Goodness, which is beyond all things, runs through and penetrates all essences, from the highest and most venerable to the lowest . . . and illumines all those that can be illumined . . . to the point of being the measure of beings, their eternity, their number, their order, their enclosure, their Requisite and their completion, so it is that in its turn, also in the manner of a luminous icon of the divine Goodness, the sun of this world, immense, full and permanent light, illumines all things that can be illumined, in a distant echo of the Good.[59]

From an "obscure icon" the sun goes on to becomes a "luminous icon": not that the gap has disappeared between it and the Good, since it always remains a "distant echo" of the Good. But the

---

[57] DN, IV, 1, 693b.
[58] DN, IV, 4, 697b–c.
[59] DN, IV, 4, 697c.

iconic attribution here flows, in returning it to the Requisite, from the donation of the sun by the Requisite. The comparisons relate back metaphorically to the Requisite only that which issues from it: the debate does not have to do with an unthinkable (and idolatrous) adequation, but with the origin of the transfer [*report*], and therefore with its legitimacy.[60] Fundamentally, icons come to us, in distance, as gifts "starting from" the unthinkable. For this reason only, we are made able, starting from them, to reascend to the Requisite, in a reversion from the originated origin to the original origin, thus recognized as such: "We do not know God starting from his own nature (which is unknowable, and beyond any mind as beyond any reason), but starting from the disposition of all beings, inasmuch as it comes to us starting from Him, and inasmuch as it comprises certain icons and resemblances of the divine paradigms."[61] Now, the icons are in fact given to us since "Jesus Christ, our intelligible life, as in an icon, departs from the divine withdrawal in order, through his absolute but unconfused humanization, to take, through love for man, his figure (εἶδος)"[62] from us. The advent of the Requisite at the very heart of the requestants completes the gift of the icons by bringing the immediate mediation to its perfection. But the gift of the *Logos* does not only deliver icons as icons. Or rather, among the latter, it is necessary to place the Scriptures—*logia* delivered as

---

[60] Among others, DN, IV, 1, 693b; IV, 4, 697c; V, 7, 821b; VII, 3, 869d; III 13, 444c; CH, VIII, 2, 240a; XV, 1, 328a; XV, 2, 329a; etc. There is no icon in itself (by definition), but only inasmuch as received.

[61] DN, VII, 3, 869c–d. See also the magnificent text from DN, IX, 9, 913c: "The theologians say that to the God beyond all, as such, nothing is similar, but that it is He who gives a divine (re-)semblance to those who turn toward Him, through imitation, according to their power, of the One who surpasses all definition and reason. And the power of divine imitation amounts to returning to the Requisite all that issues from him. It is these things thus returned that must be called similar to God, and in conformity with the icon and divine (re-)semblance; but God does not in any way resemble them." "Starting from," and similar phrases: see DN, IV, 2, 696b–c; V, 7, 821b (cited in note 56 above); V, 8, 821b: "And it is from the Requisite of all things that there issue the intelligible and intelligent essences of the Angels conforming to God, the essences of souls and the natures that constitute the whole world."

[62] EH, III, 13, 444c. See DN, II, 10, 648c, where the Word made man is indeed defined as icon par excellence, that is, by reference: "The figure that makes every figure in that which has no figure, because it commands all figure; but unfigurable in that which has a figure, because it surpasses all figure."

really as the *Logos* has actually "delivered himself" (Galatians 2:20). Would the last iconic gift, which renders immediate mediation possible, and is therefore inscribed within the hierarchy as in its unique place, be revelation, recorded in the words of scripture, after having been designated in the flesh of the Word?

§ 16. The Discourse of Praise

In delivering itself, the *Logos* delivers the *logia*. We translate by "Scriptures," but it would be better to understand them as "dicts" that include before all else the deeds and the gestures, the *res gestae* of the *Logos*. Among the innumerable icons that distance gives us to render to the Requisite, we discover the *logia:* "As for the superessential divinity and its darkness, one should not dare to say or even to conceive anything outside of what was divinely manifested to us on the basis of the *holy logia*. For while the divinity has delivered itself divinely in its *logia,* the science and the contemplation concerning it remain unfathomable to all beings because it transcends them all superessentially."[63] The tradition that delivers the *logia* to us therefore does not abolish the distance that delivers them to us, but underscores it all the more, so that the *logia* should actually be received as gifts. And therefore be returned to the giver. One should not, however, conclude from this that the *logia* (in a word, the Bible) are not distinguished from the indefinite mass of gifts (factual or verbal) that reach us in distance (Being, the one, the beautiful, the good, etc.). For with the *logia,* the *Logos* in person delivers (himself); in other terms, the Requisite no longer terminates or determines distance, he is inscribed in it—as one text among others—in the manner of the requestants. To deliver the text presupposes that the Requisite delivers itself therein: "reascending as high as the ray of the trinitarian *logia* has delivered itself," "as the (trinitarian) Thearchy has itself, concerning itself, delivered in the holy *logia*."[64] The

---

[63] DN, I, 2, 588c.

[64] DN, I, 1, 588a; then DN, I, 3, 589b. The Biblical text is not first a text but the most exterior and, for us, the most visible body of the *Logos* having taken on humanity in body and soul. See, in addition to my sketch "Le verbe et le texte," in *Resurrection* 46 (Paris, 1975), pp. 63–80, M. Costantini, "La Bible n'est pas un texte."

privilege of the *logia,* and therefore of biblical revelation, over any other gift of distance stems from their investment by the *Logos.* This privilege depends, then, on the *kenosis* of the Son, and attests it in its own way. The question of the language of/about God is inscribed, here again, as a privileged case, within the play of the hierarchy, and, in it, of the presence of Christ as its motor, its model, and, paradoxically, its place. The *logia* constitute, in this sense, because they testify to the delivered *Logos,* and therefore to the Christ as immediate mediator, the foundation of the hierarchy, "for the essence of our hierarchy [i.e., that of the Church] is found in the divinely delivered *logia.*"[65] Just as in the hierarchy the Christ intervenes at each link of immediate mediation, even the most humble, so in the hierarchy each *logion* presupposes its kenotic investment by the *Logos,* the Requisite among the requestants. This coincidence indicates quite a bit: since no exception to the hierarchical status is conceivable, our discourse likewise will admit no other foundation than the *logia.* The discourse on God, held within anterior distance, presupposes the gift of the *logia:* we do not say, and never will say, anything of God that does not develop, take up—and ground itself in—the *logia.* Here we reach the decisive threshold: the Christian, in Dionysian terms, is decided according to the acceptance or refusal of the Scriptures as the sole foundation that might validate a discourse on the *Logos,* because they issue from it. "If there is someone who is totally opposed to the Scriptures, he will distance himself entirely from our way of philosophizing, and if he is not concerned with theosophy [i.e., wisdom of God], how could we be concerned to lead him by the hand toward theological science?"[66] The one who rejects the Scriptures does not refuse the image of the world that is conveyed and produced by the lexicon of any particular natural language, but the signs that the *Logos* founded by making them his own; more, he rejects the very process that institutes our requestant language within the play of distance; a fortiori, he disqualifies the process of the divine coming to recapitulate it. The Word, made man, gives to man his divinization only in giving a

---

[65] EH, I, 4, 376b.

[66] DN, I, 2, 640a. See DN, I, 8, 597b, which speaks of "making use of what was said as of a canonical rule," like DN, I, 2: "making use of this canonical rule."

pertinence to his language. In another sense than that understood by French traditionalists, it would indeed be necessary to
say that language [*langage*] comes from God, since it comes to us
hierarchically in distance. More precisely, we will not be qualified
for any enunciation concerning God, if we do not rely on the
biblical pronouncements. Nothing is more clear in Denys himself,
who weaves his own text, so tight and apparently so abstract, on
biblical themes that are literally commented on or, even more
significantly, on liturgical gestures that are perfectly understood
by dint of monastic practice. It is a question neither of reproducing the biblical lexicon, nor of claiming to rediscover therein a
privileged semantics (the *hebraïca veritas,* from Saint Jerome to A.
Chouraqui, passing through Kittel), but of receiving, at each step
along the path of thought, a biblical citation or situation, as the
naturally supernatural place where speech is authenticated. The
place from which we speak could be, if we speak of the divine,
only the *logia* where the *Logos* speaks and is incarnated. What we
find, indeed, in the *logia,* does not first consist in a defined textual
corpus, nor in a "thought," but in the nontextual *Logos* who pronounces himself there and allows himself there to be announced.
At each step, in order not to make it in the void, the theologian,
or the one who occupies his place, must be assured of a ground
that is discovered, each time, as a last-minute gift. Just as in logical
positivism there are "poorly constructed propositions," so in theology there are also propositions that make no sense, because
they do not obey the rules of theological formulation (having no
foundation in the *logia*). There is nothing surprising in the fact
that, consequently, no meaning verifies them (heresy or, what
amounts to the same, theology of self-critique). If from the beginning of the present investigation, even with regard to Nietzsche,
we have mobilized this multiform and repeated reference, it is
neither through concern with appearance nor through impu-
dence, but through rigor. It was necessary, indeed, that a theological place should offer the distance wherein there might become
visible, and then audible, what we are interrogating. The intru-
sion, in the form of citations or references, of the biblical *logia*
here finds its foundation—that, precisely, of ensuring the foundation, or, more exactly, the ground. In a sense, my argument could
begin only here, if its principle had not already governed its be-

ginning, even unfounded. And if this long beginning had not alone allowed us to end up, finally, at the principle. In a sense, it remains for us only to finish—which will require of us a bit more time.

To include the *logia,* and therefore the practice of language, within the hierarchical play of distance, amounts to treating them as an icon. The icon joins in itself the immediacy of the relation to the superabundantly advening Requisite and the mediation of an insistence that underlines the withdrawal. The icon gives only the invisible to be seen, and language would therefore have to give only the unsayable to be said. But only the invisible is suitable to the icon because it alone is to be seen; and therefore language would belong to the unsayable—since the unthinkable alone merits that a thought attempt to think it. But can language, following the example of the icon, sustain the immediate mediation? Or, in claiming to state the essence of the thing (or whatever one substitutes here, provided that it closes the thing), does it aim at the perfect and complete attainment of a referent that is exhausted by language, or that is at least adequately indicated in language? Does not the task of a rigorous language imply an adequate science? In a word, does language not claim to coincide with that which it exhausts as an object? Can one imagine maintaining distance in the process that, nevertheless, is completed when it can say that "actually the things themselves come to offer themselves to serve as a comparison"?[67] Discourse commonly makes use of a predication that concludes categorically with an attribution of a particular predicate to a particular subject, or, more formally, of x to y. The formalization here does not place in question that which it carries out more rigorously. Thus discourse crosses distance after having understood it as the gap between x and y. That the referent, moreover, might thus be reached adequately (logical empiricism) or not (closure of discourse) perhaps does not modify the fundamental question. In both cases the subject is exhausted adequately in the sum of that which is predicated of it. If, by some excess, recourse to the referent becomes impossible from the point of view of theory, along with the revoked exigency,

---

[67] Nietzsche, *Ecce Homo:* "Why I Write Such Good Books—*Thus Spoke Zarathustra,*" § 3.

there disappears a supplementary obstacle to the crossing of distance. The adequate appropriation no longer even has to preoccupy itself with a phantom referent, which a semantic transliteration dissolves in the circularity, without fault or risk, of signifieds. When it predicates categorically, language produces objects and, whatever they might be, eliminates distance through that very appropriation. What is essential here has to do therefore not with the impossibility, so often underlined nevertheless, of predicating anything of God, nor of attaining him thus as the referent that would verify or weaken a well constructed proposition. Predication would remain unacceptable with regard to the Requisite, if it were not impossible to begin with. Its impossibility (in the sense of the rigor of predicative language) guarantees for us only an idolatry—to suppose that very predication suitable. Can one make use of language in traversing distance, even in order to traverse it? From the point of view of predicative language, the impossibility seems radical.

Now, as we already saw, Denys tends to substitute for the *to say* of predicative language another verb, ὑμνεῖν, to praise.[68] What does this substitution signify? It no doubt indicates the passage from discourse to prayer, for "prayer is a λόγος but neither true nor false" (Aristotle).[69] But how, in its turn, can prayer constitute a rigorous language that nevertheless remains in distance? What

---

[68] See, note 25, the remark of Maximus the Confessor, which, for his part, H. Urs von Balthasar takes up: "When it is a question of God and of the divine, the word ὑμνεῖν nearly replaces the word 'to say' " (p. 158). Confirmation: DN, 593c–d; 596a–c; 637b; 641d; 652a; 681d; 701c; 709b; 713c (attributed to the "divine Hierotheus"); 816b–c; 820c; 824a; 868a; 872a, c; 909b; 969a, c; etc.; MT, 1025a, etc. Above all, one must consider with seriousness the antitheses used in at least two texts: "We must recall that this discourse does not aim to bring to light (ἐκφαίνειν) the superessential essence inasmuch as superessential (for it remains unspeakable, unknowable, and hence totally impossible to bring to light, withdrawing from all union), but much rather to praise the procession that makes essences and that comes to all beings from the [trinitarian] Thearchy, the principle of essences" (DN, V, 1, 816b); and "The discourse desires to praise the divine names, which manifest providence; not to pronounce (ἐκφράασαι) the Goodness that is in itself superessential . . . but to praise the Requisite of all goods" (DN, V, 2, 816c). One might remark that John Damascene himself uses, for the distance between the Requisite and the requestants, the term *to name* and not *to praise* (*The Orthodox Faith*, I, 12), which misses, in fact, both distance and the discourse of praise.

[69] Aristotle, *On Interpretation* III, 17a 4.

cannot be said must not be silenced. For it is necessary to merit a silence that holds for that very thing about which one must be silent. Denegation would here remain dishonest, through defect. It is therefore necessary to pass beyond the categorical alternative, in order to reach another model of discourse. Let us describe it as a discourse of praise. To describe it is nothing, if a theory of it, or at least its characteristics, are not outlined. It must conjoin the rigor of a precise language with the demands that ensure it distance—that is, it must maintain it and travel through it. The discourse of praise maintains distance, since "the theologians praise the Requisite as anonymous, and outside every name."[70] It is no longer a question of a negative predication, which would conclude that "God has no name," as if he could have one in a linguistically ordinary and correct way. Anonymity indicates less an inverted category than an inversion of the category. The absence of names turns into the name of absence, even the name of the Absent. First, because distance opens up: the name of the Absent gives itself to be believed when the failure of names betrays the distraction of possible meanings, which grows in the measure that they approach the unique pole; the abdication of meaning gives to be thought the sense-less direction of an excessive signification. Anonymity betrays in its way the excrescence of signification over possible statements and meanings: anonymous because no name lifts that anonymity, but above all because anonymity becomes a name through excess. Anonymity does not make the signification that it avoids disappear, but designates it as strictly anonymous. Such a designation of the anonymous by the anonymity that leaves it anonymous introduces the play of the icon—of the invisible. The anonymous leaves us without a name, as one is left speechless—in astonishment or rapture. Between these two acceptations (failure of names, the aim of signification), a day is prepared, and distance rises up. The paradoxical diction of the anonymous ensures the direction toward distance: each naming is engulfed by the in-draft of distance in anonymity and there alone finds its rigor—its signification. Perhaps one would have to hazard that signification and meaning here grow in inverse proportion. Only the impoverishment of meaning renders

---

[70] DN, I, 6, 596a; see VII, 1, 865c and II, 5, 644a (cited in note 34 above).

possible the attainment of signification, since it alone begins to acknowledge the depth of anonymity as anonymity. The iconic depth of language issues, then, from distance, which it highlights by renouncing the category and its affirmation in favor of a "praise as . . .": the signification aimed at is finally set off against any meaningful adequation of the predicate to the subject, in working them through the obvious *index* of inadequation of an "as, inasmuch as, ὡς." It falls to signification to achieve unspeakably (by definition) the pertinence that meaning acknowledges not ensuring. Such a transference of pertinence properly announces distance. Maintained, it becomes possible to journey through it. The distance that distracts meaning also gives rise to it. The in-draft of distance multiplies meaning [*sens*] in the name of the meaningless [*l'insensé*] that remains infinitely to be signified. The same distance that masks the excess of signification (anonymity) provokes the excess of meanings and the multiplication of names: "he who is praised by multiple praises and named by multiple names, the unspeakable and the anonymous; he who presents himself to all and whom all allow to find, the ungraspable, which no investigation tracks."[71] Because anonymous, one and the same meaning-lessness [*in-sensé*] gives rise to an infinity of praises—thus distance, now ensured of its irreducibility, can be endlessly traversed. Hence the reappearance of the Requisite, who commands the ambivalence of a discourse located in distance: "He who truly precedes is multiplied according to all the knowledge of beings, and is well praised in this regard as *having been,* as *being,* and *as having to be,* as *having produced itself,* as *having to produce itself.* . . . For it is not this without also being that, nor thus, without being able also to be otherwise, but it is all things as the Requisite of all."[72] From the point of view of the Requisite, anonymity and polyonymy go together, as two banks of the same distance. It remains for requestants to speak a language that sees, in order to respect, this fundamental equivalence. Clearly, it is a matter of praising. To praise the Requisite with an infinite praise perhaps ensures the rigor of theologically well-constructed propositions: "Since, as the subsistence of Goodness through its very

[71] DN, VII, 1, 865c.
[72] DN, V, 8, 824a–b.

Being, it is the requisite of all beings, it is necessary to praise the principal Goodness of the Thearchy [i.e., *Trinity*] starting from all the requestants," "to praise the revealed providence, worker of Goodness, supereminent Goodness and Requisite of all goods," "it is necessary to praise, in an absolute manner, all these things of the Requisite that surpasses them all."[73] Praise plays the role of a language appropriate to the distance that iconically comprehends language itself. —It remains to specify a crucial point: instead of using the logical operations of affirmation and of negation, Denys utilizes the operation designated by "as"; whence a proposition of the type "*x* praises the Requisite as *y*," where "as" is not at all equivalent to "as if, *als ob*," but to "inasmuch as," and where the Requisite is especially not identified with *y*, which is not predicated categorically of the Requisite; *y* indicates the relation under which *x* aims at the Requisite; *y* thus presupposes distance and therefore refers back first to *x*. To conceive the exact function of *x*, it is again necessary to specify: each *x*/requestant aims at the Requisite under the relation in which the latter remains inherent to the former (*interior intimo meo*), without claiming, however, to predicate categorically of the Requisite that in terms of which the aim aims at it. This means that, for every requestant *x*, there exists at least one determination *y* in conformity with which the Requisite can be praised. This means that *y* aims at the Requisite, but describes the requestant *x;* however, *y* relates itself to the Requisite in that it is this relation that constitutes the only stake of the statement. To the reserve of the "as" (nonpredication) corresponds the attribution of praise. Thus the *x* remains an occasion of error if a metalanguage does not come to highlight explicitly, in the "as," the mark of the status of enunciation, and to manifest therein that praise describes the requestant and not the Requisite, in order thus all the better to designate the aim in it of the Requisite by the requestant. The complete formula would therefore be: for every *x*, there is a *y* that characterizes it in such a way that, in stating "I praise you, Lord, as *y*," *x* makes request to it as its Requisite. Or again, the proposition of the language-object "*x* states *p*, where *p* = I praise you as *y*" becomes explicit and correct only if a metalan-

---

[73] DN, I, 5, 593d; then DN, V, 2, 816c and XII, 3, 969c. See XII, 4, 972a, etc.

guage locates in "praise as . . ." the mark of a status of enunciation, which itself announces the relation of request between x and
the Requisite under a certain relation y. Whence, in Denys, similar formulas: "The sages of God, starting from all the requestants,
in multiple names, praise the Requisite as good, as beautiful, as
wise, as loved, as God of gods, as Lord of lords, as Holy of holies,
as eternal, as being, as author of the centuries, as giver of life, as
wisdom, as spirit, as *Logos,* etc."; "This Good is praised, by the
holy theologians, as beautiful, as beauty, as love and as loved, and
[i.e., as] all the other names, provided that they are indeed suitable to the splendor that effects beauty and is adorned with
grace."[74] A statement is made, but always understood within a
metalanguage that implicates the speaker in the very determination of the statement. The latter, however, does not admit any
truth table, since it is not a question here of T and F, and since
the speaker above all does not intervene in order subjectively to
ensure the statement (proposition) that it commands an only subjective truth or falsity. The relation between the speaker (metalanguage) and the statement manifests in fact a wholly other
objectivity, even if it does not bear on any object. A relation manifests itself between the speaker (a requestant) and the statement
(a request), where the "as" indicates that the request (for example, "I praise you, Lord, as beauty") wells up from the requestant
(the connoisseur of beauty) in order to target a third point on the
straight line that is determined by the first two, a point situated
infinitely beyond the segment of the line that they suffice to determine. The relation between the metalanguage and the statement,
like the play of their implication, manifests distance. The self-
implication does not presuppose any subjective reduction, but
takes up the subjectivity of the speaker within the insurpassable
aim of the Requisite. Thus he speaks in distance.[75]

---

[74] DN, I, 6, 596a–b; then DN, IV, 7, 701c. See VI, 1, 856a; VIII, 1, 889b; XII, 1,
969a.

[75] The function of the *as*/ὡς will be clearly thematized by Gregory of Palamas:
"However, even though vision is above negation, speech, which is its interpreter,
remains below the negative way: it progresses in making use of examples according to its capacity; this is why to the words used there is most often added a ὡς,
which expresses similarity, for the vision is unspeakable and surpasses any naming" (*Défense des saints hésychiastes,* I, 3, 4, trans. J. Meyendorff [Louvain, 1959],
vol. 1, pp. 114–15, mod.).

Would it not be necessary to conclude that we are just awkwardly delimiting, under the phrase "discourse of praise," what one usually means by a performative? When x praises y, and because the praise (and its y) is determined by the performance of x, one could conclude that the praise is performed as soon as the speaker states it. You *are* praised, since I *say:* "I praise you." Two remarks, however, call this easy and apparently satisfactory solution into question.—The performative presupposes a minimal qualification of the speaker, who authorizes the performative corresponding to the statement: only the justice of the peace can perform the "I declare you husband and wife," the auctioneer the "Sold!" the lover the "I love you," the policeman the "In the name of the law I arrest you!" Now, here, *every* requestant must perform the request. Who, or what, will ensure a qualification that is universal and infinitely varied according to the infinity of names (y', y'', y''', etc.) that support praise? With the request we reach such an extension (which goes as far as beings lacking *logos*, and even beyond beings, since Goodness goes beyond Being), that no distinction, no privilege, could selectively qualify so or so as one fit as a requestant, since all make request by definition. One can see that the request, in order to be performed, here depends on more than the requestant, who cannot and must not make request except in that which commands and precedes it, in the anterior distance, the Requisite. The marvel—that each term is discovered *in fact* qualified to perform praise—makes all the more evident the absence of justification of such a power—save through the Requisite itself. The Requisite alone, inasmuch as it admits, precisely, no predication, and hence inasmuch as it exceeds the statement and its performance, summons the requestant to make its request. If performative there must be, it would come down less to the requestant than to the Requisite: it is enough that it pronounce its *logos* from all eternity in order that distance (the world, if one wants) should be—that is, in order that requestants should traverse it by their multiple praises. It is enough that the Requisite "speak" in order that the distance of all logics respond to it. The performative, taken as a model for the discourse of praise, is rejected or transferred through the transfer of the qualification: far from the requestant being able, through its own qualification, authoritatively to perform its statement, he receives that qualification previously from what his statement aims at without predicating anything of it. This ecstasy, in which he who states finds himself in advance taken up by what the statement, without predication, aims at, confirms that no subjectivity burdens the language of praise: to be sure, y directly qualifies x and not God, but that x is, in each y, y', y'', and on their occasion, radically invested by distance. What raises the nonpertinent enunciation to a nonpredicative aim is nothing other than distance: as an anterior gift, it is distance that qualifies the requestant on the basis of the paternal Requisite. Such an investment disqualifies the subjectivist reduction of the language of praise as much as its assimilation to a simple performative. —On the other hand, it is necessary to note that the performative treats language as a practice: language performs an act, which says nothing, but which still indicates. Language marries, sells, loves, arrests, etc. It terminates, then, outside of a statement and claims to produce itself as a referent. The performative offers to language the privilege of action: to silence itself in order to do. When words (we) make things, they no longer state any meaning. They speak not in order to say anything but in order to act. The performative dispenses with speaking and, once accomplished, dispenses with commentary. The discourse of praise, on the contrary, maintains the propositional statement, even though it refers it back to the very act of praising. The metalanguage indeed sets out both the requestant and the Requisite within the request (traverse of distance) in a kind of performance. But the aim would relate no name to the Requisite if the statement disappeared in the performance. The excess of the proposition over the requestant (hence over the metalanguage) alone permits the setting into operation of the request. The more praise is performed, the more its statement becomes irreducible to it. Or again, praise does not attempt in the performance of the requestant to resolve the statement into a fact, and to crystallize linguistic discursivity into a point of actuality; on the contrary, it leaves in suspension the statement that the performance aims, in some way, to detach from the speaker, to hypostasize, or at least to structure rigorously enough for it to support the hyperbole of the distance of Goodness. Praise indeed functions as a performative ("I praise you . . ."), but as a performative that, instead of making things with words, elaborates with words gifts ("I praise you as y, y', y'', etc.) Praise plays as a performative all the more that it more radically sets the statement outside of the one stating. On this condition alone, the statement assumes enough consistency to merit the dignity of a gift—to traverse distance. Consequently, at the limit, the discourse of praise does not reabsorb the statement within its performance by the speaker, but absorbs the speaker in the performance of the gift through the statement. Such an ecstasy of the speaker who relies on his own product in order, in giving it, to give himself with it (in a "short ladder" to oneself that does not cease not to land, and that continues to grow longer to the point that one finally recognizes in it Jacob's ladder, where angels climb and descend) manifests nothing less than the kenosis proper to distance. The discourse of praise plays, then, beyond any performative, among three terms: the propositional statement (language-object, "I praise you as y, y', y'' . . ."), the requestant, and the Requisite which only a metalanguage can set in place, but without which also the language-object, abandoned to itself, becomes a predication that is as impertinent as it is idolatrous. The irreducibility of the three terms to one another prohibits taking recourse to overly easy models (such as the performative) and attests, through their insurmountable separation, that distance remains to be traversed, without abolition.

In order to move forward in the definition of the language of praise, perhaps it would be necessary to consider it as follows: "Instead and in place of the turbulence of hypotheses and explanations, we want to establish the calm examination of the facts of language" (Wittgenstein).[76] The facts of the language of praise require that one no longer see in it a predication, that one not distinguish the speaker, the statement, and the unthinkable aim, that one admit that an aim remains possible beyond signification. This work of specification alone permits one to bring out the language of praise as such. It seems, then, that it is necessary to admit an infinitely diverse use of words, under the apparent uniformity of their propositional usage. Thus the language of praise admits certain characteristics that allowed Wittgenstein to establish "language games." For example, signification is not determined

---

[76] Wittgenstein, *Zettel,* § 448.

within a simple relation of the concept to the object, nor by an elementary proposition, but by the regulated ensemble of other significations, of semantic values, and of the meaning effects of a homogeneous language—with the result that propositions can function correctly without any of their significations being attested by (empirical or quasi-empirical) verification; thus an imperative or indicative proposition is not verified by any empirically confirmable *Sachverhalt,* and yet it states a meaning in producing a signification for its terms. The language of praise utilizes unverifiable significations but, through the intention and the "form of life,"[77] delivers an intelligible and in fact understood meaning: the usage of linguistic praise is not founded in an absurd empirical verification of the Requisite, but in the quasi-liturgical "form of life" that establishes it in distance, for a request, in the manner of a requestant. Distance spares the signification of the Requisite a verification because the requestant delivers himself entirely to the usage of distance. The proposition goes beyond the state of things, the usage of signification, its verification—with the result that truth values, especially contradiction, no longer found the validity of all propositions. Praise is neither true nor false, nor even contradictory: it answers to other uses. Its linguistic specificity on its own is ensured only in recognizing the irreducible diversity of language games:

> You speak of all kinds of possible language games, but at no time have you said what is essential to the language game, and hence also to language. To know what is common to all these processes, and what makes them a language, or parts of language. Consequently, you accord to yourself precisely that part of the investigation that caused you the worst trouble, that is, that which concerns *the universal form of the proposition* and of language. And here is what is true. Instead of according something common to everything that we name language, I say that there is common to these phenomena not the least thing that authorizes the use of the same word, but that they are *related* one to another in different ways. And it is by virtue of this relation or of these affinities that we name them all *languages.* I want to try to explain this.[78]

---

[77] *Philosophical Investigations,* I, § 19.
[78] Ibid., I, § 65.

On the basis of such an irreducibility, the language of praise can deploy, apart from a slight affinity, the laws of its own rigor, without being defined in the manner of a simple weakening of the rigor of predicative language. In short, the language of praise plays its own game, which remains to be understood on its own basis. Rereading Denys, I have attempted an outline of this. I leave it and suggest to others, more competent and rigorous, to continue or to take up again the inquiry into the play of language exercised by praise. This aim finds an explicit although fugitive warning in Wittgenstein, who inconclusively concludes a list of language games by "Translating from one language into another.—To solicit (*Bitten*), to thank, to curse, to salute, to pray (*beten*)."[79] Praying, which is understood in the sense of religious prayer, includes in itself the request that demands, that gives thanks (without cursing), and recognizes the one who is aimed at. Prayer can play as a language game, that is, reveal the rigor of a language of praise. It is not a question of glossing ad infinitum and a little too easily on *das Mystische*, the "mystical," of the *Tractatus*. Not only because there are baptisms that are a little forced, which resemble apostasies of their celebrants, but because the *Tractatus* ends up in an apophasis that is itself insufficient: concerning that which cannot be spoken, perhaps it is not exactly necessary to be silent—as will attest the multiplication of language games. It is not a question of reestablishing a theology that is oblique and vaguely ashamed of remaining on the margins of formal rigor and verification, but of meditating on the form that our rigor must take in order to accede to theology and, far from verifying its signification, to verify ourselves in it.

This is also why it is perhaps necessary to speak not only of

---

[79] Ibid., I, § 23, to which one might relate this sequence from the *Notebooks:* "The meaning of my life, that is, the meaning of the world, we can give the name of God. And associate with this the metaphor of a Father God. Prayer is the thought of the meaning of life" (from 11 June 1916). Prayer, meaning of the world that escapes predication, God as Father, and even, in a sense, "metaphor"—we rediscover the co-occurrences of distance. See also *Philosophical Investigations,* II, X (the language game of faith/belief), *Conférence sur l'Ethique,* French trans. (Paris: Gallimard, 1971), pp. 151–52 and 158: "If there is speech, that itself is an element of religious action and not a theory. Hence it doesn't matter at all whether the speech is true or false, or whether it makes no sense"); and *Leçons sur la croyance religieuse* (ibid., pp. 112, 115).

"theology as grammar,"[80] but inversely of a grammar as founded in theology. For if a definitively plural grammar (no metalanguage, or at least an incompletion of formal systems) makes language play infinitely in languages, this is because the very essence of language, comprehending us and anticipating us by its overflow, comes to us, in distance, as a fact—that is, a given, a gift. An animal endowed with languages, man perceives distance therein. Thus one must not only recognize in the language of praise one of the innumerable language games; it would undoubtedly be necessary also to inscribe the play that pulverizes language into language games within the distance that disappropriates us of language itself, of its mastery as of its singularity. This overwhelmed disappropriation refers then to the discourse of praise, which there validates the privilege of putting distance into play exemplarily. In this sense, language games depend on the language of praise. If, within the present strategy, a reading of Denys opens us to this unique conclusion, perhaps we would have to consider with less scorn the secular opinion that makes of Denys both a Father of the Church and, in a sense obviously neither chronological nor naively deceived, the sole convert of Saint Paul, following the discourse to the Athenians.

The sole one, with "a woman, by the name of Damaris, and a few others with them" (Acts 17:34). What did those others understand? Not, to be sure, what the Dionysian corpus elaborates, but what is taught by the practice of the language of praise. Ecclesially, the language of praise brings together two words and two prayers: the *Pater,* which establishes the speaker in a filial site, introduces him into a distance that is traversed, in opposite directions, by the demands ("May . . .") and the gifts ("bread, forgiveness, strength, deliverance from evil"). In fact, the demands coincide with the gifts, for we ask the Father to exercise the distance of his Name, his will and his kingdom, and hence we make requests to him as such, and not for ourselves; when we ask for ourselves, the gifts manifest our kenotic and fulfilled filiation. Even more, the words that establish distance and us in it are given to us by the *Logos* himself: "one of his disciples asked him: Lord, teach us to pray, as John taught his disciples. And he said to them:

---

[80] *Philosophical Investigations,* I, § 373.

When you pray, say . . ." (Luke 11:1–2). *Logia* given by the *Logos*,
manifesting the paternal distance in demands that coincide with
gifts, the *Pater* establishes the language of praise in its site and
constitutes the requestant in a request to the Requisite as . . .
Whence the second prayer, which gives back to the Requisite the
gifts and the names that He ensures us in distance: the *Credo*,
which predicates nothing of God but attributes to him the words
and facts (the Hebrew *dabâr*) through which the Requisite revealed distance to us "economically" by sovereignly traversing it.
The Trinity there finds itself organized and praised on the basis
of the Christic revelation,[81] that is, on the basis of the manifestation, in the Christ, and as the conditions of his visibility, of the
Father, of the Son, of the Spirit and, in them, of the Church.

---

[81] H. de Lubac, *La Foi chrétienne: Essai sur la structure du symbole des Apôtres*
(Paris: Aubier, 1966).

Interlude 3

OUR CONCENTRIC AND CONCERTED JOURNEYS have ended up putting into play what I call "distance" without ever giving any definition of it. If such a clarification is missing, however necessary that might be at first, must one not see therein the avowal of an impotence, if not of an impossibility? One would quickly suspect distance to have played only to the benefit of certain ambivalences that are enough to place in doubt its rigor and unity. First, distance does not intervene in Nietzsche, Hölderlin, or Denys as a signifier of the discourse considered; it is introduced therein from the outside in order to back up an interpretation. Distance belongs then to the metalanguage of the interpreter and carries out his *coups de force;* far from tempering the arbitrariness of the readings, it makes that arbitrariness possible, because, more deeply, it depends on that arbitrariness. In short, the hermeneutic anteriority and exteriority of distance free it from any definition having to do with the "language-object" (or what is supposed to be such). Because it would define, distance would not be defined. Released tactically from definitional origin, distance becomes only the more suspect of an irrational lack of definition—of a vague terrorism. Next, by what right does one speak of *a* distance? Supposing that, in each of the three corpuses considered, there operates a rigorous hermeneutic instance, by what right does one then superimpose these three operative instances within a single assertion named distance? The evident heaviness of the interludes, like the difficulties of the introduction (§ 3), betray fairly well a clear difficulty in justifying the cohesion and suitability of the subsequent journeys. If a "distance" guides the interpretation of each of them, can one accept that these "distances" coincide among themselves more than the corpuses under consideration are connected to one another? In a word, can one postulate the unicity of the hermeneutic concept, precisely there where the interpretations and their materials seem irreducible? In view of this double difficulty, distance could well have not been defined, because no definition delimits that which remains too imprecise, equivocal, and metaphorical to sustain the rigor of a conceptual formulation. Since it never reaches the dignity of the concept, distance never arrives at any definition. Finally, can the supposed distance be deployed with enough sufficiency that it is so without being exposed to multiple reinterpretations? What does it become if logic takes it into view as one relation among others, and equally formalizable? What does it become if it is approached by a dialectical thinking, which would recognize easily in that intimate separation one of the moments of the doctrine of the concept? What can distance claim to say in face of metaphysics itself, as soon as one substitutes for the overly convenient metaphor of the idol the question of Being? Indeed, one could treat of distance within the sole field opened to thought—that which is opened by and opened as Being; in this context, it becomes highly probable that distance will rediscover a place, clearly defined, among other concepts, without any prevalence. It remains therefore to test distance through its confrontation with the question of Being, and that which, metaphysically, has been able to issue therefrom. The insertion of distance within the question of Being, or its disengagement from that very question, therefore redoubles the initial question—that of the marches of metaphysics. It remains that in order to speak in face of or outside of Being (if one can dare to say it this way), distance will have to explain itself in relation to what one calls the "overcoming of metaphysics." Within that explication, it would be necessary nevertheless to aim at something else, infinitely more delicate: the situation of distance in relation to Being. And to do this, the function of the *idol* will perhaps no longer suffice as it sufficed for metaphysics.

Distance and Its Icon

> The icon, which is the same as the prototype, nevertheless differs from it.
>
> Gregory of Nyssa

> Dum silet, clamat, et dum clamat, silet; et invisibilis videtur, et dum videtur, invisibilis est.
>
> John Scotus Eriugena, *De Divisione Naturae,* III, 4

§ 17. DISTANCE, DIFFERENCE

THE CRITIQUE OF DISTANCE as of a purely rhetorical and not at all conceptual theme, as pertinent as it may be, misses two of distance's characteristics that, from the beginning of our argument, govern it. First, distance has a definition. Second, it remains indefinable by definition. Distance can be defined in several equivalent statements; among others, alterity alone allows communion, and nothing of that which distinguishes separates without, by that very fact, uniting all the more. Or again, between God and man, incommensurability alone makes intimacy possible, because withdrawal alone defines the Father, just as the paternal withdrawal alone saves for man the sumptuous liberty of a son. Or finally, that which makes "God" available either to qualify or disqualify him offers only an idol of the spectator and is confused with the spectator in a fantasmatic identity. Distance as di-stance therefore means: duality alone allows recognition, communion progresses with the separation wherein gazes are exchanged. Di-stance: only he can become my neighbor who remains forever outside of me and my doubles. Only he can stand with me who stands before me. The struggle with the angel is not identical with communion (as the negative claims), nor does it contradict it (as is supposed by any indistinct harmony), but prepares the blessing that completes it. Distance buttresses the one against the other until they bless one another. Or more, since, if I am the one, the Other here is God, I give the blessing to God only after having struggled enough to understand that that struggle itself was blessing me. God blesses in making me stand before Him: the struggle here finds its truth in creation. The more that some separation opposes a distant one, the more distance blesses. Distance can therefore deploy its rigor to the point of a definition. For that, it is necessary to recognize it as undefinable, or rather as undefined. For it gives rise to an indefinite succession of definitions, which are linked to one another without any closure ever being able to exhaust the subject. Neither a subject of discourse, nor an object of science, distance removes itself from definition by definition. Indeed, it ensures communion only between terms whose separation it provokes. Now, among these terms, one interests us directly, since we ensure it, we who are speaking here. As for the other, we can approach it only within a communion that is traversed by separation all the more in that it is a matter of distance. The definition of distance defines us as one of its terms, and therefore removes us from the other, at the very moment when it exerts its attraction. The other, infinitely foreign, disappears in his very apparition, is defined by the indefinite itself. No image, no concept, nor any denial of image or concept is suitable to or frees the unthinkable. Of distance rigorously approached, one of the terms becomes rigorously unapproachable. It becomes so all the more insofar as distance offers itself in its most definite rigor. Thus could one speak of an asymmetry of distance: its definition concerns two poles, or better, it gives rise to and guarantees them. But this definition is stated only on the basis of one of the two poles—our own, which is humanly defined. The separation that unites will therefore affect the other term with a lack of definition all the more insofar as, precisely, that lack of definition properly qualifies, within distance, the intimate alterity of the terms. No third, neuter (Levinas), and colorless pole could offer itself to express distance equitably. Moreover, supposing that such a pole were to present itself, as various forms of hastily representational thinking will not fail to propose, it is not distance that it would think. For distance opens the separation that unites only on the basis of a term that is discovered there, or better that discovers there its own horizon: distance is discovered only like a path is cleared, starting from a site, but not like one reads an itinerary on a map, in the elsewhere of a neutralized representation. Because it deploys its rigorous definition, distance therefore reinscribes that definition in one of its terms; it subjects it to its perspective and plunges it totally into its constitutive asymmetry. By definition, the definition is subjected to that which is defined in it: the definition is still comprehended within distance; it is stated only at the heart of the intimate listening that it illustrates and that puts it in perspective starting from a site. Distance does not allow itself to be represented, even in its rigorous definition, unless its representation allows itself to be introduced into the asymmetry of distance.

Di-stance that no representation can display: this double characteristic of distance awakens an echo—an echo of the ontological difference such as Heidegger approaches it. It even seems inevitable to pose a brutal question—does not distance, for the most part and excluding a few adjustments (to be located in what follows), amount to the ontological difference? Distance, as distance, underlines separation only in order to save its intimacy. The ontological difference, for its part, distinguishes beings, taken in their massive and unavoidable facticity, from the Being that can be confused with one being or another all the less insofar as it governs, saves, and unconceals each of them. Within the most trivial evidence of beings is revealed, without giving itself to be seen as a being, that by which beings can haunt us with evident presence, with their present evidence—Being itself. The Being of beings appears only on the basis of the difference in which brute beings allow to be uncovered in themselves the "nothingness" of the Being without which they nevertheless would not themselves be uncovered. The difference manifests beings all the more insofar as it condenses their ontological halo; it allows the latter to be sensed only by assigning it all the more to its ontic "nothingness." The difference only harmoniously distinguishes the ontic from the ontological:

> If Being, in the sense of the uncovering Coming-over, and beings as such, in the sense of arrival that keeps itself concealed, realize themselves as different, they do so by virtue of the Same, of the dimension (*Unter-Schied*). The latter alone grants and holds apart the "between," in which the Coming-over and the Arrival are maintained in relation, separated one from the other and turned one toward the other. The difference of Being and beings, as di-men-

sion (*Unter-Schied*) of the Coming-over and the Arrival, is the *uncovering and concealing Conciliation* (*entbergend-bergende Austrag*) of the one and the other.[1]

The difference does not mark an antagonism between Being and beings so much as it definitively deepens their irreducible Fold (*Zwiefel*) in order thus to conciliate them more intimately. Difference: a span that passes from one term to the other, in the sense that the arch of a bridge spreads its span from one piling to the other. *Aus-trag: Tragen* only replaces *ferre*, in order to put into play the span from one term to the other, beyond a dual exteriority (*di-, Aus-*). The basis of the difference resides less in antagonism than in the equilibrium of pressures. Distance maintains the duality of weights (*di-*) only by thrusting them one against the other, in order to stop, with an immobile and obstinate shock, in open sky, their two falls (*-stance*). When therefore the ontological difference exposes itself as a re-port (*Aus-trag, dif-ference*) that conciliates Being and beings more radically than it polemically opposes them, we rediscover therein the communion that is ultimately aimed at by distance. That the terms of the conciliating difference (Being, beings) do not coincide with those of distance (God, man; Father-son) must be clearly marked, to be sure. But do these relations not become all the more strangely familiar insofar as in them are posed together terms that are all the less identifiable? Even more, to speak of "relations" with regard to distance seems as incongruous as with regard to difference, since the one and the other agree again in this, that they alone render possible and thinkable all relations, opposition, and composition—on the basis of their original conciliation(s) (*report, di-stance, Aus-trag*). Does distance conciliate like (ontological) difference?

Distance is defined only by removing itself, as we saw (§§ 13–14), from any definition that would claim to ensure a neutral understanding of it, and to represent it as an accessible object. Now, the ontological difference, for its part, rejects the clear and dis-

---

[1] *Identität und Differenz* (Pfullingen: G. Neske, 1957), pp. 56–57 = *Questions* I (Paris: Gallimard, 1968), p. 299 [Stambaugh, 65, mod.]; on the Conciliation (*Austrag*), see also p. 60 = p. 302, and *Unterwegs zur Sprache* (Pfullingen: G. Neske, 1959), p. 25.

tinct representation of its stakes [*enjeu*] as of its play [*jeu*]. Of its stakes: the difference between Being and beings does not offer itself to be conceived uniformly. In it, beings can give an object to knowledge, which thus relies on a tangible, available, and, in a word, comprehensible material. Beings support representation. Being, on the contrary, "is" not in the sense that beings are; it fringes beings with the halo of an invisible light that no prism comes to decompose into colors that are elementary and visible like a being; Being—a pure nothingness of beings[2]—does not cease to disappear in the measure that beings appear, which appear, however, only in the measure that the withdrawal of Being is assigned to them. Being never appears except in the withdrawal that renders (in-)visible the beings that are themselves visible. Asymmetrical, the difference conciliates the haunting advance of beings with the saving withdrawal of Being, the representable with the unrepresentable:

> We speak of the *difference* between Being and beings. The step back goes from what is unthought, from the difference as such, to what is to be thought. What is to be thought is the *forgetting* of the difference. The forgetting here to be thought is the veiling of the difference as such, thought in terms of λήθη (concealment); this veiling has in turn withdrawn itself from the beginning. The forgetting belongs to the difference because the difference belongs to the forgetting. The forgetting does not happen to the difference only afterward, in consequence of the forgetfulness of human thinking.[3]

The forgetting does not result from a psychological inadvertence, and it results even less from a collective failure: it flows constitutively from the ontological difference itself, which stages Being only starting from beings, as the (unrepresentable) Being of (representable) beings. For Being appears only when the inapparent and invisible Nothing surfaces, as is shown by the lecture "What

---

[2] See "What Is Metaphysics?" in *Wegmarken* (Frankfurt a/M: V. Klostermann, 1967), pp. 1–19 = *Questions* I, pp. 47–72.

[3] *Identität*, pp. 40–41 = p. 285 [Stambaugh, 50–51, mod.]. See also "The Anaximander Fragment," in *Holzwege*, p. 336 = French trans., *Chemins*, p. 297: "The forgetting of difference, with which the history of Being begins, in order to be accomplished in it, is not, however, a defect, but the richest and most vast event, that in which the Hesperian History of the world occurs and decides itself. It is the advent of metaphysics"; p. 340 = p. 301.

Is Metaphysics?" Supposing, indeed, presence as the privileged temporalization of Being, it falls to beings to concentrate that presence in themselves, without Being ever being able "to be" in accordance with that presence. Forgetting is not added to the ontological difference, but constitutes its reverse side: the destinal decision to think Being as the Being *of beings* provokes the forgetting of the difference, since, at bottom, the difference itself already forgetfully ruled Being. Forgetting constitutes the stake of the ontological difference, and, as destinal stake, it steals it away from any representation (since representation, understood at least according to its modern essence, issues from that forgetting, far from compensating for it, or even just conceiving it). As for distance, its stakes fall, analogically, within the alternative between misunderstanding and recognition. By ensuring intimacy only at the price of separation, distance always risks falling to the level of a simple absence, being able even to reach the trivial point of a (non-Nietzschean, nor rigorous) "death of God." At stake finally with distance is its own conceptual validity: either it is itself missed, by misunderstanding the separation as a desert of absence, and disqualified entirely, by not reaching the Father in his invisibility; or it is constituted, in recognizing that only the salvific withdrawal of the Father can qualify a son. Distance must go beyond absence; or rather, it arrives at its own rigor in "believing, without having seen" (John 20:9) that the absent one, at bottom, presents the paternal figure of God. It must lead the son to inhabit it as a fatherland, far from losing himself in it as in a borderless prison (thus §§ 8–12). Distance ceaselessly risks being misunderstood, just as difference tirelessly attempts to be forgotten. That the specific trait of the one consists *in not* being misunderstood, whereas the lot of the other destines it to forgetting—this is what opposes them less than this similar stake brings them together: the relation to their respective invisibilities decides their whole coherence. Respect for the invisible decides on the fate as much of difference as of distance.

As for their play, they also play in the same way, against all representation and all speech. The ontological difference can never become an object for representation. Indeed, it could do so only if the difference were captured in a relation, which the representational understanding could make play freely, and which it would attribute, next and in other terms, to the play of Being with beings. But precisely, if the difference were added to a representable given, it would be added to beings, a difference of beings. But what is at issue with those beings? Beings are that which is. That which, thus, is in beings, Being, appears immediately as the Being of those beings. The difference plays therefore between Being and beings even before there might intervene the representation of the difference and its definition by the understanding. "Always already there," the difference precedes its representation, since no objectivity, no representation, no understanding is deployed except starting from the Being of beings, conciliated with beings in their Being.[4] Difference, allowing Being/beings to play ("unfolding" Being/beings), commands in advance all thought, which subsequently tries only to conciliate (itself with) that conciliation. Constitutive of the thought whose openness to the Open it alone ensures, the ontological difference escapes representation all the more insofar as it grounds the thought that might, subsequently, think representationally. Such an anteriority ends up offering itself in and as language. Language does not express the ontological difference like one of its possible statements. But, in every possible statement, the difference does not cease to speak. Language only ever speaks following the difference, for the Conciliation alone opens the place where speech might play. Issuing thus from the difference, language never states it, but is effaced so that the difference might be pronounced in and upon it. Distance (we saw in §§ 13–16) also escapes all representation, since every representable object, like every representing subject, already depends on a definitively anterior distance. More, the paternal horizon of distance removes itself, by definition, from any inquiry that would claim to objectivate it. That of which it is a question here is, precisely, the unobjectifiable in the unthinkable that surpasses even the negation of the thinkable, the un-representable that escapes even the nega-

---

[4] *Identität,* p. 54. See "Time and Being," in *L'Endurance de la pensée: Pour saluer Jean Beaufret* (Paris: Plon, 1968), text and translation by F. Fedier, pp. 66–67: "This is why the thinking that represents and gives reasons answers to the *Ereignis* no more than the saying that simply states" (reprinted in *Questions* IV, p. 46); *Gelassenheit* (Pfullingen: G. Neske, 1959), p. 41 = French trans., p. 195, in *Questions* III; *Unterwegs zur Sprache,* p. 25.

tion of the representable. But again, language itself issues, with the *logia,* from the distance that dispenses it in order to give it over to an absolute praise. Unavoidable, but unquestionable, language speaks only within the distance that precedes it, and endlessly recedes from it, like so many questions that it will never be able to allow to be formulated. Here again, language does not express distance, since it expresses itself in distance, just as it receives itself from distance. As to representation and language, therefore, distance and difference play their respective games in a comparable manner. Through Conciliation and distance, through their stakes [*enjeu*] as through their play [*jeu*], distance seems to rediscover the traits that assure the undefining definition of the ontological difference. Must one, for all that, confuse them, and annul the irreducible separation of distance over against the ontological difference?

It is necessary to return here, before concluding too hastily, to the discordance that we located above: what is proper to distance consists in not being ignored, whereas the lot of ontological difference destines it to forgetting. Indeed, the ontological difference conciliates Being and beings only by first approaching the Being *of beings* (see § 2), that is, in avoiding to begin with the frontal and fontal question concerning Being as such, which perhaps aims first at the tie between Being and time, and therefore at the privilege of the present within ontological temporalization: "If the ontological difference which appears here is the greatest danger for thought, that is because it *always* represents Being, within the horizon of metaphysics, as a being; then the question concerning beings as beings, that is the metaphysical question, has another meaning than the question of Being as Being. One can express this negatively by saying that the question of Being as Being is not an empowering of the Being of beings."[5] The ontological difference increasingly underlines that Being is distinguished from beings, but that distinction does not ask, precisely, after Being *as Being.* Thus the difference does not cease to forget Being in the very measure that, insistently, it questions starting

---

[5] "Séminaire du Thor," protocol of 4 September 1968, printed in *Questions* IV, p. 237; see "if metaphysics indeed questions in the direction of the Being of beings ('What is being in the way that it is?'), it does not question Being itself," pp. 236 and 240–41.

from beings. Ordained radically to its own forgetting, the ontological difference endlessly produces metaphysics, because it
nourishes the essence thereof. It is necessary to note, of course,
that metaphysics differs from the ontological difference in that it
traverses the "fold" of the difference without thinking it as such:
"Metaphysics would be, in its essence, the unthought, because
withheld, secret of Being itself"; it would remain within the ontological difference in keeping the latter totally "unthought"—this
unthought itself leading the destiny of thought to its metaphysical
face: "Because the thinking of metaphysics remains involved in
the difference which as such is unthought, metaphysics, by virtue
of the unifying unity of the Conciliation (*Austrag*), is both ontology and theology in a unified way." What belongs properly to
metaphysics becomes its very failure to think difference proper—
metaphysics, or difference that is unthought because deported
to the exclusive benefit of the beings whose present appearance
conceals the very apparition and the withdrawal—Being—that
brings it about.[6] It remains that, if "our thinking is free either to
pass over the difference without a thought or to think it specifically as such," when it risks undertaking the step back outside of
metaphysics and with a view toward the difference as such, it
would be necessary not to infer therefrom that, inversely, metaphysics failed to think the difference only by a regrettable, contingent accident, and that a sound speculative mind could recapture
it:

> The step back goes from the unthought—from the difference as
> such—toward what it is necessary to think. That is, toward the *forget-
> ting* of the difference. The forgetting that it is necessary to think
> here is the veiling thought on the basis of λήθη (occultation), a
> veiling of the difference as such, a veiling that for its part has, from
> the origin (*anfänglich*), withdrawn itself. Forgetting belongs to the
> difference because the latter is tied intimately to the former. The

---

[6] Respectively, "The Word of Nietzsche 'God is dead,' " in *Holzwege*, p. 244 =
Chemins, p. 217 (see *Wegmarken*, p. 223 = *Questions* I, p. 305); then *Identity and
Difference*, p. 63 = *Questions* I, p. 305 [Stambaugh, 71, mod.]. On metaphysics as
"unthought difference," see ibid., p. 40 = p. 285, p. 52 = p. 295, p. 63 = p.
305 ("In the measure that metaphysics thinks being as such in its totality, it
represents being to itself with a view toward that which differs in the difference,
without having regard for difference as such"); then p. 65 = p. 307.

forgetting does not come to obfuscate the difference after the fact,
as the result of a forgetful character of human thought.[7]

The stakes of contemporary thought become to think nonmeta-
physically the difference as such; but these stakes appear as a task
and a test for such thought only inasmuch as, precisely, the passage from the difference toward metaphysics and what it leaves
unthought had nothing accidental about it, but came from an
historial rigor whose constraints we barely measure. The ontological difference as such undoubtedly does not coincide with the
onto-theological constitution of metaphysics; but its historial passage in the latter ties it rigorously because historially to onto-theology; inasmuch as metaphysically unthought, the difference
nourishes the primacy of beings within the question of (the)
Being (of beings), and therefore also leads necessarily to a privileging of the beingness of beings up to the form that marks their
completion, the most being of beings, the supreme being: "Inasmuch as Being is deployed as the Being of beings, as difference,
as Conciliation (*Austrag*), then and in the same measure, the separation and the mutual relation of grounding and accounting for
endures, Being grounds beings, and beings, as what *is* most of all
(*das Seiendste*), account for Being," "the onto-theological constitution of metaphysics stems from the prevalence of that difference which keeps Being as the ground, and beings as what is
grounded and what gives account, apart from and related to each
other."[8] As soon as, metaphysically, it is deployed in the very forgetting of what differs in it, the difference gives rise to and confirms the onto-theological constitution of metaphysics. The more,
then, that metaphysical thought is established within the unthought ontological difference, the more it constitutes (or is constituted according to) onto-theology. Now, as we saw (§ 2), onto-
theology makes the question of the Being of beings culminate in
the supreme being, to the point of giving to the latter the form of
causa sui. This completes the idolatry of God metaphysically. The
ontological difference, unthought, thus allows to be elaborated a

---

[7] Respectively, *Identity and Difference*, p. 55 = p. 297 [Stambaugh, 63] and pp.
40–41 = p. 285 [Stambaugh, 50, mod.].

[8] Ibid., pp. 61–62 = French trans., p. 304 [Stambaugh, 69, mod.], and p. 63
= French trans., p. 305 [Stambaugh, 71], then the whole conclusion of the text.

conceptual and representable idol of God, conceived on the basis of the being that accuses Being, and as the supreme being that consecrates the forgetting. Difference works under the metaphysical yoke for the supreme being and its idolatrous representation. Distance attempts not to yield to the idol, even supreme. Difference thus contributes, through its very forgetting, to the onto-theological constitution that distance tends to revoke in the name of the Ab-solute unthinkable. Even if the distance to be thought and the unthought difference seem to proceed in parallel fashion, their authorities are radically opposed, and at two levels: first, in that the one allows to grow stronger the idol of the *causa sui,* which the other does not cease to disqualify by virtue of the Requisite (Αἰτία). Next and above all because, at the foundation of this opposition, one can discern already another: the difference thinks "God" on the basis of the question of Being (thought metaphysically or not perhaps does not matter), whereas distance, by a step back outside even of the question of Being, claims to think the unthinkable in a more desert-like way, and therefore more originally. Can this claim be, if not justified, at least formulated?

But here again it is to the ontological difference and to Heidegger's thought path that it is necessary to turn. In a text contemporary to *Sein und Zeit* (1927), Heidegger shows how the analytic of *Dasein* precedes and determines the conditions of the being that affects the Christian event—"christianness." In a word, the analytic of *Dasein* indicates, ontologically, a pre-Christian datum and content whose "christianness" marks only an ontic corrective. If the rigor of theology is measured by the vigor of the ontic corrective that it imposes on the beings concerned by it, that measure will be defined in its turn only by the gap between the ontic corrective and the ontological analytic of *Dasein.* Thus, because "christianness" never intervenes except for an ontic variation, *Dasein* must ontologically constitute the invariant. "Christianness" becomes the ontic variable of an ontological invariant, *Dasein.* Theology formulates that variable and measures its deviations, just as philosophy proceeds to the analysis of the invariant and identifies it in its possible avatars.[9]

---

[9] *Phänomenologie und Theologie,* text and French translation in *Archives de Philosophie* 63, no. 3 (Paris, 1969), pp. 356–95.

Beyond the opposition between "christianness" and theology, what seems decisive here is the fundamental condition that is set, once and for all, for the question of God: God will never be able to appear within the field of questioning thought except under the mediating conditions first of "christianness" and then of *Dasein*. This, no doubt, means first that God plays only ontically (here through an "ontic corrective") upon the foundation of a *Dasein* about which *Sein und Zeit* straightaway shows that it is for this being alone that Being is at issue: the supreme being of metaphysical onto-theology finds its hermeneutical (ontological) place only within the primacy of *Dasein*, in the sense that *Dasein* alone exists. The question of God is hence transported from the beginning not only outside of the "God" of onto-theology, but also outside of any being that does not exist in the mode of *Dasein*. This means that every God possible, including any God outside of onto-theology, will be approached only on the basis of *Dasein* according to a definitively established distribution of roles: God, a being, *Dasein*, the being who is hermeneut of Being; God *regresses* to the rank of supreme being, that is, to the rank of a being who is inferior in the sense that, in its Being of beings, Being is not at issue: theology is limited then to an ontic variable—first subjection of God to Being. This means, next, that God intervenes only as one being among those that the Being of beings conciliates according to the ontological difference. God is only "God"; if he no longer intervenes except as a supreme being, this is in order to appear all the more as an inferior being; "God," under this second condition, is subjected entirely to an idolatrous precondition that deduces him, through intermediaries that are analyzed at length and precisely itemized, on the basis of Being (that is, of the *Dasein* that keeps Being) as one being among others. Indeed, a deduction—in the Kantian sense of the term, almost—rigorously ties Being (and therefore *Dasein*) to "God." The insistence and permanence of the texts that express this reduction seem remarkable:

> The thought that thinks starting from the question bearing on the truth of Being questions more originally than metaphysics can, it is only starting from the truth of Being that the essence of the sacred can be thought. It is only starting from the essence of the sacred

that the essence of divinity is to be thought. It is only within the
light of the essence of divinity that that which the word "God"
must name can be thought and spoken. Is it not necessary first to
understand carefully and to be able to hear all these words, if we
wish to be, as men, that is, as ones who exist, in the position to
experience a relation between God and man?[10]

One sequence rigorously ties, as interconnected conditions, God
to the divine, the divine to the sacred, the sacred (*das Heilige*) to
the intact (*das Heil:* the safe): "That which is no longer intact as
such puts us on the trail of the intact. Appealing to it, the intact
signals toward the sacred. The sacred religiously binds the divine.
The divine renders close the God." Prior to the question of the
"death of God" was the question concerning the metaphysical
figure (onto-theology) that rendered it possible; in the same way,
the question of a "return of the gods" or of a "new God" must
fade before a more essential question: "Where must he (i.e.,
God) turn during his return, if first (*zuvor*) an abode is not prepared for him by men? And how could an abode in the measure
of the divine be found for God, if a brilliance of the divinity has
not first (*zuvor*) begun to shine in all that is?" The lack of God
refers back in fact to an extinction of the divine: "Not only have
the gods and the divine fled, but, within the history of the world,
the brilliance of the divinity has also been extinguished."[11] The
deduction claims to deepen the question of God with that of the
divine in general; that of the divine is valid in its turn only as a
vestige of the intact (*das Heile*), which itself is received safe and
sound only by a safeguard that ensures the Open; the Open, in
its turn, conjoins—in a mode ignored precisely by the ontological
difference and its conciliation—the earth, the sky, the mortal,
and the divine only on the basis of the clearing of Being. That
which the lecture on "The Thing" names the *Geviert*, the *fourfold*
if one dares to translate it thus, would not comprehend the divine

---

[10] "Letter on Humanism," in *Wegmarken,* p. 182 = French trans. in *Questions*
III, pp. 133–34; likewise, "the sacred, the sole essential space of the divinity
which in its turn alone accords the dimension for gods and God, comes to the
brilliance of appearing only when, previously (*zuvor*) and in a long preparation,
Being has itself been clarified and experienced in its truth," p. 169 = p. 114.

[11] "Why Poets?" in *Holzwege,* respectively, pp. 294, 249, and 248 = French
trans. in *Chemins,* pp. 260, 221, 220.

among that which it dispenses if the God did not first amount to the divine and if the divine did not have to be understood by full right as a being: "For the God himself, if he is, is a being, stands as a being in Being, in the essence of the latter which arrives on the basis of the worlding of the world."[12] God must be understood as a being, and his arrival (what commonly and metaphysically one names his "existence") depends on the possibility that the world keeps of worlding, and therefore of offering the place—the Open—where the advent of any particular being remains possible. God has perhaps "ontically" created the world, but, without any doubt, it is the world that, as "living world" and bringing about the Open, ontologically works the advent of the God within the divine, through the sacred, according to the intact. It is no longer a question here, of course, of the idolatrous "God" of onto-theology. However, it is perhaps still a question of an idol. That the least of idols should arise changes nothing concerning the idolatry: "God" is in the mode of a being. Of "God" one can announce "in advance" (*zuvor*) that he is—in the manner of a being, and therefore that nothing could be expressed about him that would constitute an exception to the Being of beings. That the latter be understood metaphysically or not changes nothing concerning the fundamental decision: just as onto-theology produces an idol of "God" as *causa sui,* so a thought of the "new beginning" will receive "the God" only in the measure of the "divine abode" (*Aufenhalt,* in the sense that the "Letter on Humanism" comments on the Heraclitean ἦθος) that it is able to prepare for the God. The gap between a metaphysical thinking and a nonmetaphysical thinking of the divine matters less here than their full agreement in thinking God idolatrously as that divine being that is allowed by the divine dignity of Being: always more radically than "God" in "God" appears the Being that attests its divine dignity therein as in one being among others. "God" becomes the radiant idol where Being brings about for us, within the *Fourfold,* his divinity.

---

[12] "Die Kehre," in *Die Technik und die Kehre* (Pfullingen: G. Neske, 1962), pp. 45–46. See also p. 46: "If God is God, he arrives on the basis of, and within, the constellation of Being." Likewise the enumeration of beings, among which are the angel and God, all equally comprehended within Being ("Letter on Humanism," in *Wegmarken,* pp. 161–62).

This "God" remains an idol, the highest and the most difficult
to produce, the most glorious and the most salvific for human
Dasein; its advent would undoubtedly drive *Dasein* wild with happiness, but it would still be the matter of an idol. Must one, then, in
order to escape it even before it has arisen, risk drawing an extreme conclusion: God is not a being, which Being precedes, governs, and dispenses? Perhaps indeed it is necessary, as brutally as
possible, to posit that Being and God are two, and that idolatry
threatens the greatest (Heidegger, but also Saint Thomas)¹³ as
soon as they brush against the assimilation of the two. Perhaps it
is necessary to renounce thinking God on the basis of being, not
only when onto-theology, concluding that "God is dead," leaves
no other respectable choice for the believer; but even and as well
if the "other beginning"¹⁴ comes to populate the world overabundantly with "new gods" (Nietzsche) or with a new "abode" for
the divine. Perhaps it is necessary, backing our argument by the
very circularity of its references, to take seriously what the distance of praise (Denys) gives to be thought: that Being (but also,
let us note, the One, Goodness, or the Truth) does not offer any
essential name of God, and therefore that God becomes thinkable only once the unthinkable is accepted as the place, condition, and measure of the Ab-solute. Perhaps finally only a thought
without postulate, not even that of respecting the conditions that it
would believe itself able to establish for its own logic, can begin
vaguely to prepare itself for that of which it is a question when it
says: God. There is more: what would be the case with a "God"
treated as a being? Heidegger says that theology considers the
"way" by which "christianness" sublates (*aufheben*) the human
being and pre-christian terms.¹⁵ Without any doubt. It remains

---

¹³ The legitimacy of this rapprochement comes not so much from certain dec-
larations made a little quickly by Et. Gilson in *Etre et essence* (Paris: Vrin, 1972),
appendix II, as from a study as serious and pertinent as that by J.-B. Lotz, S.J.,
"Das Sein un das subsistierende Sein nach Thomas von Aquin" in *Martin Heidegger, Zum siebzigsten Geburtstag Festschrift,* p. 180 ff., where the doctor meets the
demands of the thinker in that he does not fail to recognize (does not forget)
the ontological difference.

¹⁴ "Another beginning": see, among other texts, *Nietzsche* (Pfullingen: G.
Neske, 1961), vol. 2, pp. 29, 262.

¹⁵ *Phänomenologie und Theologie,* p. 386; theology considers the *"Existenzart"*
(pp. 368, 374) of "christiannness," its *"Seinsart"* (p. 376), *"Existenzweise"* (pp.
366, 367), its *"Wiesein"* (p. 384), in a word its *"Weise"* (pp. 370, 372); only this

that "christianness" does not transform only the way of the human being; or rather, that transformation is effected first, before the disciple, by the Christ himself, which does not mean nothing. One can of course speak, as of a coherent and equivalent whole, "of the divine among the Greeks, among the Jewish prophets, in the preaching of Jesus";[16] but it would perhaps be necessary to understand that equivalence as Hölderlin understood the fraternity of Christ with Hercules and Dionysus—as a cumulative, paradoxical, and inaugural heritage (and Heidegger undoubtedly understood it thus; see § 10). In this case, if the divine assumes the face of the Christ, the God-man, the "way" in which he affects human being risks taking on the infinite seriousness of the Incarnation: if God invests the human with all of his greatness, without reserve, abandoning himself to human being from the depths of distance—it is not only human "ways" that God assumes, but humanity itself; it is not the ontic "way" of a particular being, but the fundamental constitution of *Dasein* that he puts on and renews. Kenosis coincides perfectly here with recapitulation: in abandoning himself in humanity and in sacrificing thereto the insignia of divinity, God takes possession of humanity magisterially, fundamentally, and as his good. In this case one must pose two questions. First this: does the Christ, through the magisterially recapitulative kenosis, content himself with an ontic and ontically thinkable event, which modifies after the fact certain ontic determinations of *Dasein* ("content"), without thoroughly affecting its most intimate constitution, or does he undertake, through an original and terminal advent, to invest not only a particular being (his own humanity) but indeed the Being of beings with a new dimension? Without yet outlining what "new dimension" might mean here, and without even deciding whether the question must have an answer, let us dare a prior question: do the Incarnation and Resurrection of the Christ affect ontological destiny, or do

---

"way" gives to the "pre-Christian content" a new ontic orientation accorded to faith as a "re-birth," but dependent on the invariant of its ontological determination. One should not, however, fail to note that the interpretation given here would be completely reversed if *Weise/Art* had to be understood in the sense of Maximus the Confessor's τρόπος (see J.-M. Garrigues, *Maxime le Confesseur: La charité, avenir divin de l'homme* (Paris: Beauchesne, 1976) p. 100 ff.

[16] Letter to Buchner, in *Vorträge und Aufsätze* II, p. 57 = French trans. in *Essais et conférences* (Paris: Gallimard, 1958), p. 220.

they remain a purely ontic event? Next this other: an objection to the ontological independence of God ensues from the undeniable anteriority of the "divine abode" that would receive him; but precisely, in what way does God depend on the abode that humanity (under any particular figure of the history of the world) prepares for him? In fact, an idol depends entirely on this precondition, since the idol reflects it, lends it a name, and finds its own face in it. But the Jewish announcement and the Christian revelation set in place, on the basis of a critique of the idolatry off of which modern thought does not cease to live, a coming of God among his own that is attested even when "his own did not receive him" (John 1:11). Far from the lack of "divine abode" limiting or prohibiting the manifestation, that lack becomes the condition of such manifestation—as a destruction of any idol prior to the unthinkable—, the characteristic—God alone can reveal himself when and where no other divine being can remain—, and even the highest stakes—God reveals himself in stripping himself of the divine glory. The God who manifests himself as Jesus-Christ depends on no "divine abode," precisely because He strips himself of divinity in the sense that men conceive it. On the Cross, as in the condition of the Nazarene, what "divine abode" was offered so that God should there be suitably (that is, divinely) received? None, and God was not suitably received there. But does God desire our suitability, and does he make of it a precondition for his coming? Would it not be necessary to learn from God himself what suitability means, in the sense that, as we are told, "it was suitable that Christ should suffer and thus walk toward his glory" (Luke 24:26)? Who can and must decide concerning the divine and divine suitability, God or *Dasein*? Kenosis, disdain, and rejection dismiss the condition of a "divine abode"; more, they contribute to establishing the figure of revelation as the paradox in which humiliation and misrecognition become the screen and the theater of the ἀγαπή (Spirit) of the Father for the Son, and of the Son for the Father. The condition of the revelation of the Father in the figure of the Son, or better, its stakes and its completion consist precisely in the failure and collapse of any "divine abode": in the darkening of the sky, where no azure outlines the glorious figure of any Greek god, the Christ dies and the trinitarian distance reveals itself forever. This is indeed why the figure of revelation is deployed equally as a figure of concealment, and hence of judgment (John, Pascal, etc.), for it gives itself to be seen and received even when the most elementary conditions ("existential dimension," "existential concept")—"divine abode"—come to be lacking. The kenosis sets no condition for revealing itself, because in that revelation it gives itself and reveals nothing other than this unconditional gift. Our lack of respect, in a word, our "unsuitability," even grounded in ontological destiny, cannot set any condition upon this gift without precondition. For the mystery consists precisely in this: God loves those who do not love him, manifests himself to those who turn away, and all the *more* that they turn away.

Through this double attestation, God takes his distance from the idol of him proposed not only by the ontological difference but also, more simply, by Being. God withdraws in the distance, unthinkable, unconditioned, and therefore infinitely closer. Distance takes its distance from the ontological difference and from the Being that, among other things, it manages. Distance therefore cannot be formalized on the basis of difference. Is it necessary to hope nonetheless to formalize it through a critique of ontological difference, put into question as still idolatrous? We believed so, and attempted to do so.

§ 18. THE OTHER *Différant*[17]

Distance remains at a distance from the ontological difference because Being, its epochs and its destiny, perhaps do not constitute a precondition for God or for his coming. The setting in place of each being, including the supreme being, certainly issues from the conciliation, and therefore from the ontological difference; but can God be understood on the basis of Being (even if it is a matter of Being as Being) any more than he could be recognized in the supreme being (conceived as *causa sui*)? If God

---

[17] *L'Autre Différant,* translated here as "The Other *Différant,*" can be taken to mean either "the differing/deferring other" or "the other differing/deferring [thing]." [Trans.]

should not be thought as a being (even supreme), would this not be because not even Being offers any site that by right receives him? What would remain of God that does not fall already to the rank of an idol if, before and more profoundly than he, Being ruled him? For as much as Being commands the appearing of beings, "God" included, it invests them silently and, as for "God," contradicts him radically. God becomes "God" again, inasmuch as from metaphysics the thought of Being as Being keeps only this minimum postulate: God, if he is, is; or rather: if the cause of God must become a thing of thought, it is necessary first to inquire into Being, since it is a matter—quite obviously—of a being. Being here neutralizes God as "God." It neutralizes, in that the foreignness of God (although "patriotic" in the sense of Hölderlin) is erased, or disqualified, by a more intimate authority. It is neutralized above all in the sense that Levinas has so powerfully understood it: "Materialism is not in the discovery of the primordial function of sensibility, but in the primacy of the Neuter. To posit the Neuter of Being above the being that that Being would determine in some way, unbeknownst to it, to posit essential events unbeknownst to beings, is to profess a shameful materialism."[18] The Neuter, whatever formulation it adopts, and therefore also Being, undertakes the reduction of God to a common denominator, or rather, since God is usually understood as "God" (a supreme being), the reduction of the Other [*Autrui*]. The other [*l'Autre*] can appear as such only if no intermediary instance marks out the unfathomed gap that renders the Other possible; ontology, understanding every happening in advance as a being, prohibits by that very fact the recognition of the Other as such: "We radically oppose . . . Heidegger, who subordinates the relation with the Other to ontology . . . instead of seeing in justice and injustice an original access to the Other, beyond all ontology," "to subordinate the relation with *someone* who is a

---

[18] E. Levinas, *Totalité et infini* (The Hague: M. Nijhoff, 1971), p. 275. However, to qualify Heideggerian thought as "materialism" seems all the more surprising insofar as Heidegger determines the essence of materialism on the basis of metaphysics: "The essence of materialism does not consist in the affirmation that all is only matter (*Stoff*), but much rather in a metaphysical determination according to which every being appears as material for work (*Material der Arbeit*)" ("Letter on Humanism," in *Wegmarken*, p. 171).

being (the ethical relation) to the relation with *the Being of beings* which, impersonal, allows the grasping, the naming of beings (to a relation of knowing), subordinates justice to freedom."[19] The Other gives himself to be encountered in a relation that approaches me immediately, naked, face to face; ontology substitutes for that encounter the knowledge of a relation of beings to Being: a relation to be cognized as a knowing, which does not include me among its terms, but offers me an object to represent. There is therefore a double neutralization of the Other by the Neuter; first, the Other no longer reaches me directly, since he is first related to the Being where he appears as a being: the relation curves from the self to Being, the other no longer invokes me face on but, as in profile, presents me only its relation to Being. Then the Other, taken up within the relation that curves toward Being, becomes an object of knowledge for me, inasmuch as he enters into relation with the Neuter itself (Being): far from summoning me to an encounter, he undergoes a summons to be known that I can address to him. I keep, or rather I thus withdraw myself from the unrestrained and unmediated openness to the Other: a nonontological dimension closes from the moment that Being neutralizes beings, forbidding that an ethical openness precede, without proceeding from, the ontological relation. E. Levinas sometimes names that openness, precisely, distance. That an object should be and remain at a distance from me prohibits me from appropriating it, consuming it, and therefore from annihilating it within the Same. Thus, outside the economic, but starting from it, a distance is carved out where the spatial gap renders alterity thinkable, where "the 'distance' in relation to the object surpasses . . . its spatial signification," where the thing and the object become themes for a gaze, in a "distance more radical than any distance of the world."[20] Distance, which thematizes the thing, to the point of granting it a finally ethical irreducibility, does not only prohibit a possession; it reveals that a relation, other than possession, can be established with that which, then, finally becomes other: an other that offers itself, and therefore is not to be touched, nor tasted, nor possessed, because in it there

---

[19] *Totalité et infini,* respectively, pp. 61, 16.
[20] Ibid., p. 184.

opens "a distance more precious than taction, a non-possession more precious than possession, a hunger that is not nourished by bread but by hunger itself."[21] Distance therefore does not open in order that one should cross it; but nor in order that one should not cross it; in order to begin to conceive what distance gives to be thought, it is necessary to consider that in it, since it is not a question of possession, "distance is uncrossable and at the same time crossed,"[22] in a word, traversed. The Infinite, like the Other, gives itself in a distance that desire does not abolish (like a provisional separation), but before which it does not recoil either (like a formidable caesura): distance, and therefore the Other, is reinforced all the more insofar as one does not cease to traverse it as the other in which, in a utopia, the most intimate presents itself. Only now can one return to God, starting from the distance where the Other arises, for "divinity keeps a distance."[23] In admitting distance, we are admitted to the sole place that the divine can recognize as its own, or, more exactly than this "neuter," the Other, who brings it about. Distance delivers access without conditions or precautions to the Other, God beyond all ontology. Thus distance would be delivered from the ontological difference, and the ethical injunction would carry the day over the care of Being. Onto-theology would yield to a dramatics of the Other.

Approached thus, distance passes beyond ontology only within the opposition between ethics and ontology, which itself relies on the difference between Being and beings. But here the dignity of beings carries the day over ("neuter") Being:

> *Being* before *beings,* ontology before metaphysics—is freedom . . . before justice. It is a movement within the Same before obligation with regard to the Other. It is necessary to reverse these terms, . . . the comprehension of Being is already said to the being that rises up again behind the theme in which it offers itself. This "saying to the Other"—this relation to the Other as interlocutor, this relation with a *being*—precedes all ontology. It is the ultimate relation within Being. Ontology presupposes metaphysics.[24]

---

[21] Ibid., p. 154.
[22] Ibid., p. 33.
[23] Ibid., p. 273.
[24] Ibid., pp. 17–18.

Obviously, in being displaced from Being to being, the privilege consecrates the preeminence of the latter, as Other, only by inverting the ontological difference, and hence in consecrating it. Even if one concludes later that existing "can go beyond Being,"[25] it is still with the goal of an "ultimate relation within Being" that existing is deployed to the benefit of being, that ontology yields to metaphysics. One can uncover in this ambiguity the symptom of a considerable difficulty: the condition imposed on the divine/ the Other by Being does not disappear if one appeals against it only to a particular being. First, because one risks thus remaining, with a mere inversion, within the ontological difference, and hence within onto-theology. Next, because, if one speaks of it as of a being, the Other seems insufficiently determined: its constitutive indeterminacy, far from demonstrating its rigor (as would have been the case if the reference to being itself had disappeared), accuses it of ambiguity. In particular, the relation to the Other is thematized on several occasions as a relation. By what right does one here use a category eminently ordained for ontology in order to attain that which, par excellence, is supposed to escape ontology? In a word, the dominance of being over Being undoubtedly does not suffice to pass beyond ontology toward the Other, because that dominance presupposes, again and in its own way, the ontological difference. The way in which E. Levinas's nevertheless profoundly meditative text sometimes treats all of this summarily, and always quickly, would confirm it sufficiently, and it would be surprising were it not known, ever since Plato's ἐπέκεινα τῆς οὐσίας and the Plotinian excess of the One over Being, that being never escapes the Conciliation of Being as little as when it claims to undo itself therefrom by a final leap. The case is the same here as with Kant's dove: in undoing itself from the air that resists it, it would fly *less* quickly and *less* high. However, would a thinker like E. Levinas lead us into an aporia? Undoubtedly not, for at the unspoken foundation of his argument, Jewish thought sustains the discourse pronounced, and it pursues the unavoidable and ancient polemic that unites it with Greek thought: at bottom, that which speaks in *Totality and Infinity* is not being, nor phenomenology, but, through them, the word of the

---

[25] Ibid., p. 278.

prophets and the revelation of the Law; one would miss everything in not hearing them there, present as a second voice. However, it is necessary to recognize an aporia: but among thinkers,
the aporia is the most precious good. For an answer can always
deceive or collapse. But a question, when its irreducibility is assured, becomes the solid point where thought experiences, more
than its strength—the legitimacy and the stakes of thought. If an
aporia is found here, we would already have received much from
the thinker, if we have learned to formulate it more rigorously.
The aporia, since there is one, could therefore be constructed as
follows: beings do not depend uniformly on Being, since the
Other and its ethical justice transgress the ontological Neuter; it
is not, however, a matter of inverting the ontological difference
in favor of a primacy of beings over Being. Or again: distance is
not to be confused with the ontological difference, but it does not
refute it either, nor does it reject it. How to admit a distance that
passes beyond the ontological difference, all the while remaining
homogenous with it? Or again: distance is not freed from the
ontological difference by inverting the relation of its terms (moreover, it could not substitute one primacy for the other unless the
Conciliation could be understood as a primacy, and nothing
seems less sure), nor by camping on its terrain. It could therefore
free itself therefrom only by ceasing to play on the field and with
the terms of ontological difference, in order to reinterpret it, in
situating it on another terrain of difference. This exterior terrain
exceeds the exteriority of E. Levinas, it seems, in that it would
not mobilize, following its example, Being and beings, but would
reinscribe them in a place of exteriority, in a grid of separations,
a combination of differences that, together, would situate and rel-
ativize them. The ontological difference would remain, but as
transgressed. At least that's how it seems.

As long as it remains ontological, difference perhaps conceals
its scope, unless it misses its own rigor—in restricting itself, precisely, to a property. It would be necessary to regress outside of
the appropriation of the difference to its ontological propriety in
order to glimpse that in it another difference differs/defers [dif-
fère]. J. Derrida has attempted to risk this other "step back" with
an insistence that is even more rigorous than diverting, perhaps
less disconcerting than itself disconcerted. There again, we will

have less to repeat or to find fault [*redire*], in the double sense of the term, than to learn, even and above all from questions. To think difference then: difference does not only separate two terms, which it would set apart from one another; it also records and provokes separation on the basis of *différends* (motives for combat). To this first (but already double) sense, where one sees a difference of spacing, is joined a second, which is ignored by what one could almost name the "vulgar concept" of difference. Namely, the retard, delay, or detour that does not immediately deliver the presence of present being, but substitutes for it a particular instance that assures its lieutenance: the difference of temporization. Spacing is doubled by temporization because in the one and the other one hears a verbal form differ/defer— precisely, differing/deferring. What, in these differences, makes the difference (to speak like sportspersons who, after all, know, without realizing it, how the term remains "immediately and irreducibly polysemic")?[26] Answer: the differing/deferring itself that differs/defers there ceaselessly and equivocally; "it differs/defers" verbally even if a particular *différend* or particular *différends* is/are lost amidst the chassé-croisé of their polysemy. At least, and (we will see) at the most, it is necessary to invoke, as the sole substantive, the verb itself, taken in its participial form—differing difference. There is nothing stranger about the *a*, which indicates the present participle, than about the ὄν/being, which indicates the verb and substantive, with the slight exception that the present participle of εἶναι crosses and superimposes them exactly in the same orthography, whereas the differing (*le différant*, participle) does not coincide perfectly with difference (*la différence*, substantive); this is registered in the compromise différ*a*nce,[27] where the participle (verb) imposes its vowel but supports the consonant of the substantive. The graph loses its orthonomy, admitting a double fault. But the irregularity sets things into play since it

---

[26] J. Derrida, "La Différance," in *Marges de la philosophie* (Paris: Editions de Minuit, 1972), p. 8. As is known, this text had already appeared in the collection *Théorie d'ensemble* (Paris: Editions du Seuil, coll. *Tel Quel*, 1968).

[27] Following established practice, I leave the French *différance* (difference, deferral, etc.) untranslated, along with the related *différend* (difference of opinion, dispute, etc.). The verb *différer* I generally translate in its double sense as differ/defer. [Trans.]

allows one to divine the irreducibility of the differing/deferring [*différer*] (the *différant* of the *différance*) to any one particular difference or other: "What is written *différance* would be the movement of play that 'produces,' through what is not simply an activity, these differences, these effects of difference."[28] What is not simply an activity; *différance*, indeed, must not be understood as a cause that, short of them, would produce effects, which one would name differences. *Différance* does not exercise causality any more than differences are produced as effects. If, as usage shows, "the ending *ance* remains undecided *between* active and passive," then *différance* differs/defers itself as much as the differences to which it gives rise, since it differs/defers—is differing/deferring—in them and as them. *Différance* is expressed according to the middle voice; *différance* speaks as well in a neuter voice, between differences, to be sure, but in them and without transcending them, at the level of differences. In making the difference, or rather such or such difference, *différance* does not produce any effect (difference) other than itself: it differs/defers in and as a particular difference, or rather differs/defers from itself therein. To the question "What makes the difference?" we have still given only a "logical" answer. It remains to answer "physically"—or rather to show the "physical" validity of the "logical" answer. Logical, because with language we are dealing with the sole λόγος that remains for modern thought. To put it plainly, since we "dwell first within the semiological problematic,"[29] a return to Saussure: in the *Course*, the sign, in its two faces (signifying, signified), is not at all defined intrinsically or independently of other "images" (signifiers) or "concepts" (signifieds). In fact, each concept is defined by an extension that is delimited, from the outside, by concepts that border, exceed, and surround it; in a word, a particular concept is defined only by the differences that it maintains with other concepts. Likewise for mental images (sig-

---

[28] "La Différance," p. 12. See also "In a classic conceptuality and with some classic requirements, one would say that 'difference' designates the constituting, productive, and originary causality, the process of scission and division whose different things or differences would be the products or constituted effects" (p. 9). But, to this "classic conceptuality," it is necessary to add the ulterior reservations, which make (would make) one "speak of an effect without cause, which would lead one very quickly to speak no longer of effects" (p. 12).

[29] Ibid., respectively, pp. 10, 11.

nifiers). Saussure concludes that "in language there are only differences." Difference, here, does not register a new concept, but reveals a "symmetrical play of differences. Such a play, difference, is no longer then simply a concept but the possibility of conceptuality, of the conceptual process and system in general."[30] *Différance* produces infinite differences whose cross-checkings cover the system of language; it produces the system of differences in producing itself therein. For here *différance* differs/defers as well in distinguishing (sign as placeholder of the referent) through temporization. Behind, or rather within, the system of language plays *différance,* which differs/defers without limit, without design, and without privileging any term. Other paths can show how speech and writing, as other things that differ, can be added to the *différance* that differs/defers (itself) (in) language. The regulated play of *différance* can, in the end, be recognized in any semiology, provided that it admit no other semiology that that ruled by *différance.* "We designate by *différance* the movement according to which language, or any code, any system of references in general is constituted 'historically' as a tissue of differences."[31] The play of *différance* does not indeed privilege any "meaning," or hence any term of the *différend,* since it falls to *différance* to produce both. The perfect equality of the differed/deferred differences ensues from the universal validity of the *différance* that differs/defers therein. That one can locate *différance* already at work in certain differences mobilized by Hegel, Nietzsche, Freud, and Levinas (and why omit Marx here?) confirms, as an indication, that, not being reducible to any particular concept, it can compel them all the more indifferently insofar as it differs/defers them all—that is, makes them differ among themselves, but also temporizes, in them, the advent of its play. For, as *différance,* it temporizes its own *différance:* it presents (or gives in present being) of itself only its trace.

Différance differs/defers (itself) in its differences. The latter would appear as effects only if the cause could be understood as a prior cause. However, every difference mobilizes, in its substantive, the play that *différance* plays (verbally) therein: the gap that,

---

[30] Ibid., p. 12.
[31] "Ousia et Grammè," in *Marges de la philosophie,* p. 76.

differing/deferring thus, distinguishes difference from *différance*
cannot refer to any cause, any meaning, any essence: every substantive priority would miss by that much the impersonal verbality
(it differs/defers) of which it is a question, exclusively. This other,
which nevertheless offers only a verbal trembling, a silently pro-
fered slipping, and a regulated disturbance, must never, however,
become any*thing* other than what it differs/defers. And this because in differing/deferring it, that other differs/defers itself. Indifference thus commands *différance*, and in two ways, moreover.
As trace: absence of what will never be and never was present,
namely, the other that differs/defers, but not as something; presence nevertheless of that which instantly designates an absence, a
trace that "it differs/defers" here and now without any "other"
presenting itself, nor even being present enough so that one
might thematize its absence. Beyond both absence and presence,
the trace demonstrates the indication of *différance;* an indication
that indicates nothing, a trace of no path, toward no trail, it "produces itself as its own effacement."[32] The trace is defined and
completed in its own disappearance: *différance* manifests itself all
the more insofar as to the question traced by each difference—
"What is it that differs/defers?"—only the impersonal can respond, all the more insofar as the question thus disappears. The
trace thus becomes itself when it no longer marks but the trace of
an anonymity (neither absent nor present): what is proper to the
trace is to reject any principle, any origin, any depth of the text.
"No depth for this bottomless chessboard," because "the trace of
this trace that difference (is) could above all not appear or be
named *as such,* that is, in its presence. It is the *as such* that precisely and as such slips away forever." The undecidable anonymity
of the trace prohibits one from finding for it any other transcendence than that of "a writing without presence and without absence, without history, without cause, without *arché* and without
telos."[33] It is necessary to admit that we have only the trace of
différance, and therefore the vestige of an effacement; now,
" 'there is no name for this': read this proposition in its plati-

---

[32] Respectively, pp. 22, 77, and 78; see also pp. 73–74.
[33] Ibid., p. 28.

tude."[34] The platitude of *différance*, since the trace removes any name for it, disqualifies any identification of it, and finally fills any of its depth. Nothing appropriates *différance* to itself because, as trace, *différance* offers nothing to the least appropriation. The trace therefore marks the platitude of *différance*, which becomes indifferent to names. Hence the indifference of *différance* to that which it differs/defers: as perhaps in the "abyssal thought" of Nietzsche, "it is on the basis of the deployment of this same as *différance* that the sameness of difference announces itself." That the Same should reappear here, when it is nevertheless especially a question of "the other,"[35] would be surprising only if one did not understand the other in its leveled platitude. *Différance* fills its depth in renouncing any "transcendental absolutely" and extends its differing/deferring indifference to the infinite polysemy of differences. Everything, indifferently, is organized in a differing/deferring system (in the sense of desiring machines). In this semantic-less polysemy, no dominance (among others, of a supreme being, or of beings) remains susceptible to privilege, since none of the differences that would render it possible maintains the least surplus over the others. The play of writing differs/defers without truth or falsity: "*Différance* in a certain and very strange way (is) 'older' than the ontological difference or the truth of Being," "difference is perhaps older than Being itself," " 'older' than Being itself, such a difference has no name in our language."[36] Beyond onto-theology and Being/beings (ὄν), difference differs/defers (itself) indifferently (in) their difference, without having to grant it the least privilege, and above all not that which it would refuse to itself. The ontological difference would thus constitute only a particular case of a *différance* that, before and around it, differs/defers in an indefinite, insignificant, and bottomless chassé-croisé. To a regional ontological difference, one must not prefer any more essential instance; one

---

[34] Ibid., pp. 18–19. Perhaps only, for the Eternal Return could not be understood without the will to power, which, in a sense, to be sure, differs by *différance* in evaluating beings, but which, for that very reason, plays the game of an ontological difference. Then, ibid., p. 17, n. 1.

[35] Ibid., respectively, pp. 23, 77, and 28.

[36] Ibid., p. 29.

must only adjoin thereto, in order to surround it, situate it, traverse it, and pass beyond it, the indefinite network of differences
where *différance* differs/defers (from) (itself) without privilege,
priority, or dominance. Being/beings can be located as one of
the possible centers, equal to all the others within the differing/
deferring network, whose indefiniteness can admit, at every point,
another center. To disappropriate the ontological difference of
difference, to reappropriate difference in a perfect indifference
to *différance*.

Thus *différance* seems to offer to distance the traits that distance
claimed to conceptualize of itself: to pass beyond the Being of
beings, not only by inverting the ontological difference, but by
marginalizing it in favor of an "older" difference. But the indifferent leveling exercised by *différance* over the ontological difference does not only play against "that other face of the nostalgia
that I will call Heideggerian *hope*" for the proper word that suits
Being; it claims to undo as well what it already no longer conceives but as "*nostalgia* . . . myth of the purely maternal or purely
paternal language, of the lost fatherland of thought."[37] This
means at the least that the paternal question, in the sense that
anterior distance is finally named the distance of the Father, is
reduced to "nostalgia" and, perhaps more banal, to the nostalgia
for the proper, original and absolute language. In rejecting such
a nostalgia, has one finished with the paternal element of distance? Has one even approached it? Before responding to such a
question, it is first necessary to test the terrain where it is posed:
that of a surpassing of the ontological difference, an enterprise
that, from the beginning, attracts us in the highest degree. Now,
this surpassing that rejects proceeds by a transfer of properties.
Indeed, *différance* begins by inheriting traits that are characteristic
of the ontological difference. It is not by chance if the problematic of the trace arises entirely from a reading, remarkable by the
way, of "The Anaximander Fragment,"[38] where it is the very text
of Heidegger on the trace (of the ontological difference) that is
convoked in order to allow its own disqualification by the same

---

[37] The texts, commented on on pp. 24–29, are found in *Holzwege*, pp. 335, 336,
339–40, and 337.
[38] "La Différance," p. 23.

trace, whose disappearing anonymity could not be attributed to Being/beings. More generally, in having no proper essence or concept or definition, *différance* takes up on its own account the constitutive impossibility of a representation of the ontological difference (see § 17). This transfer is not inconsequential: the ontological difference perhaps finds itself here placed, conveniently enough, in the situation of representation, as an object for thought; also conveniently enough, thought ceases to find therein that which, in the forgetting itself (and its trace) of Being (of beings), governs and anticipates it. Otherwise, how could one say that "the deployment of *différance* is perhaps not only the truth of Being or of the epochality of Being"?[39] This "is . . . not only" presupposes a relation of exteriority and of representation with the Being of being that, far from being permitted by difference, renders it possible, since it frees for it, and in advance, the traits of the ontological difference. The same question can be formulated otherwise. Can one keep the (undoubtedly nonconceptual) terms of *trace, forgetting,* and *difference* outside of the Being of beings where, to begin with, they appear? *Trace* and *forgetting* exercise their respective redoublings and tie their interlacings (forgetting of forgetting, trace of the trace, trace of effacement, etc.) only in a precise place: the Fold of the ὄν, where the obsessive presence of the being-present manifests and marks Being as well; or better, the more Being provokes beings to visibility, the more beings omit it, or invoke it as a being. Only the Fold of Being/beings saves, without any cleverness of thought or virtuosity of style, the possibility of a forgetting, of a trace. Thus both forgetting and the trace belong still to that of which they forget the trace: the Fold. The Fold, in its turn, remains, at the heart of forgetting, only inasmuch as Being and difference, remaining unrepresentable, could disappear, by the very fact that a thought obsessed by being lacks the representation of them. If, on the contrary, one tries to set the trace and forgetting into play outside of the Fold, and hence of ontological difference, what shelter will allow the trace to be valid still as trace at the moment of its effacement? Of what,

---

[39] Heidegger, *Identität,* p. 53 ff. The complete silence of "La Différance" and other texts concerning that of which one nevertheless cannot stop thinking in reading them—*Identity and Difference,* precisely—seems fairly revealing to us.

rather, will the effacement be a trace, now that the effacement of Being in being itself no longer shelters within the Fold? Answer: the effacement of the trace remains the trace of *différance*. But what is the relation of *différance* to the ontological difference? The ontological difference is inscribed, in full equivalence, within an indefinite polysemy of differences: could it be so if one did not first admit that difference is specified in comparable differences, among which is the ontological difference; and then does one not expose oneself to the critical demonstration that *Identität und Differenz* opposed in advance—namely that difference does not precede, like the genus its species, possible differences, among which would be the ontological, but that on the contrary Being/beings "always already" produces difference; in a word, can one differ/defer without and before the Fold of Being/beings?[40] We are, by the transferred attributes of *différance,* led directly to the omitted center, so to speak, as soon as Being/beings there became the object of a representation: outside of the thought of Being/beings in their difference (called ontological), what basis can thought find for itself, including that thought which claims to differ/defer by an autonomous *différance?* In principle, one will respond to this question that *différance* rejects any "natural" basis, as it disperses, within the equivalent isotropy of tropes and of places, any "paternal" site. —In fact, two remarks come to tackle in a roundabout way the "bottomless chessboard" of *différance.* First, *différance* plays with difference, but also with the differing/deferring, the play of the substantive, of the verb, and of the ambivalent present participle; thus it obviously imitates the play of the ὄv, a present participle whose ambiguity conjoins and disjoins at once the verb and the participle. Difference therefore attains the utopic site where it finally transgresses the ontological difference only in reproducing—with a slight double error, we saw— the Fold of the ontological difference: unless one sees there a miraculous coincidence, one would have to acknowledge a paradox. By paradox, I mean an aporia produced by the system itself: rejecting the anteriority or primacy of the ontological difference presupposes nevertheless that one still attribute to the new instance the characteristic spoils of the preceding, or more, that the

---

[40] "La Différance," respectively, pp. 16 and 10.

founding gesture reproduce, no doubt with a slight deviation, the dismissed instance. One could thus ponder the following: *différance* finally subverts the ontological difference only inasmuch as the trace—marking what it does not represent—remains apparently indifferent between them; inasmuch as their "attributes" (trace, forgetting, difference, -ance) also seem equally attributable to one or the other, and finally inasmuch as the nonrepresented *différance* wins out over an objectified ontological difference.

Now, we have seen that the trace could perhaps not be transposed outside of the Fold of the ontological difference, the other "attributes" could perhaps not be either, and finally the ontological difference cannot be represented or objectified. What originality can still ensure for *différance* a nevertheless original indifference? For despite its indifference, *différance* must indeed admit that it is "older" than the ontological difference: is this not again an anteriority comparable to the one that has just been censured? The principal trait that avoids the equivalence of hypotheses concerning the anonymous trace, as concerning the other "attributes," will be that which *différance* does not borrow from the ontological difference; namely, quite obviously, the Saussurian definition of the sign by the chain of differences ("values"). Of that, to be sure, there is not a word in Heidegger, who obstinately thinks language outside of any system. But this contribution itself, far from settling the question in favor of *différance,* renders its status more questionable than ever. The Saussurian definition of the sign rests itself on certain well-delimited presuppositions and decisions: the gap between speech [*parole*] and language [*langue*], the definition of linguistic science on the basis of language as object, the constitution of that object on the basis of a method, the representational interpretation of the signified, etc. To be assured "hypothetically" of these decisions is a point that the injunction to dwell "first within the semiological problematic" reinforces but does not justify.[41] For in the end the Saus-

___

[41] Ibid., p. 6, of which, "And nevertheless, what is thus indicated of *différance* is not theological, not even of the most negative order of negative theology, the latter always being busy trying to disengage, as is known, a superessentiality beyond the finite categories of essence and existence, that is, of presence, and always attentive to recall that if the predicate of existence is refused to God, that

surian discourse on the λόγος must here be justified, inasmuch as it can be situated fairly precisely, within the destiny of metaphysics; for example, as one of the fragments of the dislocation of the λόγος, after the Hegelian excess and completion of the Subject as Absolute: next to Frege and formal logic, as much as Marx and Freud, it fills a defined historical role, whose theoretical strategy can be demonstrated. Hence the recourse to Saussure, far from passing beyond the ontological difference with an unheard of contribution, delivers to the historical destiny that the ontological difference makes possible a new material (a fortiori the recourse to the other "indications," Hegel, Marx, Nietzsche, Freud, calls for the same remark). Without any doubt, the purely taxonomic and differential definition of the sign, like the arbitrary relation between the sign and the thing, constitutes a moment of Enframing, hence of the essence of technology, hence of the historical destiny of metaphysics, hence, in the end, of the ontological difference itself. *Différance,* far from appropriating for itself the attributes of the ontological difference, seems to offer it a new region of interpretation. Far from surpassing the ontological place of the Fold of Being/beings, and far from reducing it to a regional difference, *différance* could indeed offer itself to the ontological difference as a new ontic regionality waiting to be situated. Along with *différance,* which works in them in its way, linguistics, semiotics, and logistics would also await such a situation.

---

is in order to grant Him a superior, inconceivable, and ineffable mode of Being." What is meant by "as is known" here? We have seen that, precisely, the so-called negative theology, at bottom, does not aim to reestablish a "super-essentiality," since it aims neither at predication nor at Being; how, a fortiori, could it be a question of existence and of essence in Denys, when he still speaks a Greek original enough not to have either the idea or the use of them? Further on, the sequence "*Différance* is not only irreducible to any ontological or theological—onto-theological—reappropriation—but, even opening the space in which onto-theology—philosophy—produces its system and its history, it comprehends it, inscribes it, and exceeds it without return" explicitly misses an astonishing equivalence among theology, onto-theology and philosophy. These identifications had, moreover, to intervene, so that *différance* not risk being outflanked by the Unthinkable. But then it is necessary to pay for that security with an idolatry borrowed fundamentally from the ontological difference: namely, that God can be conceived only in it, as a supreme being. The quick and brutal liquidation of what one registers polemically under the name of "negative theology" has no other function than to secure *différance* from the rear, against a nonidolatrous (nonontological) face of God. Perhaps E. Levinas remains, here at least, outside the reach of J. Derrida.

One perhaps escapes the ontological difference as little through *différance* as through the Other. It remains that *différance* coincided with the ontological difference on one point, against the thought of the Other as a recourse beyond the Neuter. What J. Derrida rejects, under the name of "Heideggerian hope," is that, within language, Being might paternally regulate, situate, and measure that which differs/defers. *Différance* must break with Being in order to differ/defer in full equivalence and indifference. One therefore rejects the privilege of an ontological difference inasmuch as the Father is thus outlined in it. To eliminate any paternal site, it is necessary to reject the ontological difference. In strictly Heideggerian terms, we saw that it is perhaps the ontological difference and the onto-theological constitution that reject the freedom of God over against Being. The refusal of the ontological difference in the one case, and its assertion in the other, aim at the same goal: to reduce to the Neuter, to neutralize the distant irruption of the Father. Whence a new equivalence, this one strategic, between *différance* and the ontological difference, as opposed to the unconditional recognition of the Other (distance, in Levinas's sense). —However, this alliance in favor of the Neuter rests on a compromise: the ontological difference requires "God" to pass by way of Being, because it thinks "God" as a being; it thinks him, therefore, again under an idolatrous condition. *Différance*, to the contrary, in neutralizing Being/beings, neutralizes the ontological Neuter itself, and neutralizes it in the second degree. It therefore eliminates the thought of the "God" being. But all theology as well finds itself assimilated to onto-theology. Even more precisely (with a remarkable correctness, in fact, one does not fail to pass through this obligatory place), "negative theology" finds itself, by a surprising *coup de force*, reintegrated within onto-theology.[42] It then becomes easy and logical to eliminate any other God, since onto-theology here exhausts all theology. The onto-theological Neuter thinks the ontological idol "God" (and even awaits his nonmetaphysical face).

---

[42] "Temps et être," in *Questions* IV, pp. 18–19 = "Zeit und Sein," in *L'Endurance de la pensée*, p. 22 ff. See, for commentary, *Questions* IV, pp. 63, 71–74, 300. Of course, the analysis of "*es gibt*" appears well before, parallel to the ontological difference, before relieving it, thus in "La Thèse de Kant," in *Questions* II, p. 115 = *Wegmarken*, p. 306, and *Unterwegs zur Sprache*, pp. 194 and 253.

The differing/deferring Neuter eliminates, beyond that idol, any other advent of God (with or without quotation marks). The alliance of the Neuters is undone therefore for a new strategic intention: *différance* rejects any God/"God," in face of the "God" of the ontological difference and of the ontic primacy of the Other (E. Levinas). But precisely, that intention provokes an immediate and ultimate reversal of the alliances: *différance* rejects any idol (even if, eliminating in advance a beyond or a this side of idolatry, it remains negatively), just as the Other claims to pass outside of the (idolatrous) neutrality of ontology. On the contrary, ontological difference indeed admits "God," but only under the idolatrous figure of him given by onto-theology, indeed, the condition of Being. The "Greek" primacy of Being suffers the double and disconcerted assault of an unequally "Jewish" speech. This new alliance must not dissimulate the fact that in a sense *différance* goes farther than the request of the Other: the latter, we saw, inverts the primacy of the ontological difference in favor of being, and it remains inscribed in that difference, even if, obliquely, the being-Other attempts to remove itself therefrom. A residual idolatry still affects the Other. On the contrary, *différance* eliminates that residue in attempting to pass beyond the ontological difference as such. It still remains idolatrous itself, no doubt, but negatively, in rejecting under the vague term "negative theology" the possibility of any non-onto-theological theology. Derrida's path therefore leads us further forward, certainly not in the way of an answer, but in the seriousness of the question. But it is in these questions first that the seriousness of thought is experienced.

Our question was formulated, let us recall, as follows: what theoretical rigor can one grant to distance? To begin, it was suitable to put it into relation with the ontological difference (Heidegger). The idolatrous function of the ontological difference, but also of what its overcoming left possible, prohibited finding in it the very rigor of distance—whence two attempts to, in aiming at distance, critique and "surpass" the ontological difference. First, if we might put it thus, "vertically," in favor of a being, no longer supreme, but Other. Then, "horizontally," in favor of an "older" *différance* that enframes it, situates it, and exceeds it. These two advances instruct us as much by their aporias, restrictions, and obstacles as by their appearance of critique or their conquering rigor. There issues from these, in fact, two lessons. First, that one does not leave ontological difference in contesting it, no more than one makes the step "outside" of metaphysics in "overcoming" it—in the one case the ontological difference is inverted (and not overthrown), and in the other generalized (at the risk of being banalized). Thus one remains all the more inscribed within the ontological difference insofar as one travels through it and pulls it in every direction. Next, and for this very reason, neither *différance* nor the Other avoids the onto-theological idolatry, since *différance* sees in it the only "God" possible (negative idolatry), whereas the Other does not entirely withdraw from it the privileged being (residual idolatry). We have therefore not progressed at all since the paradox expressed before this journey: how, without claiming another site than the Being that conciliates beings (with itself), not to conceive God idolatrously as a being, even supreme? Unless we have better understood that one can neither dissolve nor overcome this paradox; distance would have nothing other to think than this paradox, but it alone could confront it. It would have as its task to think how we have a site in Being as not having our site. We? At least those who recognize first that God has a site in Being as not having his site. The formulation of the question, precisely because it attains the rigor of a paradox, fixes the constitutive term of that which it would be necessary to understand precisely not as a solution (for the solution dissolves the question, instead of responding to it with an appropriate word): "that those who use/maintain (χρώμενοι; τὸ χρέων, *der Brauch*) the world, (that they maintain it) as (ὡς) not maintaining it; for the figure of this world is passing away" (1 Corinthians 7:31). Would distance overcome the ontological difference and the Being that is figured metaphysically in it, hence also their idol, not by leaving it, critiquing or inverting it, but by remaining in it—as not remaining in it?

§ 19. THE FOURTH DIMENSION

To pursue distance, we took difference into view, along with its results and theory. Not having progressed thus by one step toward distance, we are looking for a certain position toward the ontological difference that does not claim in illusory fashion to withdraw everything from that difference, but that, restraining us, allows this result (*re-saltare:* to rebound) to accede, through it but outside it, to distance. Now, the impossibility noted up to here indicates to us how to progress. If difference has not yet allowed any result, this is perhaps because the ontological difference constitutes only the last word of the question that it nevertheless opens. The ontological difference is comprehended, at least *for us* who have to conquer it through a "destruction of ontology," within the metaphysics that is produced by its forgetting and that remains tied to it. Thus, the thought that attempts to think Being in its essence ends up leaving aside the ontological difference as such, in order to take up its stakes under the other formulation of the *gift.* Or rather of the *es gibt,* which we translate—or rather do not translate—by an *il y a,* where there lacks precisely the connotation of the *Geben,* of the *giving:* it would be necessary to transpose, and to ask, before a given, or a datum (for a problem, a question, an enterprise) how that given is given, and above all whether its character as a given has any relation with its manner of Being the particular being it is. One can undoubtedly hear in this "There is (a given)" only its tangible product—presence, which is achieved in a particular—present—being. But then, in fact, one misses that as which the being-present offers itself to presence, that is, its arrival in presence. More essential to the present than its presence seems to be the gift of the present, or better the present that makes a present of itself. If present indicates, besides the being that mutely imposes itself, the very movement of presenting itself, hence of giving itself as a present, it is necessary to understand the being itself starting from this gift, which becomes possible only by first hearing, in the "There is (a given)," the giving arrival. Hence,

> Now it is a question of thinking properly this letting-be-deployed-in-presence (*Anwesenlassen*), that is, the measure in which place is given to the deployment in presence (*Anwesen*). To give place, i.e., *to let be* the deployment of Being, makes that which is proper to it appear, in that it carries it to the non-withdrawal. To let be the deployment in presence means: to free from the withdrawal, to carry into the Open. In "free from the withdrawal" there plays a

giving (*Geben*), that, to tell the truth, in the *letting*-Being-deploy-it-self, gives the deployment, that is, Being.[43]

It is a question of meditating not *what* there is but that there is a "There is" that gives what there is only as, precisely, a given that it abandons; one would be rid of this given a bit quickly in noting that it could have not been given, for thus one lowers the abandon of *letting be* to a contingency; and moreover, in fact, the given is given. It remains therefore to experience it as given precisely in that it is given, as nonavailable precisely in that it is nevertheless available in our familiarity. To receive the given as given amounts finally to receiving the *giving* as the manner of the given, no longer only as the origin or the ontic event of its presence: more than a matter, the given is registered as a manner of Being—as the manner of Being. Even massively secured in its ontic presence, the given lets tremble (or vibrate) over it the *giving* that, alone, lets it be. Through the giving, Being befalls being as the abandonment or the letting that abandons or gives it to itself. In this very withdrawal, it manifests its donation. To conceive the present not as a presence but as a gift through which there does not cease to pass donation, which, in letting it be, accords Being as an abandonment or as a releasement. It remains therefore to think the gift.

> The lecture titled "Time and Being" questions from the beginning concerning that which is proper to Being. It is revealed there that Being as well as time *are not*. It is in this measure alone that the step might be won in the direction of the *there is*. The *There is* (*Es gibt*) is commented on first in the perspective of the giving (*das Geben*), then in the perspective of the *It* (*Es*) that there is, that gives. This *It* is interpreted as the event (*das Ereignis*).[44]

It remains to follow the scheme thus proposed. Here, the *giving*, which man first perceives according to donation (*Gabe*): without that donation, man could not accede to his essence: "If man were not constantly the one who receives the donation (*Gabe*) coming

---

[43] *Questions* IV, p. 55, see p. 300, which comments on "Temps et être," p. 18 = *L'Endurance*, pp. 22–23.

[44] "Temps et être," respectively pp. 29–30 = *L'Endurance*, pp. 40–41 (see *Wegmarken*, p. 106 = *Questions* II, p. 82, "La Faveur de l'être"), p. 19 = pp. 24–25; p. 23 = pp. 30–31; p. 26 = pp. 34–35; p. 31 = p. 42.

from the presence of the *there is,* in watching out for what appears in the letting-the-deployment-advance (*Anwesenlassen*) . . . man would remain excluded from the reign of the: *there is Being.* Man would not be man." This means not only that donation befalls man as that which qualifies him, but above all that, in donation, it is necessary to be watchful, more than for the given donation (the gift), for the donation that gives, that is for the *Geben.* The thought that thinks in the metaphysical mode busies itself with freeing up being for itself, and how could it avoid doing so, when it thinks through representation, and Being is not representable because to begin with Being *is not?* To the contrary, the thought that regresses from metaphysics in passing beyond the ontological difference applies itself to maintaining donation within the donating gesture itself, without the latter ever withdrawing itself, like a tide that withdraws from a shore and leaves dead what it abandons there:

> The giving that plays in withdrawal within the very freeing of the withdrawal. Being, as the donation of this There is, belongs to the giving (*Geben*). Being as donation is not pushed outside of the giving: thus Being as deploying-itself-in-presence (*Anwesen*) finds itself transformed. As deploying-in-presence, it belongs (to be sure) to the freeing outside of the withdrawal, all the while remaining (nevertheless) maintained as the donation of the latter in the giving.

To think donation always within the giving is undoubtedly to pass beyond the ontological difference and the forgetting adjoined to it, since "at the beginning of Western thought, Being is indeed thought, but not the *there is* as such. The latter withdraws in favor of the donation (*Gabe*) that there is, a donation that, in the future, will be thought, and thus conceived, exclusively as Being with a view toward beings." Metaphysics masks the giving, obsessed as it is by the donation of present beings. Only a correct understanding of the *giving* would allow one to complete the ontological difference, but also to undo oneself from its forgetting; but that understanding requires pushing the paradox of a reciprocal belonging where, nevertheless, giving and donation do not cease to detach themselves from one another, through a detachment governed all the more by the hold of the giving over donation. Heidegger inscribes this paradox, a first time here, in black and white: "That which is appropriated properly to Being, that to which it belongs and where it remains held back (*einbehalten*) is shown in the *there is* (a given) and in its *giving* understood as destining (*Schicken*)." Being never attains its own inalienable property better than in that which properly returns to it—giving, in the *there is,* being as a donation. In this gesture, Being at once departs from itself, in a donation that obfuscates it at the risk of maintaining itself (metaphysically) outside of the giving, and imparts to itself a withdrawal, in vulgar terms an absence, that signals it perfectly to itself; as gift, Being departs from donation, and this departure belongs to it as the most proper part that it could ever impart to itself. The departure of the giving in donation must become for us what is most proper to impart to Being. To impart to the giving the gift, precisely because it does not cease to depart from it: for such a partition—letting-be-in-presence without advancing itself in the presence thus left or abandoned— characterizes the *giving* of Being in that which it most properly possesses. On this condition, donation will no longer be confused with the being that is thought in forgetfulness of its Being, as a present being. Through the play that shares out [*répartit*] that which imparts itself and that which departs, donation is illuminated by a double thrusted presence: for assuming that "every presence (*Anwesen, an-wesen, proe-s-ence*) is not necessarily the objectified presence of a being represented as present now (*Gegenwart*),"[45] donation can refer ceaselessly to that which continually gives it—the *giving*—without ever presenting it otherwise to thought than in its unrepresentable and undeniable absence, or better, withdrawal. Now, it is this very withdrawal that does not cease to befall us as a destiny. But, as to the *giving* that operates

---

[45] Ibid., respectively, p. 36 = pp. 50–51: "The danger grows that with this naming of the It, we arbitrarily enter into play some undetermined power whose task would be to put into operation the donation of Being and of Time"; p. 41 = pp. 56–57: "without being mindful of it, we have represented it (i.e., the It) as something present, while we nevertheless attempt to think the Being of presence as such"; and p. 37 = pp. 52–53, to which one might compare the "Letter on Humanism": "*there is Being: 'es gibt' das Sein.* This 'there is' does not translate exactly *es gibt.* For the *es* (it) that here *gibt* (gives) is Being itself," in *Wegmarken,* p. 165. It is undoubtedly necessary to ponder here the identification of the *Es* by *Sein,* or rather it would be necessary to assess the fact that this identification does not allow one to name the *Es* any more than it is possible to *name* Being.

in the *There is* (a given), does it not admit a verbal subject and, thereby, a first instance that would take upon itself, on its own basis, to effect causally the gift of a donation? It is necessary here not to yield to the illusions of grammar, a science about which one knows that it was constituted only after, and on the basis of, the metaphysical deployment of Greek thought. The *It*, indeed, does not name any "indeterminate power," since it is no more a question here of power (*Macht*) than of making (*machen*) something, but indeed of giving the donation of a given. Nor is it a question of a "something represented as present," since the donation must remain in a definitively nonpresent *giving*. No doubt more legitimately, once the quadruple dimension of time is taken into view as "porrection" (*Reichen*), one can suppose that time interferes with the Open of Being, in a word, that perhaps "true Time appears as the *It* that we name in saying: *There is* [*Il y a, Es gibt*] Being." However, the *It/Il* of the *there is/Il y a* (a given) remains indeterminate, since Time itself befalls us only as another of the donations of the *giving* (unless this is the same as Being). The "porrection" of Time indeed convenes with the destination of Being starting from the sole *There is/Il y a:* the *It* (*Il, Es*) therefore remains totally "indeterminate, enigmatic."[46] It would therefore be time to transform, if not the question—how do things stand with the *It/Il?*—at least the means by which we might correspond to it. We were seeking, indeed, a grammatically identifiable "subject"; it remains to be known whether the grammatical injunction must count as law, and whether it is not necessary to recognize here one of the "impersonal or subject-less sentences."[47] Through

---

[46] *Questions* IV, pp. 72–74, see the long parenthesis from the lecture, ibid., p. 38 ff. = p. 52 ff.

[47] *Temps et Etre*, p. 39 = pp. 54–55. The absence, which only advances, confirms the *giving* in anonymity, in the sense at least that names characterize beings (according to the language of the representation of objects). But the *giving* nevertheless does not lose its property (Being), as J. Derrida attempts to indicate (see § 18), in order to become différance: for the impossibility of representing it, its anonymity, then, properly characterizes the withdrawal of Being, as *giving*. That a withdrawal arrives, it is not sufficient to register it as *différance* in order that one not still be able to ask: "What is this withdrawal? (or *différance?*)"; or better: "From where can this withdrawal with neither name nor property arrive, and how can it always already *be there?*" Or rather, the effacement of the trace still demands a status and an origin anterior to the indifferent equivalence of the origins that it seems to authorize.

this grammatical disengagement, it becomes possible again to think the definitive anonymity of the *giving*, an anonymity that precedes, announces, and governs it. What would an identity of the *It/Il* signify, when the *It/Il* announces that donation still inhabits with its presence a giving that, by definition (we mean to say that it is in this way that it defines the presence of donation), absents itself therefrom: "The *It* names . . . an advancing of absence, *ein Anwesen von Abwesen*."[48] The anonymity of the *It* concentrates in a grammatical function that itself which gives itself to be thought in the *There is/Il y a* (a given)—the obsessive withdrawal of the giving in donation.

Withdrawal? To arrive at this withdrawal, it is necessary to recall that the indeterminate anonymity of the *They* finally finds its place (but not its name) in that whose intersection it assures: there is— Being, and there is—Time; Being, as destining (*Geschick*), hence *giving*, and Time as the quadri-dimensional, hence as "porrection" (*Reichen*), intersect or match one another (including in the detective sense of the term: they each say a lot about the other) in the same *It/Il*, which would be equivalent *both* with Being *and* with Time, as of Time *and* Being. The play of the *and* rejoins that of the *It/Il*, "as a result of which the *It* that gives in the *es gibt Being, es gibt Time*, is attested as *Ereignis*."[49] Our aim here cannot be to theorize or to elucidate what Heidegger means by *Ereignis*— supposing that such an enterprise would make any sense. We will limit ourselves to underlining one of its traits, namely, the apprehension of what the *Ereignis* gives to be comprehended. In fact, outside the appropriation of man to it, the *Ereignis* admits another singular property, withdrawal (*Entzug*). This withdrawal already governed the economy of the *giving* (we saw above); here, it plays explicitly: "The destining in the destiny of Being was characterized as a giving wherein that which destines is itself suspended, and, in that suspension (*Ansichhalten*), withdraws from disclosure."[50] The *giving*, in the manner of which *there is*, delivers and gives the given in donation—being—only by not giving itself

---

[48] Ibid., pp. 40–41 = pp. 56–57.

[49] Ibid., pp. 43–45 = pp. 62–63 and 64–65, which one could supplement with p. 23 = pp. 30–31; p. 26 = pp. 34–35; etc.

[50] Ibid., pp. 43–45 = pp. 62–63 and 64–65, which one could supplement with p. 23 = pp. 30–31; p. 26 = pp. 34–35; etc.

therein: only thus, far from losing itself as a being, does it preserve itself as Being; in this way, then, preserved as Being, abandoning its gifts, it can fill man with its withdrawal. Each of the three dimensions of time, thought "authentically," is taken up within the fourth, which, far from counting among the others, opens to them the "approaching proximity" (the *Nahheit*) where they can deploy their play. The "porrection" (*Reichen*) that thus extends itself and strains itself in order to present time to its essence is neither present, nor past, nor future, all the while manifesting itself each time as the reserve that renders present, past, and future possible: "Reserve and restraint (*Verweigerung* and *Vorenthalt*) show the same trait as the suspension in destiny: namely, self-withdrawal (*Sichentziehen*)."[51] Time and Being withdraw themselves from that which they thus make possible in the "porrection" and the *giving*. But, one will ask, what could be more foreseeable and natural than their forgetting by metaphysics in favor of the present and of the being, which themselves do not withdraw at all, but do not cease obviously to arrive? How to envisage another destiny for thought, than the forgetting of that very thing which makes itself forgotten through the withdrawal? How would the withdrawal that removes itself not provoke its removal? Being and Time, destiny and "porrection," withdraw in concert because the *Ereignis* appropriates them one to the other. It is therefore to the *Ereignis* that, finally, the questioning must be addressed: retiring, does the *Ereignis* not expose itself by full right to a placement in withdrawal, which metaphysics would accomplish without failing, but, on the contrary, in accomplishing what the anonymity of the trace and the continuous withdrawal of the *Ereignis* allow—or even call for? The inverse alone is correct: it is necessary precisely not to remove this withdrawal, since it is it alone that properly characterizes the *Ereignis:* "In the measure, however, that the ways of *giving* determined by it (destining and 'porrection') rest in the movement of making befall itself in its propriety (*Ereignen*), it is necessary that the withdrawal (*Entzug*) belong to what is proper to the *Ereignis*," "to the *Ereignis* as such belongs disappropriation (*Enteignung*). Through it, the *Ereignis*

---

[51] Ibid., pp. 43–45 = pp. 62–63 and 64–65, which one could supplement with p. 23 = pp. 30–31; p. 26 = pp. 34–35; etc.

does not abandon itself, but on the contrary safeguards what is proper to it."[52] This is how, generally, the paradox is expressed in which Heidegger's approach perhaps culminates. The *Ereignis,* as that which is appropriated in it, Time and Being, withdraws from what it prepares and ensures: it enters into withdrawal all the more that beings and presence enter into view and visibility. Metaphysics, quite naturally, concludes from this that the anonymous can be abandoned to anonymity, difference to *différance,* the trace to the effacement that it traces of itself; nothing would any longer be suitable, nothing would any longer be appropriate to the withdrawal of the *Ereignis,* if, precisely, the *Ereignis* never attained its property as much as in this very withdrawal. The whole property of the *Ereignis* consists in giving the proper: to give the proper, where Being and Time accede to their own property, respectively, destining and "porrection"; or again to give the proper where Being and Time accede to their reciprocal appropriation in the *Il* (*y a*) that properly proposes and disposes them each in their unique correctness; to give the proper, finally, where Being and Time appropriate being to its essence, that is, by maintaining donation in the immobile and frozen trembling of the *giving.* In short, the property of the *Ereignis* culminates in the property that it ensures and gives (or abandons). To itself the property of the *Ereignis* appropriates nothing (that an abandon or a withdrawal would lose), but appropriates to itself that which, only then, can become other than it, Being, Time, beings. The *Ereignis* attains its property in disappropriating itself in order thus to appropriate to itself that which there finds what is proper to it. Far from the withdrawal deciding its absence, and confirming its anonymity, it manifests its insistent, silent, overabundant, and humble advance. The withdrawal presides over the advance, and coincides with it, because no advance other than appropriation is suitable, and because the appropriation appropriates nothing to itself except to let each "thing" reach what is proper to it. If we do not conceive this coincidence, that is because, metaphysically, we see only being, or rather we see only being as the sole property, that is, we conceive being as the appropriation of a foundation, because,

---

[52] Ibid., pp. 43–45 = pp. 62–63 and 64–65, which one could supplement with p. 23 = pp. 30–31; p. 26 = pp. 34–35; etc.

more intimately, we understand property not as access to the proper, but as the assumption of a function. This, moreover, is why we appropriate being to ourselves in representing it to ourselves as object. And, to be sure, for the representation that takes possession, the *Ereignis* remains absent, anonymous, and vain, since all representation fails in face of it. But is not claiming to represent the *Ereignis* already to miss what is proper to it, and, thereby, to miss what is proper to us? Hence the *Ereignis,* which in this completes and passes beyond the ontological difference, never reaches what is proper to itself as much as in disappropriating itself, since it is in this way that it makes "something else" reach what is proper to it. The *Ereignis,* in abandon, ensures the *giving,* and in the *giving* gives it to be thought. Its "absence" covers over its highest "presence," its withdrawal coincides with its proximity—since only that withdrawal ensures us of reaching the "approaching proximity, *Nahheit.*"

Evidently, we rediscover something like a formation of distance. Two ways of proceeding propose themselves here, which are as hastily thinkable as they are quickly expressible. On the one hand, one can say that, if similar formulations intervene for themes as distinct as the trinitarian relation of the Son to the Father in the Spirit (or, what amounts to the same, the relation of divinization) and the *Ereignis* (as the truth of ontological difference), they prove thereby a lack of rigor in their definition; "distance" remains an equivocal concept, which, too loose to characterize a precise object, is for that very reason suitable to several. But we have said that here "object" and "definition" could not intervene, since with the *Ereignis* it is a question of that on the basis of which all knowledge is defined, and since with the distance of Goodness it is a question of an absolute paternal anteriority; the critique has lost its object as soon as it has believed itself able to exert itself on an "object." Or else, on the other hand, one can say that the correspondence of the formulations establishes the identity of the *Ereignis* and paternal distance; that is, creation corresponds to donation (*Gabe,* being), and the Father exercises (as *Es, Ereignis*) the *giving* (*Geben,* Being). But setting aside the expeditious triviality of this approach, which recuperates as abusively as it idolizes naively, one forgets that the *It* could be identified neither with a "something" (present being)

nor with an "indeterminate power," nor even with Being
(whether subsisting or not). Between these two ways, which
should one choose? But first, is it necessary to choose one? It is
indeed a question of putting into a certain relation distance and
the appropriated withdrawal of the *giving*. Instead of choosing
between abusive identification and logicistic antagonism, would it
not be suitable to establish a more measured relation—measured
according to that which it is a question of thinking? Could one
not make distance (and the appropriated withdrawal) play with
regard to and between distance and the appropriated withdrawal?
One would then say—one would then risk saying—that distance
maintains with the *Geben* (appropriated withdrawal, *Ereignis*) a relation in which the more the irreducibility is marked between a
radically theological thinking and a thinking that aims at Being
as Being, the more their reciprocal suitability grows. Between distance and the *Ereignis* there intervenes no similitude, nor any dis-
similitude either, since no directly measurable relation joins
them; but an indirect relation is established: the *Ereignis* enters
into distance from distance. It is no more opposed to distance
than it is composed with it; it is disposed over against it in the
intimate alterity and separated communion that distance mobilizes. It is therefore a question neither of an identification nor of
an analogy in the current sense of the term. For if one said, for
example, that the relation of the *Ereignis* serves as *analogon* to the
trinitarian relation, that *analogon* would still remain to be measured, and it would hence expose itself to all the extreme varia-
tions one might wish, oscillating between extrinsic equivocity and
brutal univocity. Here, the relation of analogy that (dis-)joins the
appropriated withdrawal of the *Ereignis* and distance does not rest
indeterminate, precisely because it is inscribed within the terms
that it (dis-)joins—namely, as distance. Distance, beyond the filial
adoption that straightforwardly receives the believer, approaches
us doubly: in the experience of that which, in the *Ereignis*, reveals
itself as a withdrawal that appropriates in disappropriating itself,
of course, but also in the patiently acquired measure of its
(dis-)similitude with paternal distance. This double movement
alone allows one to avoid two pitfalls, all the more dangerous in
that they seem crude.

  First, idolatry: if distance finds itself placed in unmeasured relation (theologically), it is exposed to an identification with a particular instance (the appropriated withdrawal of the *Ereignis*) that, not drawing on metaphysics, pertains only that much more to Being (as Being) and therefore exposes itself to a new idolatry: in the best of cases, it would be a question of Saint Thomas, in the most current and worst of cases, a question of "Christian philosophies," whether explicit or ashamed. It is suitable then that distance should invest and measure the *analogon* that distance maintains with the appropriated withdrawal. Next, indecent theologization: so often rejected by Heidegger, it would risk, as the victor vanquished by its victim, seeing its analogue take possession of the relation of analogy; for why would the appropriated withdrawal of the *Ereignis* not recognize in the relation of analogy that which is appropriated to itself only on the basis of that withdrawal? The way in which, with Thomist commentators and others, particularly with Cajetan and Suarez, the theological analogy (coming originally from the *Divine Names* of Denys) was little by little reduced to a particular case of a whole, radically nontheological, theory of analogy should serve as sufficient warning; it would not have taken the incomparably powerful modern conceptualizations (Hegel, or formal logic) long to formalize, dialectize, or reject the relation between distance and appropriated withdrawal, if distance were not redoubled so as to invest and measure it. It remains to be known whether distance itself can manage this, or rather, since there is no doubt about that, whether we have known how to think it powerfully enough—concerning which, obviously, doubt is permitted: hence, redoubled distance sets the appropriated withdrawal at a distance from distance.

Can one, if not justify this placement in distance (according to what norm?), at least give an exposition of it? One undoubtedly risks expositing badly that which exposes itself to too much risk. Let us attempt, nevertheless, an outline. —The relation between the appropriated withdrawal and distance can be developed on the basis of the preceding analysis (*Entzug*, withdrawal), in four moments: (a) Just as distance gives rise to a discourse of praise that forbids all predication concerning the *Requisite* by requestants, but lets a language come to the latter as a gift from the Former, so the appropriated withdrawal disqualifies all representation and definition, since it is it that renders them possible, in their metaphysical erring itself: *lack of definition.* (b) Distance withdraws from the knowledge that would comprehend it, and hence claim the right to speak concerning the *Requisite,* only in that the requestant finds himself already comprehended in a filial manner within its paternal anteriority; in the same manner, the appropriated withdrawal ensuring each "thing" of reaching that which is most intimately proper to it, in the congress of Being and Time, prepares to begin with all destining, and hence all history, and it passes beyond any comprehension that it would render possible and thinkable: *anteriority.* (c) The meditation on the congress of Being and Time leads one to comprehend Time no longer as tri-dimensional (past, present, future) but indeed as quadri-dimensional; Heidegger names this fourth dimension, which brings together and redefines the first three, *Reichen,* which is translated (by F. Fédier) as "porrection," that is, extending in order to present, where it is necessary to understand a gift that abandons that which it gives in withdrawing, that is, a gift that maintains an opening where moments and beings can advance themselves; "porrection" gives the dimension of time (the anterior gap, which allows space as much as delay): it plays as a "porrection that under-takes (*an-fangende*)."[53] "Porrection" not only takes the initiative, at the beginning, but renders possible that which it does not cease thus to take up again at every moment and in every being. It is therefore very little to say of the fourth dimension that it prevails over the others: it is necessary to conceive that it alone puts in place, measures (in the sense that one measures out to someone a sentiment, an honor, etc., that is, that one imparts and gives it to someone), and opens the dimension where the three others are articulated. The "enter-prising porrection" is thus made, in the name of the *Ereignis,* anterior and withdrawn, paternal. —Distance, on its side, can admit four dimensions, or rather four differences, the fourth bringing together the three others in order to make them permanent. If one here follows H. Urs von Balthasar,[54] one notes that distance must also pass beyond and bring together the terms of a "vulgar con-

---

[53] Ibid., p. 34 = pp. 46–47.

[54] *Herrlichkeit,* III/1, *Im Raum der Metaphysik* (Einsiedeln: Johannes Verlag, 1965), and particularly "Der Wunder des Seins und die Vierfache Differenz," pp. 943–56.

cept," that of creation. Commonly, one mobilizes for its benefit three differences; in the space of a world I find myself as a being, without cause—difference between a being and the world; being enters into difference from Being, without being able to ever attain it—ontological difference; finally, Being does not answer for the distinctive characteristics of each being—difference between Being and essence (*Wesen*). Up to here, we did not go any further than a series of metaphysical questions (and perhaps their Thomistic style). The fourth dimension, rarely appropriated to theological distance, appears when one asks about "the highest difference, that between God and the Being of beings."[55] The fourth difference, between God and Being, puts the other differences in place, because to begin with it gives rise to the (unextended, nonspatial) space where these differences, including the ontological difference, become imaginable. The fourth dimension, the last, is always the first. It is a question in fact of distance itself, such as it passes beyond every possible idol, and exercises itself as the distance of Goodness. *Fourth dimension.* (d) The *Ereignis* lets itself be characterized, in that which is most proper to it, as a withdrawal that nevertheless does not cease to appropriate in disappropriating itself, or again as a *giving* that, at the same time, withdraws from its donation and displays itself with insistence in this very withdrawal. Distance plays equally upon a withdrawal in which requestants not only experience the absence of the *Requisite* but above all discover, in the absence that abandons them, the *Requisite* that gives and gives itself. Given that the *Ereignis* and God are all the less to be confused insofar as neither the one nor the other *is* in the manner of beings, one can avoid the parallel. The differences and the *Ereignis* "become useable in an obediential fashion for the revelation of God":[56] there is an affinity between

---

[55] Ibid., p. 961. Note 4 of the section mentioned speaks of "God as the sole foundation / sufficient reason (*zureichende Grund*) of Being as well as of being" (p. 954). The repeated mention of God or of the theological instance under the title of *Grund* (pp. 963, 965, 975, 982, etc.) feeds the suspicion of a forceful return of the metaphysical question par excellence, and hence also of the idolatry that attaches to it. However, the very interpretation of the "foundation" thus acquired in God as a kenosis, a gift, and a withdrawal, seems to refer back to the figure of the Father too clearly for such a massive parologism to remain likely. This suspicion confirms us, nevertheless, in the recourse to an iconic relation (governed by distance) between distance and the *Ereignis*.

[56] Ibid.

the nevertheless appropriated withdrawal of the *Ereignis* and the unrestrained gift where God at one and the same time abandons the world by withdrawing from it, and, in this intimate withdrawal, manifestly abandons to the world its trinitarian basis: "The non-subsistence of the Being-Act is for God the adequate *medium* of creation, in order to produce therein and to profer the kenotic word of cross and glory, and to send and introduce it therein, as his Son, in the death and resurrection."[57] The *Ereignis* can therefore be understood in two ways, neither unifiable nor contradictory, nor competing: as such, the last word of Being, and as *medium* or *analogon* of the trinitarian play (the gift of creation referring back to and growing deeper in the original filiation). Let us remark that we have not ceased here, in freeing up the point of view of (and on) the Christ, to practice this double reading, as much in the cases of Nietzsche and Hölderlin as in the case, of course, of Denys. To free up this point of view, in order to take it, therefore did not presuppose any "critique," nor any "recuperation," but only the relation of double reading that it remains for us to define. Before going further, let us register the last encounter: the *paternal withdrawal*. These four characteristics conjoin the appropriated withdrawal of the *Ereignis* and distance. The last among them already forces us to speak about it, or to think more about it, that is, to determine the nature of this conjunction.

We have already seen that this conjunction could not be reduced either to an assimilation or to a structural parallel. More, we posited that the conjunction between the appropriated withdrawal and distance would be suitable to that of which it is a question only if it understood itself on the basis of distance—a redoubled distance, then, which presupposes the placement in distance between distance and the appropriated withdrawal. Starting from what point of view can this placement in distance be effected? Starting from distance itself, no doubt. Thus the same effort of thought would have to establish for us both distance and its redoubling. Now, to attain distance becomes possible, we saw, only in praising the *Requisite*, hence in receiving distance in order to render it all thanks. The only ones who manage this, the apos-

---

[57] Ibid.

tle Paul says, are those who are "rooted and founded in charity": if we are so, then we will have "the strength to conceive with all the saints the breadth, height, and depth" of knowing the ἀγάπη of the Christ, which "surpasses all knowledge" (Ephesians 3:18–19). We have conceived the ontological difference in its "breadth" (Being/being); then we attempted to conceive its overcoming through "height" (the Other), or through "length" (*différance*). No other dimension, it seemed, remained open to our approach. However, the Apostle mentions a "depth," which is obviously unthinkable according to the intuitive space that admits only three dimensions. It is therefore necessary to think this dimension, without place and without measure, according to another instance than space. Which one? The text answers clearly: charity; from the point of view of charity, a point of view that one can take only by establishing oneself in it and by taking root in it; taking a point of view here means conquering a belvedere, taking root here means digging out one's foundations. From the point of view of charity, therefore, a fourth dimension, in fact the first, is discovered, because, undoubtedly, it is charity in person that delivers it and delivers itself in it: "depth" (βάθος), inexhaustible, unfathomable, secret. This "depth" offers the inconceivable knowledge of that very thing from which it issues: depth, which appears only from the point of view of charity, makes charity alone appear (beyond all knowledge). "Depth" issues from charity and refers back to it—a traverse that signals toward distance. Like distance, "depth" aims at no other performance than, as ἀγάπη of the Christ (filial charity), to lead one back and introduce one into the "fullness of God" (paternal charity; Ephesians 3:19): for precisely, "the fullness of the [paternal] divinity," if one receives and conceives it on the basis of distance, "dwells corporally" in the Christ, in a filial manner (Colossians 2:9): that separation gives birth to communion and is reinforced by it attests again to distance. In order to recognize a last trait of it in "depth," one has only to remark on what unknowing is opened by knowing, "to know the ἀγάπη of the Christ which surpasses all knowledge" (Ephesians 3:19): charity goes further than knowledge, just as knowledge reaches that which it is a question of knowing only by reaching unknowing; not that it renounces knowing, only that it "knows as it is suitable to know" (Corinthians 8:2) in loving. The fourth dimension, therefore, is indeed revealed as the "depth" of distance. The placement in distance, which conjoins the appropriated withdrawal with distance, must thus be understood less as an overcoming (through "height" or "length") than as a reprise through "depth." But how does "depth" play? "Depth" intervened earlier in our itinerary (see § 1): straightaway the icon was characterized by the filial depth that traversed it, and that through it referred back to that of which it constituted the visibility. Charity, in this sense iconic, is indeed turned back, in a filial manner, to Him whom it loves and from whom it receives the very chance to love Him—the Father. Icon and charity coincide in the same reference, because this reference indicates the disappropriated property of the Son. To put the appropriated withdrawal (of the *Ereignis*) into play therefore especially does not mean that one would reduce it by force to distance; the filial reference, far from dismissing the alterity of the Son, underlines all the more his irremediable singularity; if reference there is, or better, so that there might be such a reference, it is necessary that the appropriated withdrawal remain decidedly other than distance. It is a matter of understanding, therefore, how a reference—to be simple let us say the depth of the reference—could transit the appropriated withdrawal to the point of making of it the icon of distance. This transition must indeed be understood only as a transit into distance, without transport or displacement, for distance gives itself to be traversed, not transgressed, so that one work one's way through it all the more insofar as one does not abolish it. It remains then to be seen how such a (-n iconic) reference can play on the basis of the appropriated withdrawal (*Ereignis,* and hence also Being as Being) with a view to incommensurable distance. Practically, and mobilizing reference (*Verweis*) in this regard (or *almost* in this regard), H. Urs von Balthasar defines the Christian as the one who, "because he believes in the absolute Love of God for the world, is compelled to read Being in its ontological difference as a reference (*Verweis*) to love."[58] He therefore does not only read being

---

[58] Ibid., "Der christliche Beitrag zur Metaphysik," p. 974 = "L'Apport chrétien à la métaphysique" (the sole passage translated from vol. III/1), French trans. by F. and R. Brague and J.-J. Becquet, in *Résurrection* 37 (Paris, 1972), p. 87. See also *Verweis, verweisen,* pp. 961, 962, 977, 978. On these questions, see

in general as a gift where God would fulfill him ("God" being
confused tactically with Being, the most metaphysically in the
world); he reads ontological difference, hence also the Being of
being (in its Being), as that which, through a certain reference,
gives to think in the direction of love. On several occasions we
have just seen how distance and withdrawal accomplish a similar
gesture of abandon and of gift. Something else must be approached here: the placement in distance of this similitude; in a
word, it is necessary to bring to light the gesture of gift and abandon that makes these two gestures of abandon and gift suit one
another. For that, it is not sufficient to speak of "love in the ontological difference" and of "the Being given/presented by God,"
for one must still understand how "the Being presented by God
(is) plenitude and poverty at the same time."[59] Plenitude and poverty: their coincidence indeed decides the distance at work; plenitude, because the appropriated withdrawal of the *Ereignis,* which
appropriates to itself all the more insofar as it does not appropriate to itself that which it lets reach what is proper to it, governs
beings as a whole, and accords them to us without end, since with
measure: this poverty delivers and appropriates all ontic plenitude. Thus can we recognize here already the rigor of that which
presents itself all the more insofar as it withdraws, that which gives
itself over [*s'adonne*] to itself all the more insofar as it abandons
(itself in) its gifts. The poverty of the *Ereignis* fills every man who
lets himself be appropriated therein. The Christian, like every
other, cannot avoid conforming to it, that is, acceding to it. More
than any other also, he measures the stakes of this plenary poverty, since he recognizes in it a paternal withdrawal, experiences
abandon in it as filial, in a word, discerns distance in it "in an
enigma as in a mirror" (1 Corinthians 13:12). But the overdeter-
mination of the *Ereignis* by the stakes of distance does not only
enrich this play of plenitude and poverty. Or rather, the more it
enriches it, the more it seems that the play of the *Ereignis* impover-
ishes it in face of the stakes of distance. One remark here: Heidegger, it is known, repeats insistently that the believer can indeed

---

also the essay, so often penetrating in its very oversimplicity, by K. Hemerle,
Thesen zu einer trinitarischen Ontologie (Einsiedeln: Johannes Verlag, 1976).
    [59] "Der christliche Beitrag zur Metaphysik," respectively, pp. 965 and 956.

follow, formulate, and even sense the question concerning Being as Being, but that he can never engage himself in it absolutely, because another authority absorbs him, reassures, and upsets him—faith, salvation, and certainty itself. Now, here again, poverty and wealth go together: to be sure, the Christian experiences an "indifference to the whole of Being,"[60] because its play remains abysally distinct from trinitarian distance (and therefore from Creation); but it is for this very reason that it is necessary to *intensify* one's vigilance in the place of the *Ereignis,* instead of following the destining of Being, from afar, with the blasé boredom of a "suave mari magno" that a theological ground would sustain (as if distance gave assurance). The Christian places himself at a/in distance from the *Ereignis* in multiple ways through this "indifference": he experiences first that the *Ereignis* appropriates only in disappropriating itself and here agrees all the more with the thought of Being; next, he reproves the solitude of Being, and disqualifies any of its idolatrous pretension (see § 17), in order finally to concern himself all the more with it as with a possible icon of distance. In this sense he seems not at all indifferent to passing beyond metaphysics and its idol ("God" as *causa sui*), in order to reach difference and above all the thought of the *giving* in the *Ereignis:* at issue here is the conversion of the idol into icon. There is nothing more right than that the Christian should become in a sense "indifferent to Being"—on the condition that one understand that he will not thus free himself toward (no doubt illusory, because still ontic) positions of withdrawal prepared in advance, but doubles the seriousness of the question of Being with the seriousness of the distance that can find the icon therein. The fact that indifference and seriousness should cross in concert, like wealth and poverty, only attests that it is indeed a question of a placement in distance. For distance renders indifferent all that which it nevertheless renders to itself to

---

[60] "The Christian fact projects a light of inexorable acuity and sobriety on this very interior point, it requires not only indifference vis-à-vis all that is (like the Stoics), but also indifference vis-à-vis Being, whence springs forth, as a source, the original Words and Sayings (*Urweisungen*); an always renewed indifference, for God remains free to specify otherwise Sayings already pronounced, free to push them further, to re-employ them, to deepen them, in an unawaited, unhoped for, and unexpected way." Ibid., p. 979 = French trans., p. 93.

differ; it forces into suspension not only being in general, like anxiety, but also Being and its suspension. But then occurs the event that, precisely, makes Being an icon of distance as paschal distance (kenosis, death, resurrection). From the point of view of charity, everything enters into another light: Beings and Being itself appear, certainly not annihilated or without value (for *nihil* and *value* come to us from metaphysics), but nil in charity, inept because inapt for distance, in a word, vain. *Vain*, in the sense that "vanity of vanities, all is vanity" must be understood more or less as: "wind, nothing that holds, nothing but wind." That which reveals itself at this point to be vain (*vergeblich*)—namely, Being as well as beings—departs like wind. But the "wind" indicates also the spirit, which "breathes." Can the inanity of *Dasein*, like "wind," offer a name to the Spirit, offer its inanity (*Vergeblichkeit*) and give it (*geben*) to another authority? "If this is vain (*vergeblich*), one can forgive (*vergeben*) him, and he can receive forgiveness (*vergeben werden*). And only then can he say with the absolute Word: 'as we also forgive'."[61] The ontico-ontological inanity un-covers such a poverty to charity (distance), that charity cannot but remit it to it: to remit that inanity, that is, to forgive it, by overdetermining it with a ratification, as well as leaving it to it as its share, its wealth, and its good. The two moments coincide in distance: to for-give Being its inanity is to abandon to it its proper field as a gift where it receives itself. Being has no more *why* than the rose—but only a forgiveness can grant it that one not impute that absence to it as a fault. Only the distance that gives for noth-ing, unless for the pleasure of a grace, for-gives Being its inanity, and gives to it the chance to abandon itself to a game without reason. That vanity should become a gift without reason—only distance can give this to Being, because distance alone, which abandons itself in these gifts, knows how to recognize in *Gelassen-heit* an icon of charity. This forgiveness of inanity is no doubt suitable to the times in which nihilism makes epoch, our times. But it is valuable also, outside of metaphysics, for the slow ad-vance, across the experience of thought, toward a breakthrough of Being as Being, which, more than the Being of beings, precisely because the instance of the *why* (*causa, ratio, Grund, value,* etc.)

---

[61] Ibid., p. 982 = French trans., p. 96.

will not obfuscate it, will expose the still unheard of marvel of *Gelassenheit* toward the danger of abandoning oneself in inanity. For inanity can threaten all the more insofar as serenity and completion take hold of beings. Put more trivially, there is nothing more dangerous than a happiness that nothing can trouble, for it gives rise to the suspicion of the inanity of its very serenity. Abandon threatens all the more that which no longer has to be possessed in order to offer itself. This inanity grows with serenity. And serenity will reach us historially only with a "new beginning." Only forgiveness will allow us to receive it as a gift without abandoning ourselves to its serene inanity.

In the play of inanity and forgiveness, Being receives, as a gift, its gratuity. It thus becomes "not the light, but the witness to the light,"[62] that is, the icon of distance. And in a double capacity: in itself, Being plays according to the appropriated withdrawal of the *Ereignis* and thus, as one says, "presents some analogies" with distance. That "analogy" itself in turn finds itself taken up within distance, where Being sees its abandoned inanity forgiven. This placement in distance, in bringing about through its depth in Being an icon of distance, both maintains supremely the independence of the question of Being and holds back any threat of idolatry—which, far from weakening the rigor of such a relation, reinforces it. For what places Being in distance as an icon of distance remains first the humble and unthinkable authority of the Father.

---

[62] Ibid., p. 962.

INDEX OF AUTHORS

Cet ouvrage publié dans le cadre du programme d'aide à la publication bénéficie du soutien du Ministère des Affaires Etrangères et du Service Culturel de l'Ambassade de France représenté aux Etats-Unis.

This work, published as part of the program of aid for publication, received support from the French Ministry of Foreign Affairs and the Cultural Service of the French Embassy in the United States.